S0-BYG-076

# "ARE WE ON THE AIR?!"

*The Hilarious,*

*Scandalous Confessions*

*of a TV Pioneer*

# "ARE WE ON THE AIR?!"

## The Hilarious, Scandalous Confessions of a TV Pioneer

**Guy LeBow**

Introduction by Ed McMahon

## S.P.I. BOOKS
A division of Shapolsky Publishers, Inc.

Copyright © 1992 by Guy LeBow

For any additional information, contact:
Shapolsky Publishers, Inc.
136 West 22nd Street
New York, NY 10011
(212) 633-2022
FAX (212) 633-2123


10  9  8  7  6  5  4  3  2  1

ISBN 1-56171-049-0


Design and Typography by Kable News, Mt. Morris, IL

Manufactured in the United States of America

# Dedication

*To my colleagues . . . true pioneers who—with virtually little else than spit, rubber bands and extraordinary ardor—produced precedent-shattering TV entertainment pushing beyond the bounds of television technology of their times, setting the stage for today's epochal TV. Many of these stalwarts are gone and many soon will be. For them the following stories are told. And to Brigadier-General David Sarnoff: I promised I'd never tell . . . and I haven't yet.*

# Thanks and Special Thanks

To myriad good and earnest people from coast to coast, who often pro bono spent days of research to come up with the answers I required or the photographs I needed.

To Toby LeBow, who kept vital notes, stories and photos and memories, so important to the book. . . .

To Stephen LeBow, for producing many of my shows.

To cousin Robert Levy, who furnished my introduction to sports and politics.

To old hands, who remembered: Ed McMahon, Otis Freeman, John Tillman, Soupy Sales, Phil Rizzuto, Len Jacobs, Pat Tillman, Edward Woodruff, Gene Crane, Walter Engels, Wally Reed, John Cameron Swayze, Douglas Edwards, Freddie Bartholomew, Edie Adams, Clark Jones, Ted Estabrook, Herb Holmes, Irving Rudd, George Wyle, Dan Grabel, Ben Sckolnick, Joe Franklin, Mike Baker (president of AFTRA), Candy Jones, Henry Morgan, Marvin Pakula, John J. Giordano, Hal Brenner, Joe Berger, Ben Blank, Peggy Gannon, Mike Meltzer, Roylance Sharp, Steve Jackson, Fred Kelly, Don Dunphy, Don Ameche, Elliott Gould, Leah Breier, Joyce Randolph, Dick Charles, Paul Denis, Stan Freberg, Stan Chambers, Harry Coyle, Gus Cordeiro (WJAR), Harry Burkhardt, Ira Senz, Neil O'Donnell, Dick Smith, Bob Kelly, Herman

Buchman, Charlie Hepner, Bernie London, Mel Allen, Bud Greenspan, Les Arries, Jr., Bob Wolf, Stan Fischler, Al Rylander (Executive Editor, *The Friars' Epistle*), Lou Ames, Mac Busch, Elsa Sule, Hal Tunis, Les Persky, James Pollack, Angelo Savoldi, Bob Cochran, Howard Cosell.

To friends and colleagues, who offered creative support and help: Henny Youngman, Lou Jacobi, Joey Adams, Jerry Stiller and Anne Meara, Kay Gardella, Larry King, Sidney Zion, Bill Bell, Gary Wagner, Gene Schoor, Bob Kimmel, Jean-Pierre Trebot (Executive Director, Friars' Club), Woody Allen, Vincent Sardi, Jr., Jim Trupin, Louis Wolf, Stephen Birmingham, Nicole Gregory, Carolyn Lloyd, Cathy Christel, Arthur Hettich, Ralph Schoenstein, Lewis Frumkes, Frank Lauria, Joyce Rocca (widow of Antonino Rocca), Pat Piper (Producer, "Larry King Live"), Jack Arden, Efrim Abramson, Cameron Swayze.

To Madeleine Kelly, personal manager for Ed McMahon, for her kindness.

To those everywhere who always said, "I'll find it": Mickey Fisher (WLTW, Cincinnati), Roseli Spiers (Timex), Ed Harrison (KTLA, Los Angeles), Victoria Clayton (WCAU, Philadelphia), Fernand Bibeau (KOB, Albuquerque), Dick Sweeny (WHAS, Louisville), Barbara Ware (WNYW, New York).

To researchers, for crack work: Anne Barry, Alicia Mandl, Gerry Hirsch, Charles Sinclair.

To TV stations WNBC-TV, WABC-TV, WCBS-TV, WAAT-TV (now WNET-TV), WABD-TV (now WNEW-TV), WCAU-TV (Philadelphia), WKRC-TV (Cleveland), WBEN-TV (now WIVB-TV, Buffalo), KTLA-TV (Los Angeles), WTVR-TV (Richmond), WRGB-TV (Schenectady), KSD-TV (St. Louis), WHAS-TV (Louisville), KOB-TV (Albuquerque), WLWT-TV (Cincinnati), WMAR-TV (Baltimore).

To the *New York Post*; New York *Daily News*; New York Public Library; Broadcast Pioneers Library, Washington, D.C.; Museum of Broadcasting, New York; and *TV Guide*.

Also thanks to Suzanne Stoeckler and Kate Caren, and to Ron Mandelbaum and Howard Mandelbaum (Photofest), as well as to Gene Healy and Lee Canizales. And to those, if any, I inadvertently omitted.

To former middleweight champ Jake LaMotta and Bert Lebhar, a.k.a. Bert Lee, radio executive and sportscaster, and to TV director Jack Murphy. These three gave me my first breaks. And to Robert Wogan (Vice-President of NBC), Nick Gordon and publicist George Schreier, who helped me immeasurably in my career.

To my partners at WNWK-FM, Evelyn Jose and Emil Antonoff.

To my able assistant and program producer, John Cetta.

And finally, a special thanks to my editor and dear friend, Barbara Sue Carlin, who insisted for ten years that I write this book, and without whose continuous nagging belief in it and the most brilliant editing, this project would never have been started and surely never would have been finished.


And as one pioneer to another, I wish to honor the fledgling organization called The Talk Show Hosts of America, which includes hundreds of broadcasters coast to coast. As a charter member, I commend the efforts of both founder Jerry Williams, talker at WRKO, Boston, and President Mike Siegel, talker at King Broadcasting in Seattle, Washington, in raising the sights of the profession and in seriously reflecting what Americans think and want.

# Contents

xi

# Introduction

## By Ed McMahon

I was wondering when somebody would write this book, finally done by my colleague, Guy LeBow. To any performer who faced a camera in the late 1940s and is still getting a good check from working in front of the tube right now, he's got to say about right now, as Mr. Gleason would, "How sweet it is." What is life like on "The Johnny Carson Show" for me right now? Well, a comfortable dressing room . . . a makeup person . . . someone to worry about my wardrobe or mail . . . no cares about a teleprompter if I want it or the lights being just right or the props in place . . . and everyone involved first-class talent.

But LeBow's *"Are We On the Air?!"* sure brings back the bittersweet memories—sometimes more like nightmares! Sure, we had a lot of fun breaking the stress. Like when I was doing a daily five-minute show on WCAU-TV in Philadelphia, where I started, and the fun-loving crew signaled me to stretch my closing and just keep on going. And I kept on going. I can't at all remember what I said, but I remember sweating from every pore. And guess what? When this near-fatal trip was over, the technical boys told me they had me talking into a dead mike and dead camera. Some joke! I thought strangling was too good for that crew.

And let me tell you, it's good that nobody could read my mind when the daily goof-ups came—and I made my share too. Mistakes, accidents, errors were on the menu every day in early TV. For announcers, emcees and other performers, the daily brush with complete oblivion in the TV business usually was linked with the reliability of the guy or gal who held up the cue cards—so you could look like you were very cleverly ad-libbing. And I've always felt there ought to be a Hall of Fame for cue card holders who got the cards in order two times in a row. As for other errors of announcers, directors and technicians —accidental or otherwise—I still get big belly laughs remembering . . . But as Guy points out, where did all of us budding stars come from?

Well, friends, you name it. After the war was over, guys who once pushed pencils, worked machinery, taught schools or were technical sergeants said: "What the hell. Whatever television is, let's go for it!" Some guys like myself attended college communications classes. I did my four at Catholic University in Washington, D.C., where, incidentally, I am encouraging young people to go into broadcasting by furnishing Ed McMahon scholarships. And at graduation I thought I was ready for show biz. But you know where my introduction to being a TV emcee came from? Yes, and I'm proud of it: I was the best damn hawker of potato peelers the Atlantic City boardwalk ever had. I sold enough peelers to make 500 bucks a week. But I chucked all that top money to work for about a third as much at WCAU. Even then, I knew Johnny was going to need me someday.

Finally, let me warm you up before you hit this book—just like I do on "The Tonight Show." A little tale out of my life in the early days at WCAU:

We created a daily cowboy-type show, partly televised just outside our studio, as well as inside. Even though we were dead serious about this oat-burner, the home audiences probably collapsed when, along with the Old West dialogue and scenes, they heard the honking and screeching noises of automobiles or the roaring of airplanes overhead. But wait! It gets worse. In one scene I remember, a cowboy was pursuing a villain on horseback when the two guns he was carrying fell out of his holster. When he reached for his guns at the crucial moment—curses! They weren't there. But with the camera up close, the panicky actor made pistol shapes out of his hands, pointed his fingers at the bad guy and shouted, "Bang! Bang!" Yes, TV and I survived even that.

But that's for starters. This book takes you where no other TV opus has been before . . . so now . . . heeeere's good reading!

*Los Angeles, California*
*1991*

# Author's Preface: How I Came to Write This Book

The idea for this book about television became clearly defined, ironically enough, while I was working in Woody Allen's motion picture *Radio Days*. At its heart, *Radio Days* exemplified what turns out to be America's innocent days, trusting times and—despite the sadness and struggle of the Depression—its best times. And riding radio's transformation into the major-league days

5

of network TV came Uncle Miltie: Milton Berle, whose astounding popularity gave us more promise of hearty laughter at eye-winking deeds, of good-natured "mayhem" (pie in the face and cotton balls in the mouth), of a time when child and adult could have a good belly laugh, followed by a restful sleep, secure in the arms of a Sweet America, looked after by uncles just like . . . Uncle Miltie.

But I'm jumping the gun. I had been hired by Woody Allen to play the role of Bill Kern, which was patterned on Bill Stern, a radio star of the forties and fifties. If you sat by a radio and gave Bill sixty seconds at you, his voice marching to dramatic cadences, thrumming with feeling, your emotions were putty in his hands.

Bill once told the story about how President Lincoln, on his deathbed, asked to see army officer Abner Doubleday. And he told Doubleday that he, Lincoln, knew he was going to die, but he hoped that Doubleday would make the President's big dream come true: to keep baseball going. . . .

To get into the film character I thought a lot about Stern. He was the peephole to yesterday. I was suddenly awash, suffused, imploding with memories not only of Stern and radio, but of LeBow and TV.

In my mind, television can be divided into two periods. There is today's TV, technically adept, strictly controlled, populated with highly skilled pros. Then there was the other time, the beginning days, which I fix at from 1946 to 1954 or so. It was a kind of Dodge City in black-and-white, filled with charlatans, thieves, bunco artists, no-talents and ne'er-do-wells. And some wonderful people, too. It was many times technically impoverished and inept, uncontrolled, zany, funny, sad, innocent —and not profitable. And it was a time that will never come again.

It occurred to me that no one had ever told the story of those early days. Not really. There had been reports, studies, personal memoirs of this aspect or that, but none from the front lines or the trenches . . . how it was in sports and news and game shows and drama . . . and more. How it really was when the tube was born!

Actually, for ten years someone had been pestering me to tell this story: a writer-editor named Barbara Carlin. But I kept putting it off. Then one day I heard a guy on television refer to the "good old early days of television in the sixties." That did it! That would be like beginning American history with the Battle of San Juan Hill. It occurred to me that the ranks of us who could tell the true story were thinning. Somebody'd better get it down, I told myself. I decided to get a typewriter.

*Guy LeBow*
*New York City*
*1991*

# 1 / Screen Test: Hollywood Meets TV

News of the times . . .

**WIVES OF TV FANS COMPLAIN
MATES NEVER TAKE THEM OUT**

LOS ANGELES, July 12 (UP) — House-wives who have television sets almost unanimously complain that their husbands never take them out any more, a sociologist's survey showed today. . . .

*(1950)*

"Tell Eisenhower he can go fuck himself!"

Humphrey Bogart slammed down the car phone and glared out the limo window. Next to him the reporter hunched over her pad and scribbled intently. By her side, the hair and makeup girl found something fascinating to watch on the floor. Even I—hardened to maniacal TV directors and temperamental sponsors—felt my mouth go dry.

This was not the genial, generous person we'd been with the last few days. Where was the wonderful fellow who said, "Well, that's fine, but I think Katie really deserves it," when he got the phone call about his Oscar nomination for *The African Queen?* Or the nervous guy who asked the stylist if his wig was O.K.?

A what! All the toupees I'd seen looked just like their

nickname: rugs. But every hair on Bogart's suave head looked homegrown. He caught me staring and smiled. "Could have fooled you, huh? I found a wigmaker who discovered the secret. You want your toupee to look like your own hair would—at your age? See how my hairline recedes? Just a bit, of course." I couldn't believe this: Sam Spade doing a dissertation on toupees!

Now I was faced with the "Bogie" moviegoers witnessed from the safety of their seats. Tough. Sneering. Explosive. And in the flesh he was goddamm unnerving.

It was February 1952. Bogart was in New York on a publicity blitz for his latest movie, *The African Queen.* Loews Theaters, the movie chain that owned M-G-M, had assigned me, a seasoned TV personality, to appear with him. Three, sometimes four stops a night. Manhattan, Brooklyn, the Bronx, Westchester, New Jersey. Everywhere, massive cheering crowds as the limo arrived. It was more than mindless star mania. These people had come out despite the cold because they liked Humphrey Bogart. You could feel it, see it, hear it. Even more so in the black neighborhoods, where Bogart was welcomed like a hero. "You tell 'em, Bogie!" they shouted. "Go get 'em!"

Bogart explained later that according to studio surveys, he and Bette Davis were the two most-loved screen stars in black theaters. He thought it had something to do with their feisty roles, always bucking the system.

Backstage, more intensity. Bogart was surrounded by stagehands, and at almost every theater one would grab his hand, saying tearfully, "You don't know me, but I knew your father. God bless him." Bogart beamed while they told stories about Dr. Bogart, who had operated on many of them.

Our appearance was timed to the film's intermission— ten or fifteen minutes. I went first to warm up the audience. But they didn't need any encouragement.

Before I finished my "And, now, ladies and gentlemen, the man . . ." they were shouting his name, "Bogie, Bogie, Bogie . . . !"

What a pro. First he poked fun at his tough-guy image, telling the audience that he was a pussycat to Lauren's tigress. Laughter. Applause. Shouts of "You kidding us, Bogie?" For his finale, he did tuneless, scratchy renditions of sea chanties he said his father had taught him. Clapping. Stomping. Cheering. Standing there in his conservative dark suit he looked as smooth as a Park Avenue lawyer—but as he sang, he rumpled into the scruffy captain from *The African Queen*. He captured them forever—and for M-G-M. There was no chance anyone here tonight would miss the movie when it came around.

Hold it. . . . Why does an internationally known movie star need a television announcer on his publicity tour? The answer had been giving movie moguls killer migraines since the late forties: Television was beating the shit out of the film industry. By 1951, according to one estimate, box office revenues had fallen by thirty-five percent. Hundreds of theaters closed across the country.

Hollywood tried ignoring us—we didn't go away. They tried strangling us. Most of the studios wouldn't sell us their movies, which we needed desperately to fill air time. They put television off limits to their major stars. And a few weeks after my tour with Bogart, RKO's production chief Jerry Wald announced a campaign to entice women out of their homes—the first step in weaning them from TV. The catchy slogan was: "Get Out and Shop and Then Go to a Movie." They tried everything short of buying utility companies and shutting off the power to homes with TV antennas. Think I'm exaggerating? Jack Warner was so paranoid he wouldn't allow a TV set in a living-room scene in a Warner

Brothers film.

But yet at the same time Hollywood is praying and plotting for our demise, they see that television personalities are very popular. Like . . . stars! So they decide to use us to lure audiences back to them—the movies. They revive the Depression-era gimmicks of contests and drawings during intermissions—with TV personalities as hosts. At Loews theaters all through Manhattan and the Bronx, I conducted quiz shows on sports and movie trivia, and emceed kiddie talent contests. For prizes I handed out watches, perfume and—of all things—passes to Loews movie houses.

Hollywood then has another job for us. Studios are also losing faith in their stars' power to draw crowds to public appearances. So they add what they hate to admit is a sure draw—a TV star. Loews learned the full power of TV's punch in 1949, when for the very first time they had me publicize a movie on my own. I was to give away passes to *Jolson Sings Again*, starring Larry Parks and Barbara Hale. No mammoth publicity campaign; I announced the free tickets a couple of times on my wrestling show. That afternoon my wife Toby and I took a cab to Father Duffy Square. But it had to let us out four blocks away. An immense crowd, maybe 2,000 people, was blocking traffic. I knew I was in big trouble. Those cheap sons of bitches at Loews had coughed up a paltry twenty-five tickets!

I pulled Toby along, looking for the Loews PR guy. After I gave him hell, he was going to get us out of this. Then somebody yelled, "There he is!" and the mob turned toward us. They came from all sides, grabbing at the passes I held out, snatching at me and knocking Toby to the ground. If a big Irish cop hadn't muscled his way in and hustled us out, we would have been trampled to death. The police had no sympathy. They threatened to arrest me for causing a riot. Taken by surprise, they'd had to call in reinforcements, which were still trying to get people to go home. I found a few remaining passes in my jacket pocket and bought my freedom.

I'm not pretending that the stupendous turnout was because of me. The fact remains that, whether it was me or the movie passes, it was television that got a couple of thousand people to Father Duffy Square.

And it was television that got me in the hotseat, in the jumpseat across from Humphrey Bogart, a phone cord stretched over my shoulder and digging into my jacket— the one I had bought to be with Bogie.

"They have got one hell of a fucking nerve," Bogart growled. He finally noticed the telephone cord and freed me from my bonds.

"What's up, Bogie?" I inquired. (It had taken days of practice before deciding what to call him. "Mr. Bogart"? Nah. Too mealy-mouthed. "Humphrey"? Humphrey???!!! All my television experience boiled down to nothing in my eyes. I was going to spend two weeks with —I was still pinching myself—Bogie.)

"I am informed that Eisenhower would be pleased"— Bogart enunciated this word with that sneer we all knew so well—"if I would show up at the rally at the Garden." With the 1952 presidential election getting into gear, each side was lining up its celebs. "Like hell I will."

The reporter kept writing, but the makeup girl relaxed. It wasn't a star tantrum, after all—just politics.

Bogart explained that he was PO'd at Eisenhower for staying mum when General Marshall was accused of being soft on Communism. "Marshall's never been soft on anything," said Bogart, "and Eisenhower's a chicken-shit for not standing up for him."

This was the only hard-boiled stuff we saw. This and his anger, when the limousine took us through the depressing, winter-bleak neighborhoods of the poor. "Those bastards in Washington don't give a damn about the underdog," he said. "This country is for the rich. Don't forget to put that in," he ordered the reporter.

The rest of the time, Bogart was the antithesis of the brawling, drinking and obstreperous tough guy I'd read about in the press. Part of it was his preoccupation with his son, who was in the hospital. Bacall, who had been scheduled to appear on the tour with Bogart, had canceled. "She's got a bed in the room with him," Bogart said, shaking his head. "She refuses to leave him alone at night. Some dame. You have any kids?"

I didn't then, but Toby and I were expecting one in June. Bogart and I started kicking around names, which is how my son ended up being called Stephen Bogart LeBow—with Bogart agreeing to be his unofficial godfather.

I met Bogart every night for dinner at his favorite hotel in New York, the St. Regis, on East Fifty-fifth Street. He was prompt, and appeared shorter and slighter than the screen admitted. He was unruffled, unentouraged and unfanfared. And so damned organized that I half expected him to be carrying a briefcase, on his way to the office. And his clothes . . . You couldn't get a suit that fit like that off the rack. I knew. Next to Bogart's, my new jacket looked as if I was also wearing the rack. I promised myself that the first time I had $1,000 all at once, I'd have a suit custom-made.

In the dining room, the same table was waiting for us every night. Bogart ordered simple food and no alcohol. He didn't drink on the tour, which disappointed the theater managers, who had set up lavish bars backstage. "I'll have a soda, hold the whiskey," Bogart would say. It always got a laugh. (I remember all these details because I was the unofficial Hedda Hopper of my neighborhood in the Bronx. I had to answer everyone's questions, from the building super to the corner candy store owner. "What did he wear?" "What did he eat?" "What did he say about Lauren?" "Does he drink?") As we walked to our table, I felt the electric current generated by a star. Heads turned. Forks stopped in mid-air. The room actually turned off its sound and then came back with a buzz.

But the juice flowed two ways. I didn't tell you the whole story when I described the pandemonium for Bogart. Leaving the hotel entrance the first night of the tour, we heard a man yell, "Say, Guy. Whatcha doing with Bogie?" Bogart gave me a sidelong glance but said nothing. When the limo pulled up to the theaters, the autograph books were thrust at both of us. Calls of "Bogie, where's Lauren?" were balanced off with "Hey, Guy, is St. Francis going to win the championship this year?"

"Folks really seem to know you," Bogart said on the ride back into the city the second night. "You're in this television, right?" That was all he ever said about TV.

It was an uppercut to my ego. By now, I'd been in television for six years. I'd zoomed up fast. I'd been featured on the cover of *TeleVision Guide*, been voted one of the ten outstanding sportscasters in the country (and that included California), was charming audiences every day of the week on sports, news and quiz shows, and annoying them day and night on commercials. But to Hollywood stars as big as Bogie, television was second best.

Bogart wasn't the first Hollywood luminary I'd taken in tow. I'd been acting as bait for screen-star tours since I started in television. One of my first assignments was prettyboy Van Johnson. I'd been signed by the Dumont channel, WABD (Channel 5), to do boxing and had a fair-size segment of female fans. But being with Van Johnson was a lesson in humility. We visited the Loews headquarters at 1540 Broadway. Floor by floor, Van Johnson disrupted the entire organization. He shook secretaries' hands and they swooned. He talked to an office manager and her mouth dropped open. Women pressed their hands to their heads, bit their knuckles and acted like star-crazed teenagers.

Bogart was every bit as popular as Van Johnson, and had an even larger male following. Which presents a puzzle. If the fans were so crazy about their Hollywood stars, why weren't they plunking down money at the box office? Why were they sitting home with us mighty mites? I'd like to claim that it was our compelling television personalities that lured audiences away from films—but why lie?

TV had two advantages the movies didn't. For one, you couldn't beat us for convenience. Before television came along, you had to leave the house to see a movie, a ballgame, a play. Now here we were! So what if it rained? You were indoors. A few theater owners recognized early on that if they couldn't bring movies into people's living rooms, they could bring people's living rooms into their theaters by installing television sets. Walter Reade, Jr., owner of the Walter Reade chain in New Jersey, claimed that his theater attendance soared after he put sets in the lounges in 1948. (Those of you who never had the immensely pleasurable experience of buying a theater ticket and then waiting inside the theater, sitting on a comfortable chair in a carpeted waiting room—and being served coffee and cake—you were born too late!) And although prissy critics accused us of prostituting the air with mindless entertainment, we had it over hookers in a big way: you didn't have to pay each time you wanted enjoyment out of us.

We were free. And we were free when postwar inflation was driving prices of everything up. As a disgruntled West Coast theater manager said in 1951, "These days it costs about $5 for a couple to attend a movie. Two 94-cent tickets with all the taxes, parking expense, cup of coffee or dish of ice cream and then the babysitter!''

But even a few years later, when TV hit hard times with soaring costs and canceling sponsors, and Hollywood smelled a victory, they continued to cash in on our power. And the next time they called me, I should have stayed home. The occasion was the glitzy, Hollywood-style opening of a small radio station on Long Island. . . . Movie stars. Glamorous women. Flashbulbs. Autograph hounds. The works. The main attractions were my charges: Robert Strauss, actor, and Jayne Mansfield, sex bomb and one of America's natural wonders. It was a pisser from start to finish.

To begin with, Jayne kept Robert and me stewing in the limo for an hour and a half, before she made her appearance in a plunging gown that barely kept a grip on her breasts. Jayne never just appeared, she always "made" an appearance. Don't ask me what color her dress was. Color is not something you remember when Jayne wore it.

Strauss was furious at being upstaged. He was the STAR, having been nominated for an Oscar for his role of Animal in *Stalag 17*. Jayne gave us both a vague wriggle and a giggle and slinked her way into the limo, holding a quivering chihuahua to her breasts. Bob sat at the opposite side of the limo, leaving me in the middle.

We hadn't even reached the Queens Midtown Tunnel yet when I felt something wet on my pants leg. No mistake. That yippity-yappity chihuahua was peeing on my tux. (The first one I owned, not rented.)

For me this was *déjà phew*. A couple of years earlier, I was up at Grossinger's resort in the Catskills, introducing a round of celebs, including our Jayne. What got me that time wasn't her dog, it was her daughter, plunked on my lap by Jayne when it was her turn to entertain. And now her dog was doing it. Should I take it personally? I gave the beast a little kick (not a big one, heavens no) and it hopped like a spouting tripod over to Strauss.

"Goddamm bitch," he muttered. I knew he didn't mean me. I'd known Strauss since our high school days at James Monroe in the Bronx. I also knew he had a little of Animal in him. That dog was a foot away from extinction.

I didn't want any star-crossed scene to spoil our grand entrance. So I tried some light conversation. "Jaynie, what a cute little dog you have." Strauss groaned. "But Jaynie," I continued, "why didn't he do his business before you left?"

By now the doggie had dripped its way back to Jayne, and all nice and dry was panting on her lap, leering at Bob and me. Jayne picked him up and squeezed him to her breasts. Lucky pup.

"My baby doesn't have to dodo if he doesn't want to, does him babykums," she pouted.

"Hollywood, you owe me one," I said to myself. I pitched in for you all these years and now you've pissed on me. (But don't worry about Bob and Guy. It was a long ride out to the Island from Manhattan and our pants had time to dry.)

In a sense, Hollywood has ended up the victor over TV. Not so long ago I saw this headline in the *New York Post*:

### FILM DIRECTORS GO
### TO THE RESCUE OF TV

The story began, "TV network biggies—who've seen millions of viewers slip away in the last three years—have cast their talent nets wide for the coming season and caught some big fish from the movie business."

And you don't need any headlines to tell you what you already know: that people sitting in front of their sets these days are often watching Hollywood movies rather than current TV programs, thanks to the invention of the VCR. Did you know that TV cut its own throat in this department? In 1951, none other than the emperor of NBC, Brigadier-General Sarnoff himself, the cluck, asked his research staff to come up with a machine that would replay video programs at home!

But this book is not Hollywood's story and not just mine, either. It's the story of the maniacal directors, the temperamental sponsors, anxious announcers and clammy-handed cameramen who stitched postwar television together and created a form of entertainment that gave Hollywood a run for its money.

# 2 / "And Now a Word from Our Sponsor . . . We Hope"

"I hear science has invented a weapon that kills with sound . . . and I think it's a TV commercial."

—Paul Denis, TV critic

They should have given all of us the Bronze Star for surviving early commercials. We were cut, scalded, deboned—right before the unblinking eyes of the audience. This was live TV—and it was a risky business. Some people say that the invention of tape destroyed spontaneity in television. But remembering some of the "live"-ly disasters we lived through, tape sounds good to me.

Typical problem: this Progresso soup commercial. The plan was for my "wife" to serve me a bowl of soup, me to take a spoonful, smiling the hubby smile and saying, "This soup is delicious, dear. What did you say the name of it was?"

She'd answer with a wifely, "Oh, I knew you'd like it, darling. It's PROGRESSO!"

My "wife" was the daughter of the head of the Carlos Vinti advertising agency, which handled Progresso. A darling little thing, she was—god knows, no actress— and papa had insisted she be given a chance to get into "show business." And papa was so powerful and famous that he'd been given a Maltese Cross by the Pope. Nobody was going to turn him down. So I was stuck with her.

The first night, her hands were shaking so badly she looked like the center of an L.A. quake. And SPLASH. CRASH. The soup landed in my unsuspecting crotch. In order for the steam to visualize on screen, that soup was red hot. As Sid Caesar used to say, "Oh boyyy."

My "wife" screamed and stood there staring at me, hands over her mouth. But we professionals weren't supposed to let on that something was screwed up. (Maybe fatally this time?)

"M-m-m-m!" I said heartily as my genitalia mixed with the minestrone. "This soup is as good on your clothes as it is in your bowl." CUT, and cold towel please.

Being on camera put a hitch in doing commercials. We couldn't read our scripts as we had so comfortably done on radio. Even in front of a studio audience, we could still depend on those scripts. Now we were in front of a camera. We had to "look" at the viewers almost constantly while we were talking to them. (Couldn't they hear us if we didn't establish eye contact? They'd heard us on radio all those years.) Even more frightening, we had to do stage business—walking, pointing, han- dling products, drinking, smoking—as we delivered our lines. And we had to do it all live.

Overnight, we announcers had become actors. Staff announcers gave live performances three, four, five times a day. With no tape technology to erase the bloopers, the pressure was enormous. "If you blow it, the viewers know it," one comforting director told us.

But more crucial than the audience's response was the sponsor's.

In TV, as in radio, we understood that the commercial was KING. As it was succinctly explained by Don McClure, TV director at ace ad agency N.W. Ayer & Son, "The commercial is really the only point in sponsoring a television show at all." And the sponsors watched over every breath we took. If you gave an announcer the choice between death and blowing a commercial, he'd choose death—undoubtedly. Because here's what happened when a commercial got screwed up:

The Engineer recorded the error in his log. The Station Director and Station Producer recorded it in their logs. (Not that anyone committed the real reason to paper: "Announcer drunk." "Station went off air." "Camera wouldn't work." No, no, no. The station had to look good at any cost.) The report went to the Traffic Manager. Then on to the Sales Person, who turned it over to the Sales Manager, who in turn informed the General Manager.

This was Decision Time. Should they inform the Sponsor? Maybe his set had conked out that night, and he hadn't seen the debacle. Maybe not. The honest course was to let him know. In this case, the Station called the Ad Agency and broke the news to the Account Executive, who called the Account Supervisor, who told the Advertising Director (AD), who would decide on how to break it to the Sponsor.

Now came the heart-stopping suspense. Would the Sponsor demand a refund? The Ad Agency didn't think this was a good idea. It meant that they would have to refund the fee they had charged. So they encouraged the Sponsor to ask for a "make-good"—have the commercial redone. If they succeeded, the entire process made a "U" turn. The Ad Agency called the Station and the word was passed along until it reached the Announcer. He had to do the commercial again, for free, even if the flub was beyond his control. He did have a choice: he could quit.

(Not always did the Sponsor depend on the Station to report its crime. Some ad agencies sent a rep to the TV studio to keep an eye on commercials. At Jackson and Delaney, one of the early mid-size ad agencies to risk TV, Steve Jackson trained the most famous agency watchdog, Make-Good Mike. Day after day, Make-Good stood guard, implacable and impenetrable. His only words were: "Uh-oh, sign held up at wrong time. MAKE GOOD." Or: "Announcer stunk. MAKE GOOD." "Make Goods" made Mike look good at the agency, but made us mad. It meant extra work all the time.)

If it was tremble time for us old radio hands, it was terrifying for novices. Unforgettable is that winsome lassie who turned her words inside out. Demonstrating the marvels of RCA's new washing machine, she declared, "Here is where you put your clean wash IN, and it comes OUT nice and DIRTY." Cross my heart.

The strain seemed even worse for veterans. Taken out of our beautiful radio palaces of regal bronze and gleaming glass, we were lost in the eerily stark studios. In depressing gray and white, they had the impersonal atmosphere of airplane hangars. And they were filled with commotion. Cameramen adjusting their unwieldy instruments. Boom men pushing dollies that suspended the big, heavy mikes. Cue card holders shuffling their cards. Men chalking lines on the floor to indicate where performers should stand. Assistant producers flashing signals. Directors yelling orders. And crisscrossing the chaos were inept-looking ADs, who tripped over the wires snaking out from their earphones.

In radio, it was just us in the booth. Cozy. Engineers, directors and others supplementary to the voice stayed on the other side of the glass. In the television studio we were a mere speck on the floor—lost, unimportant, undone. There's no question that the lights and cameras and mess discombobulated us. Which must explain why radio's basso profundo announcer and narrator David Ross, whose impeccably classic delivery had won him umpteen Peabody Awards, insisted that his own name be printed on the cue cards. But not until after he bumbled: "Hello. This is . . . uh . . . my name is . . . uh . . ." And when Milton Berle was a guest of Jerry Lewis, Lewis said, "Let's sign off now," and Berle said, seriously: "This is Jerry Lewis saying goodnight." Seasoned performer Ray Doty said "Coke" very clearly three times when his sponsor was—you guessed it—Pepsi. And I goofed with a beauty. A big real estate firm proposed that veterans who bought their ranch homes would pay significantly LESS than non-vets. But as the announcer on this Sunday morning, I was wearing my get-up-early-on-Sunday-morning bitterness. I gave it my best voice, but came up with "You lucky veterans will pay MORE for these beautiful homes at Mastic Acres. Call us now!" We registered two hundred calls of boos, hisses and sneers.

Another seasoned announcer was Jack McCarthy. Nineteen hundred and ninety-one was his forty-first year as official voice of the St. Patrick's Day Parade up Fifth Avenue in New York. McCarthy was famous for holding mountains of Irish minutiae in his Irish brain, but that didn't prevent him from otherwise screwing up. One day he was late getting to the studio for a commercial. I was just starting onto the set to fill in, when he burst out of nowhere, knocked me over and delivered, "Got a headache? Smoke Bufferin."

So, you're asking, why didn't we make it easier on ourselves and read the teleprompter? I'm glad you asked that. There weren't any teleprompters the first few years. Which left it up to us to write out our own cues. Men inked lines on their shirt cuffs, women put theirs on hankies, or gloves or fans (a big number in those days), and everyone wrote on the palm of the hand. That's why so many of us used that hammy gesture: hands out in front, palms up. Or, we printed things on scraps of paper, which we stuck strategically around the set: on lamps, furniture, a box, a bottle. At the Dumont station this pathetic attempt to keep our heads above water posed an irresistible temptation to the sadistic crew. The minute we left the set, they switched our paper notes around— which we never discovered until we did the spot. Pointing to, say, a lamp, we would say, "Picture this handsome upholstered sofa in *your* home!"

And what about film? Even if there wasn't tape, why couldn't we film our commercials? There were some films and animations being done. Mostly by the big-big sponsors—Lucky Strike, Texaco, Maxwell House, Ronson among them. They paid unbelievable sums for animations. But the smaller sponsors didn't have the money—and they needed to update their spots for sales and special offers. So they depended on live announcers. And technology was against us. First, there weren't enough cameras or crew for wasting valuable space and time to film a commercial, when it could be done once, live. And not all cameras could shoot simultaneous sound. When these were out of the studio for a news story, then we filmed commercials. It was a trial.

The announcer did the commercial in front of the camera. Then he recorded sound in another studio. Next, the editor matched the words with our mouths. The hitch was that if he couldn't read the announcer's lips, the overall effect would be out of sync. Our first attempts at this match-up were mixed: sync was crazy, editors and announcers complained violently. Then we genius announcers figured out a way to solve the problem. We substituted words that the editor could lip-read. For instance, instead of "Good evening, this is Guy LeBow," I said, "Hello, I'm Guy LeBow." The mouth made more distinct shapes when forming "Hello" and "I'm." Gradually, this sync-talk became part of our regular presentation. The necessity of filming commercials changed the way announcers spoke.

When the simultaneous sound cameras were available, we could use cue cards—if someone had time to print them. But even these human-held aids were subject to "technical difficulties." At WBEN in Buffalo, the floorman responsible for the cue cards was constantly drunk —courtesy of the bottles of brew used on the commercials. So one night, viewers heard the new commercial actress say, "Always put your money where you know it's safe—knab notlimah." The floorman was holding the card saying "Hamilton Bank," upside down, but by golly, if that's what the cue card said, that was the way she was going to read it. No ad-libbing here!

At WABC in New York City, when the regular cue card girl called in sick, a cameraman volunteered his girlfriend. The AD showed her how high to hold the cards so I could read my Hayr hair-restorer copy. The director gave the signal, the tally light went on. The cue card stand-in fainted. The excitement of being "on TV" was too much for her! I had to wing it.

That faint-hearted cue card girl taught stations a valuable lesson. Soon after, WABC began testing ad-lib abilities at auditions. "Do an 'Esso' spot," we were told. (That's what Exxon used to be called.) No ad lib, no job.

That was the nub of live commercials: thinking on your feet. Dick Lane, an established movie actor, also worked as a sports and commercial announcer for KTLA-TV out in Los Angeles. Trying to lend a little sophistication to a car commercial, Dick rested one foot up on the front bumper. Suddenly the bumper came off the car. Dick lost his balance. Not exactly bulging with Mr. Universe muscles, he deadpanned, "Guess I'll have to stop taking those body-building courses."

And what do you think you would have done in Joe Franklin's shoes? Yes, the host of television's longest-running talk show, "The Joe Franklin Show" and the man known as Mr. Nostalgia, was once a commercial announcer with the best of us. Listen to Joe selling Melmac dinnerware. "This beautiful dish set is a MIRA-CLE of modern science," Joe assures the audience. "It is pos-i-tive-ly indestructible, ladies and gentlemen. It ab-so-lute-ly cannot be broken, cracked or chipped. GUAR-ANTEED to last for an entire lifetime!" But as he gestures in his enthusiasm, the entire set crashes to the floor and before the eyes of the unbelieving viewers, it breaks, cracks and chips. Joe rebounds in a sec. Sadly surveying the carnage, he shakes his head and says, "And that, ladies and gentlemen, that is what COULD happen to you if you don't buy 'Melmac' dishes!"

Franklin had barely recovered from the great fall of china when he was snafued again. A Necchi sewing machine disappeared just minutes before airtime. The floorman asked the stagehand who had placed the Necchi near an emergency exit, but the stagehand "didn't know nothin' about no Necchi." And you know where that left Joe. You try demonstrating a sewing machine that isn't there. This mysterious phenomenon —the Vanishing Product—occurred at all studios. Washers, dryers, vacuum cleaners . . . they all walked through those exits. And, we announcers were certain, into the waiting arms of the stagehands.

Well . . . thinking on your feet was a breeze compared to thinking off your feet. During a freelance stint at WABC, I hosted a movie show. While they were changing reels, I pitched Singer sewing machines. Usually I didn't leave the set between breaks, but on this particular day I had a crucial phone call to make. It was about a one-minute trek out of the cavernous studio and down the hall to the phone, but the AD guaranteed that the movie reel—Carole Lombard in *No Man of Her Own* —would run eight minutes. I dropped my nickel and committed a heinous crime for announcers: lost track of time. "LeBow, get your ass in here—you're on in twenty seconds!" the AD hollered. Jesse Owens couldn't have run that stretch in twenty seconds—and leave time to catch his breath. "Oh, shit," I berated myself. You missed a cue around here and you were out. Then I spotted a dolly—the kind they used to move heavy equipment around with. I leaped on, scootered right to my cue mark and jumped off in true Douglas Fairbanks style. Only I fell flat on my back!

The AD bent over me and wildly signaled the director: "Jesus, hold up . . . do something . . . go to black. You can't come in on him now—he's not moving, he could be hurt."

"I don't give a fuck if the bastard is dead," the director answered. I could hear him through the AD's earphones. "We are coming live—now."

I opened my eyes and the camera's red light glared malevolently at me. I wasn't going to let that son-of-a-bitch director ruin my career. LeBow was down—but not out.

Smiling into the lens, I said, "Hi! This is how relaxed you can be when you're using a Singer sewing machine."

Oddly enough, when we had spectacular screw-ups like these, sales went up! I checked several early advertisers who confirmed this. The public seemed to trust us more when things went wrong. Maybe they transferred their empathy for us to the product itself. Allow me to take you to the set of the Roto-Broil commercial for such an example. Lester Morris, a 275-pound veteran pitchman from Atlantic City, is the "Roto-Chef." He demonstrates the delicious ease of cooking a chicken in the Roto-Broil, which is an oven-broiler with a spit. Now, as it was impossible to broil a chicken in the time of the commercial, a realistic wax chicken was impaled on the spit. Per usual, Morris skewered his bird ahead of time and heaved his bulk off the set.

Enter: a BRAND-NEW stagehand. He's like a rabbit quivering in a row of lettuce. So much to do and so little time.

Furniture—in correct position? Check!

Broiler—on table? Check!

Broiler—plugged in? Check— Wait. NO!

The stagehand rectifies that error.

Commercial begins. Morris waxes enthusiastic about Roto-Broil, and at the end of the spiel he opens the broiler door to reveal the succulent chicken. It's a blob of melted wax drip-drip-dripping to the floor. Morris-the-pro can't even ad lib, he's so undone. He's going to murder the entire Stagehands Union. But before he leaves the studio he gets word that Roto-Broil order phones are ringing off the hook like never before.

As you can plainly see, back then most commercials weren't "produced," they were just plain "done." They were shot in the studio, with a cast of one, sometimes two. An announcer, maybe a pretty girl and the product. No musical scores. Who figured that someday there'd be trucks falling from the sky, Broadway-type productions for soft drinks and flying saucers landing? It was mom-and-pop production time and costs could be added up on your fingers. Two hundred dollars? For most sponsors that was pricey.

One reason for this minimalism was that the sponsor cupboard was bare. Ad agencies were caught short by the TV explosion. They didn't have the staff for producing commercials. Sometimes a client snuck around the agency and went directly to a station to buy time. But sponsors were finding that they couldn't depend on getting good, honest advice from their agencies. And the cause was money.

The average agency was billing huge amounts of moolah for network radio. They lived off their fifteen-percent fee of the product, talent and cost of advertising paid by the client. A major radio program could have a budget of a half-million dollars per show. Fifteen percent of that bought a lot of execs a lot of good living. A television show, on the other hand, could hover dismally around $25,000 or $30,000. What's fifteen percent of that? Forget it! So, many ad agencies told their clients not to buy television. "Trust us," they smiled. "It's not a good sales tool." The honest agencies, though, began to dabble in television, anticipating a day when it would rival radio's sales might. Such agencies as BBD&O, Cunningham and Walsh, Donohue and Coe, Y&R had crystal balls in their offices.

However, ad agencies made up for lost revenues—or low ones—soon enough. They billed their clients nice sums for rehearsing the commercials. You know, studio time, director and so on. But the trick was to rehearse over . . . and over . . . and over. In 1955 I was hired as the Aero Shave man for "Douglas Edwards with the News" on CBS. Once a week for an entire year, I had to rehearse for the agency. They didn't change one single word of that commercial. It was a waste of time for me, not to mention the money being thrown away by Aero Shave. To make my point, I brought my four-year-old son Steve along one day. He rattled off the commercial perfectly. "Look," I said. "Even a kid can memorize this commercial. We don't need rehearsals!"

"Are you out of your mind?" they protested. "Get out —you and the kid. Come back when you're ready to work."

The ad agencies didn't have to talk some clients out of switching to television. Many didn't recognize the immense scale of television's selling power. It's easy to call these businesses shortsighted now, but let's look at the situation from their standpoint. There weren't a lot of sets out there—by mid-year in 1948, only about 375,000. Some large companies got their feet wet in TV —like Chevrolet and Schaefer beer. You did have national sponsors such as Texaco and Esso for top-rated shows. But with the mistakes made on live commercials, they wondered, "Is this worth it?" Kellogg's Corn Flakes sponsored a Saturday-night comedy show on NBC.

The commercial had a superb announcer, Ed Herlihy! Fantastic director, Fred Kelly! (You'll hear more about this half of the Gene-and-Fred Kelly Brothers dance team in another chapter.) Gist of the commercial was this: Ed sat at a table with a bowl of Corn Flakes in front of him. The TV audience would see Ed's spoon dip into the bowl and come up laden with cereal and they would hear Ed's smooth, well-modulated voice. They would not see *him*. At least that was the script. But it got revised by a dimwit cameraman. Instead of keeping the camera on the cereal bowl, he panned to Ed—and gave viewers an unforgettable eyeful. Ed was tossing spoon after spoon of the cereal over his shoulder, at the same time as he was saying that he loved Corn Flakes so much he couldn't begin his day without them! There was a good reason that the script called for the cameraman to keep the damn camera off Ed. Ed couldn't deliver his lines if his mouth was full! The ad agency—blameless here—nevertheless got nailed by the Kellogg's execs. But in another disaster, the admen were guilty as charged.

This agency booked household-name announcer Rex Marshall to do live commercials on NBC and ABC at the same time. Obviously impossible—but did the adman notice this? Uh-uh. The harried TV director, Freddie Bartholomew (the same Freddie who'd been one of Hollywood's biggest child stars), discovered the error with only ten minutes before airtime, and called the agency. The screaming, whining adman responsible for the screw-up ordered Bartholomew to get an NBC staff announcer to stand in for Marshall while Rex performed live at ABC. Not a perfect solution, of course, but at least a reasonable one. Oh yeah? Ad execs and NBC crew were congratulating each other as the stand-in announcer intoned the commercial lines, following the cue cards perfectly. Then chaos. Calamity. And critical crisis as the substitute ended with, "Thank you . . . Goodnight . . . This is Rex Marshall speaking."

(Quick, bartender, double Scotches for everyone.)

Other sponsors saw no profit in advertising to relatively few, when they could reach hundreds of thousands daily on radio and in print. Furthermore, many potential sponsors got terrible reception on their sets. To lure them into the fold, stations practiced a little harmless deception. (So they said.) Dumont, for instance, juiced up their top-of-the-line television model and installed it personally in the sponsor's house. (They didn't inform him that even if he saw his commercial, most viewers—his potential buyers—would still be getting lousy reception.)

A further drawback to TV advertising was the black-and-white. Products with color as a selling point didn't make an impression. And packages with the color red were a problem, since red didn't visualize. But certain sponsors got around that. When I nabbed the first commercials for Ralston's Wheat Chex and Corn Chex, I saw it as a treat. I loved cereals and ate them guilelessly at the Horn & Hardart Automat for breakfast every morning. But when I hit the set, instead of the familiar bright red-and-white checked boxes, I found a pair of the dingiest you could imagine. It took the fun out of that commercial—but it had to be. In order for the box to show up as red-and-white, it had to be specially made in black-and-white. Marlboro cigarettes, packaged in lush red, used the same trick. They ordered "commercial" boxes in gray-and-white. If viewers saw what we announcers did, sales would have plunged immediately!

So, by and large, TV was a neighborhood business aiming for local trade. And local meant yokel.

Stations were crying for sponsors. And some wise guys sniffed out this pot of gold immediately. I call them the electronic medicine men, because they were like the old traveling medicine shows in the nineteenth century. Out in frontier sections of the country, clever entrepreneurs found a public starving for entertainment and goods. And with nary a demographic survey or consumer poll, they devised a surefire way to make a buck. Pitching a pitch and spieling a spiel, they sold lotions to cure baldness, concoctions to calm bowels, oils to banish impotence and creams to create youth.

In the late 1940s, there was another hungry public. This one had been squeezed by the Depression and then rationed by the War. The consumer marketplace was a deflated balloon waiting to be filled—with hot air. While the giants of industry stuck their big toe in the TV waters, these medicine men dove in headfirst. The stations snapped them up. So what if they offered crap? It sold phenomenally. Kitchen gadgets, pots and pans, furniture, watches—it was junk-o-mania. How could it not be? Many of the salesmen were recruited from Atlantic City, Asbury Park and other boardwalks along the East Coast —the magnet for shim-sham pitchmen around the country.

This super-sellathon was partly the result of so many sets being bought by people in the middle to lower classes. Eighty percent of sets in the nation belonged to these income groups, reported *The Wall Street Journal* in 1948. I can't find a better statement of the situation than this by the advertising manager of General Foods Corporation, A. M. Whitlock, who told the paper, "There's little question that television is of more value to the unsophisticated than the rich. For the first time, the average guy with a limited entertainment budget, can bring the glamour of the theatre and night clubs right into his own living room for the whole family to see." But not only glamour. Into his home came the medicine men.

Let's meet one of them in his own home. Big Max is a 300-pound pot-and-pan entrepreneur, who is a sponsor on Channel 11 in New York City. A year or so into its history, Channel 11 had been stiffed by one sponsor too many. When it came time to collect from the business—after the spot had been on the air—the business had gone out of business! So Channel 11 now collects in advance, in cash. And it's time salesman Ben Sckolnick's duty to collect from Big Max this Friday afternoon, as Big Max's spots go on Friday and Saturday evening. Mrs. Big Max lets Sckolnick into the apartment, a grand penthouse whose last tenant was the musical genius Jascha Heifitz. The place is now cluttered with cartons of pots, and the only music around is a strange chant over by the window. Big Max is doing an Indian rain dance. "It's snowing, it's snowing!" he's singing and panting and sweating with all his chins and his pot bellies quivering and his pots rattling in their cages. "Don't ja get it?" he says to Sckolnick. "Those chumps'll be stuck home in front of MY SPOTS all weekend. I'll make a fortune!"

Very true. Television proved itself as a selling machine. Sight plus sound added up to astronomical figures. Some medicine men made millions. Fortunes. Earl Scheib—"We'll paint any car, any color"—started his empire on the tube. The wacky used car salesman "Mad Man Muntz" switched to TV and grew even richer. Some of these mini-Rockefellers went on to Hollywood. I did commercials for an ad agency owned by Les Persky. Persky is now one of moviedom's most successful producers. Recognize the title *Hair*? Or *Equus*? That's

Persky. He learned his wheeling and dealing in television. Little Les was the consummate producer-entrepreneur-director.

Coaxing me into a car wax commercial, Persky sent his spindly, soft arms flailing in every direction. "Tougher! Harder! More intense . . . and at the same time . . . gentler and warmer." I worked for Persky for three or four years, so I must have been as crazy as he was. He was unstoppable once he got a client. In 1954 he upstaged national elections with his client Roto-Broil. This was the first year the networks were covering the congressional elections on a large scale, and Persky realized he could make Roto-Broil, already a big company, even bigger. He bought NBC from 6:30 to 9:00 p.m. He bought CBS from 11:00 p.m. to midnight. And when he learned that CBS had no sponsors after that, he persuaded them to let him run Roto-Broil until 5 a.m. By two in the morning, Persky was harpooning anyone he could to go on the air. Roto-Broil's owner, Albert Klinghoffer, did a spot for him. (But Albert's brother, Leon, was too shy to appear on camera.*) Persky even tried to talk New York Governor-elect Averell Harriman to do a pitch for Roto-Broil. The next day the *New York Times* commented in this vein: "It's not clear whether Democrats or Republicans won the election, but we're rather sure that Roto-Broil did."

Small stores took a chance on television, too. The rates were low and the bigger department stores weren't muscling in. Local companies like Ripley Clothes, a "nothing" men's suit business, started advertising on TV and mushroomed from one store to sixteen in two years.

---

*Does the name Leon Klinghoffer sound familiar? Tragically, he did appear on television some thirty years later, when he was murdered by terrorists aboard the ill-fated cruise ship *Achille Lauro.*

Sunset Appliances expanded its five stores to twenty-five —an empire. But some companies hadn't been hit with the King Midas virus. I hosted a kiddie Western film show as "Cowboy Guy" for Gold Seal Dairy. This outfit had done so well on TV that it had expanded beyond its wildest dreams into a nightmare. It was outgrowing the manageable, friendly size that the owners liked. Will you believe that they canceled their sponsorship? When I had to turn in my "Cowboy Guy" hat, I was sorry to lose a sponsor, but part of me was cheering Gold Seal on for valuing something more than the Almighty Buck.

The pay scale for commercial announcers was generally about three degrees above zero then and we were fond of bitterly pointing out that these outfits couldn't have made their mints without us. Today you're used to seeing company owner or presidents sell their own products on the air. But in the beginning most hucksters were pros. Like Joel Holt, the King of the Call-Now commercials. Put Holt and a sales pitch together and there was bound to be excitement—and not always involving sales figures. On one commercial, the camera was to "accidentally" come upon him while he was engrossed in working at a desk. You know the setup. The announcers starts up and says, "Oh, hello!" Which is what Holt did—but he jerked his head so hard his toupee flopped down over his eyes. Did that embarrass him? Not enough to quit TV.

Joel had nearly given his life in the line of duty, at the tender age of twenty-five, for a kitchen chopper. I was hosting yet another movie program and King Joel was the demonstrator. Perhaps I've given you the idea that Holt was an ordinary pitchman, but nothing could be more wrong. Holt wasn't merely an announcer. He was a member of that announcer subspecies that was more like magicians. They could rat-tat-tat their lines while they showed audiences how to assemble toys, work vacuum cleaners and . . . use choppers.

"Even a child can work this amazing kitchen instrument that cuts meal preparation time in HALF!" Joel orated in a mere two and a half seconds. Then I chimed in, "Yes, ladies and gentlemen, this incredible new chopper is like ten kitchen utensils in one!"

King Joel, a tall, handsome blond, held court behind a table lined up with cabbages, tomatoes, onions, eggs and carrots. His hands moved faster than a speeding bullet as he guillotined a cabbage in his revolutionary shredder. But this day not fast enough. I heard a slight intake of breath. Blood was running down the chopper onto the table. I moved closer to Joel and snuck a glance out of the corner of my eye. He'd cut off part of his little finger.

"See for yourself that the blade never loses its sharpness," said Joel as he continued mangling the cabbage.

More blood.

"Thanks to the wizardry of modern science, this blade never dulls."

The vegetables were starting to swim in the red stuff. I was starting to get sick.

My turn. "This incredible kitchen chopper—ten utensils in one—is yours if you call IL 9-9999 now. Call now and receive a free gift, plus this three-in-one pan and a free cookbook! Yes, a cookbook! Call now, that's IL 9-9999 for this incredible offer while they last!."

Joel was slumping now and ghastly white, but still gripping his chopper. One of the AD's pried it from his hand and clamped a tourniquet on the finger. The floor crew got Joel out to a taxi and he fainted before they got to Bellevue.

But the viewers never saw any blood. Remember—red didn't show on the screen. King Joel knew this and wouldn't stop in the middle of his demonstration. The pitch was everything.

It was guys like King Joel and me—I'll take the blame too—who pioneered the CALL NOW! pitches you suffer from today. We crammed 100 words into 30 seconds. We shouted. We screamed. We pounded again, again and again. Because that's what we'd learned from radio.

Studies done for radio had proved that words had to be repeated several times for people to really hear them. And television brought another dimension to this torture: sight. Scientific research indicated that an image had to remain on screen for at least six seconds to be noticed by the mind. That's where the cards came in with their flashing telephone numbers and addresses. But six seconds wasn't long enough for sponsors. If the public needed six seconds to notice, why not eighteen seconds to remember forever?

Our crass huckstering didn't faze the public. To them, television gave products cachet overnight. Tuesday you'd never heard of Excel watches, as I'll call them. By Thursday, Excel was modestly calling itself the "World's Greatest Watch"—and getting away with it.

The public was helpless. No consumer protection. No Ralph Nader. Only the electronic medicine men. And some of them were greedy. Each time I hear a politician or businessman bleat that business can regulate itself without government interference, I remember the fledgling days of television commercials. I also remember ABC program director Paul Mowrey's 1947 prediction that television would dictate "absolute honesty" for advertising, because viewers could see products for themselves. To quote Ralph Kramden, "Har-har-harrity-har-har!"

Right off, TV and advertising figured out how to use sight to dupe the public. Take your standard floor wax commercial. Funny thing how those floors gleamed like glass. . . . It could happen that an assistant director, such as Herb Holmes, might be working on a TV crew that might be working on a commercial for, say, Beacon Wax. To "help" the wax shine beautifully, a layer of glass might be placed on top of the Beacon-Waxed floor.

Or, let's look at the imagination that went into bamboozling women about a cosmetic from Charles Antell, a "miracle" cream that made crow's-feet vanish instantly. The miracle wasn't the product, it was the commercial. To produce it required no less than one of the Westmores, Hollywood's makeup dynasty. Westmore carefully painted the crow's-feet on a beautiful model's flawless face. Next, he and the technical crew worked for days on the type of lighting needed to accomplish the "miracle" and make the lines invisible. On the actual commercial, people saw the model's "unsightly" lines, saw Westmore rub the Antell cream on them, and then (as some studio lights came up and others went down) they saw the lines vanish RIGHT BEFORE THEIR EYES!

As for the electronic medicine men, they didn't even bother with these elaborate disguises. They had their own techniques for suckering you. Let's say you see a product on TV. Storm windows for $7. Or a sewing machine, $26. Wow! Cheap! Catch is, a salesman will come to your home. In two minutes, the guy's your best friend. He tells you confidentially that you're such a great person, he doesn't want you to be stuck with the product you saw on TV. It's inferior. No, he's going to put himself out and sell you a superior product . . . for five or ten times that much. Or maybe you send away for product. But it never arrives.

Arthur Godfrey was innocently involved in such a scam in 1951. His sponsor, Lipton Tea, offered a kitchen knife in exchange for 50 cents and a Lipton Tea label. Godfrey did his usual irresistible pitch, 164,000 orders came in, and waited. Turns out the advertising man in charge of this promotion had diverted the money to a new Caddy convertible, a new suit and a trip to Palm

Springs.

Or maybe you go to a store to buy the product. You're greeted with "Gee, we don't have that model in stock now, but I happen to have one you'll like better. It's a little more . . ."

I was unknowingly in on a medicine-man pitch for Excel watches, at Channel 11 in 1948. One Saturday after hosting the matinee movie, I went downstairs to the Automat with fellow announcer John Tillman, a.k.a. the Alabama Assassin, for coffee and banana cream pie.

Tillman got his label because he was from Alabama and he possessed a sixth sense about who was going to get canned. He'd casually drop in on the victim, ask to "borrow" a lamp or something and then keep it when the guy got the ax. After a while, when you saw Tillman heading for your office, you started packing. But the Alabama Assassin had the best-furnished office of any of us.

The Automat at Forty-second Street and Third Avenue was downstairs in the Channel 11/*Daily News* building. (The *Daily News* owned television station Channel 11.) In 1948, successful professional people weren't ashamed to carry their own tray with food on it. The Horn & Hardart automats were some of the best places in town to be. Everybody ate there. (When I worked at radio station WMGM in my pre-TV days, Rudy Vallee used to invite some of us younger announcers for an evening out with him. First stop, the Automat, to "dine," and then a 25-cent movie. Rudy was so cheap, we heard, that he had a sign in his bathroom at home, reminding guests not to use too much toilet paper.) Anyway, two elderly ladies in their late sixties approached our table, and Tillman and I stretched into our fan smiles. He and I had a nice cutthroat competition going about who especially was favored by little old ladies, or LOLS, as we called them. But not this day.

"You boys ought to be ashamed," admonished LOL Number One. They were dressed to chill in navy blue suits, navy blue hats with navy blue veils and Dr. Scholl's sensible shoes.

"Excuse me, ma'am?" The Alabama Assassin's accent was honeyed with respect.

"We thought you were such decent boys," remonstrated LOL Number Two.

My piping-hot coffee froze with fear. All performers' contracts carried a morals clause. No fistfights, shoplifting, adultery or any other actions that reflect poorly on the sponsor—or you're out.

Tillman tried again, more respectful—and much more worried—this time. "Ma'am, I assure you both that my colleague and I don't know what you mean. Have we seen each other before?"

"We've seen you," was the answer. "You sold us those watches."

That was true. We were selling Excels—and wearing Excels. Gratis, of course. And ours kept time on a dime. I showed my watch to both LOLS.

"Don't try to fool us," said LOL Number One. "We took ours to our local repairman and he told us, 'Ladies, you've been robbed. These watches have no movements.'"

The pie bet was off. Tillman and I practically ran to the program director's office and gave him the bleary news. It turned out that our LOLS were right. We'd been had. The Alabama Assassin, Channel 11, me—and thousands of honest citizens.

Excel had delivered watches with superb movements to station execs and personnel, but the ones shipped from their warehouses to customers had rinky-dink movements or possibly none at all. The watches were taken off the air. And about a year later, stations began demanding that sponsors put money in escrow. If the product did prove defective, the television station could make good. That was only a stopgap. The public was taken and retaken. By 1954, the New York Better Business Bureau geared up for an investigation, and a March 14 *New York Journal American* headline blared:

### DRIVE IS OPENED
### ON TV HUCKSTERS

You can be sure that most of the gentlemen referred to in the headline were lolling on their yachts, yukking it up over the newspaper story.

(The papers never got this story about an inside huckster. A TV exec who jerked around honest sponsors in New York City, little stores and small companies who trusted him. This was the Channel 11 general manager, G. Bennet Larson. He sent his time salesmen like Ben Sckolnick into the field, ordering them to promise whatever was needed to clinch a deal. Don't worry, he told them, I can get out of anything you tell them. And he did. He promised sponsors a certain number of spots, or certain times for spots, and never delivered. When Larson retired from Channel 11, the time sales staff received letters from many sponsors to the effect that "Thank God, that snake and *&$##xx&&** is gone!")

To go back to our commercials . . . No LOLS were used on them. "Where's the beef?" with eighty-something Clara was a concept thankfully far in the future. We got gorgeous, young, big-eyed, perfect creatures who filled bathing suits, stroked refrigerators, smiled invitingly at pots and pans. And some TV show hostesses like the now-syndicated columnist Cindy Adams (a stunner!) and Faye Emerson did their own pitches. From time to time, one of our refrigerator models was Jacqueline Susann, a dark-haired aristocratic beauty. None of us could believe that it was Jackie who wrote *Valley of the Dolls* years later. Studio gossip was that she was as cold as the fridge she demonstrated.

The announcer would say: "With this beautiful new refrigerator you get a freezer . . ." (Jacqueline would smile generously and point, palm up, at the freezer.)

". . . two drawers inside . . ." (She'd graciously open the door and gesture grandly at the crisper drawers.)

". . . and," the announcer would finish, "you get everything, including the fine design of this blahblah refrigerator." (Jacqueline would slowly sweep her hand up the length of the appliance.)

"She gets paid for this?" we announcers asked each other.


I did sports and news and game shows and interview shows and whatnot on old-fashioned TV. But nothing was as big a challenge as pioneering live commercials. There was an immense problem in becoming accustomed to showing up on screen. This sounds farfetched today. You own videocameras and can tape—and then see yourselves—on your TV sets at home. But put yourselves in our shoes. We had to remind ourselves constantly that people could *see* us.

In 1948 the first New York Knickerbocker basketball games were being telecast and Stan Lomax, a heavyweight announcer of the day, was the sportscaster. Sponsor: Old Gold cigarettes. Lomax smoked incessantly as he called the game—but it was a pipe.

These days, the main camera shoots from behind the sportscaster, looking over his shoulder. So he sees the same view the audience does. But nobody understood that necessity yet. Lomax called the game with the camera facing him from across the court.

Break for commercial. Lomax was waxing eloquent about Old Gold—and he was terrific! But at the same time he was puffing on his pipe. It never occurred to him that the camera was picking him up. Old Gold threatened to cancel if Lomax wouldn't give up his pipe. He threatened to quit. They said go ahead. "I'll give up the pipe," he offered grudgingly. "But I won't smoke those crappy cigarettes." And he didn't.

And if we did recall we were on camera, we didn't fully understand the impact of the visual on the public. The ad agency had brainstormed a new angle for my hockey sponsor, Schaefer beer. I would wave a "magic wand" over a glass of beer, as I described this magical brew. (Corny?) They even had a special "Schaefer magic wand" made for me. (Corny.)

Commercial times. I couldn't find the damn wand. Like Lomax, my mind was on the game. Not the product. Not the fact that I was on television. So I did what seemed to be the smart thing. I picked up a pencil and waved it over the beer, delivering my new "magic" lines. But we got letters. I was called jerk, weirdo and stupid for attempting to fool the public with a pencil. Viewers watched every move we made.

Sponsors too. Their motto was "Seeing Is Believing." If the public SAW the announcer using the product, they'd be more motivated to buy it. So we had to smoke, drink, eat, button, unbutton on camera. Some of us, like the Alabama Assassin, had never smoked a cigarette in our lives. But on a Friday afternoon, the ad agency gave John Tillman a pack of Parliaments, the official Parliament ashtray with the distinctive Parliament "V" and told him to start puffing. Oh, God. Tillman couldn't inhale without choking and tearing. He made smoking so undesirable that single-handedly he could have ruined the tobacco industry.

Saturday morning he called the account exec in despair. "I can't do this," he said. "Why don't you get Paul Henreid? He can light up two at once."

"Too late, John. It's the weekend. And we want

YOU." (John's dark good looks and smooth voice had made him a killer salesman on the air.)

Tillman didn't sleep that night. But early Sunday he had a vision. He called the agency exec. "Will you buy this?" he asked hoarsely. "Camera comes in on me. I light up. I take a draw. While I hold smoke in my mouth, camera pans to ashtray. I blow smoke into ashtray and put cigarette down. Camera follows tight on my hand to show only smoke, ashtray and 'Parliament' logo."

Ingenious! But Tillman still threw up before each commercial twice a week for thirteen weeks—and this for a thirteen-second commercial.

Drinking was another minefield. At that time we were allowed to drink alcohol on the air. But try taking a manly sip of foam-topped beer and not ending up with a white mustache. Once I got the hang of it, though, I became known as the best beer salesman on television. I did hundreds of commercials for Pabst Blue Ribbon, Rheingold, Schaefer and others. But the rewards of neat beer drinking were offset by my wipeout with wine. And naturally it had to happen while I was hosting a show with Eddie Fisher, Milton Berle and a constellation of stars I wanted to impress.

It was a matter of digestion. Manischewitz had a wine that was a killer. I'd take a sip, restrain a belch, say "Excuse me," and continue while the director died. "Son of a bitch, LeBow," he hollered. "Can't you drink without that belching? You're murdering the commercial." I tried. At home, my wife tried to de-belch me with practice drills. Deep breath out. Sip. Slowly. But the belches reached disgusting decibels. The camera crew took bets on how many belches I could produce in one spot. Why Manischewitz stood by me, I don't know. I was hoping they'd dump me. Anything was better than humiliating myself in public.

One night my director approached me, carrying a

bottle. The guy was smiling! "We won't have to hear your fucking belches anymore!" he said. "From now on, you're drinking this." "This" was grape juice. The same color as Manischewitz's purple popper. And, as we all forgot, made from the same thing as wine: grapes. I popped a big one that night, and from then on it was colored water. To this day, I don't like red wine.

Not until chance brought a brilliant director to Channel 11 did commercials get some real class. A refugee from Hollywood, ex-child star Freddie Bartholomew taught me, and others, how to conduct ourselves more naturally in front of the camera, how to "relate" to it, to be "at home." That was his professional contribution. He added life to the station in other ways, as you'll read in the special section on Freddie B.

Gradually there was a lull in the screaming commercials. The head of Channel 11 ordered: "Stop shouting! We're supposed to be guests in people's living rooms!" Oh, sure, there was some modicum of sympathy for the public. But the real turning point was because of the competition. "Do it like Godfrey," we were told at auditions. Godfrey made you think he had stumbled across a product—and he was simply passing his observations along to you. He talked in a quiet, intimate manner that women went crazy for. And he sold big.

Sponsors loved Godfrey. Doing commercials was an art, not just a job, people were realizing. Commercial announcing schools sprang up. The prime teacher of conversational commercials was Betty Cashman, who ran her own school. Her trick was to get the announcer to connect with the audience by believing that he was talking to one person, a little old lady sitting on a porch in Iowa. After a time, we announcers began identifying ourselves with the Cashman Code. "Have you met the little old lady from Iowa?" If the answer was, "She's great. She listens to every word I say," we knew we'd met a fellow graduate.

As sponsors became more powerful, they wanted more control over us—their mouthpiece. When we auditioned for a new commercial, we had to fill out a form indicating the commercials we'd done in the past six months. If we'd done a juice commercial, landing a job for another liquid—even a beer—was impossible! We couldn't sell milk to kids if we'd sold beer. If we'd sold Soup A, we were out of the running for Soup B. And if you lied on your application, God help you. An aggrieved sponsor was a vicious sponsor who wouldn't hire you again.

But job control wasn't enough. Sponsors interfered in our private lives. When Hudson automobiles signed me as their boxing announcer, their honchos huddled with me and said, "Guy, we think you should own one of our cars."

I knew that car companies didn't hand out their autos to announcers. And I certainly didn't make enough to have two cars. "I have a car," I told them. It was a Dodge, four years old but very dependable. Hudson was a relatively inferior car. Not a lemon. I just preferred the Dodge.

The honchos hemmed. "You see," they explained, "we think you'd present a much stronger image if you drove the car your audience sees you selling."

I didn't see why I should have to spend my money just because I was being hired to do their commercial. That was like paying them back for hiring me. But they were adamant. The best I could do was get them to "give" me a car for one-third of the cost. But a new car is a new car, and I drove around feeling pretty snazzy in my blue Hudson. Then a newspaper ran an exposé about sponsors. Among the guilty, according to this article, was the president of Hudson. He was driving a Cadillac. To hell with you bastards, I said. I ditched the Hudson and bought a Packard convertible. No sponsor was running my life again.

Well . . . not quite. Sponsors had as many holds as an octopus. If you were doing Parliament, you'd sure as hell better not be spotted in public with a pack of Camels. If you sold Schaefer beer—that was the only beer you could have, whether you were having more than one or not. I didn't leave my house without double-checking that I was taking the RIGHT product with me. Those sponsors had spies everywhere.

But to enjoy the true flavor of early sponsors, you have to meet Joe Rudnick, owner of the Sunset Appliance stores and sponsor of wrestling on Channel 11. Gentleman Joe and Channel 11 almost parted over a natural event: an eclipse of the moon on April 12, 1949. Nature had the audacity to schedule this eclipse during a wrestling show—without conferring with Rudnick first. Channel 11 wanted to preempt the match to telecast the rare event, the first total eclipse of the moon since 1844.

Gentleman Joe wasn't having it. He stormed up to the head offices at Channel 11 and caused an ungentlemanly ruckus amongst the Brooks Brothered execs with his cheap suit, Brooklyn accent and scruffy shoes. One B. O'Sullivan suspended breathing every time Gentleman Joe was near him.

As the wrestling announcer, I was asked to be in on this bout. Gentleman Joe's bow tie spun like a pinwheel as he threatened to pull out his sponsorship "for good!" B. O'Sullivan pleaded as to how an eclipse didn't happen every day. Another exec ventured a compromise: five extra spots—free—if Rudnick would just let them do the eclipse. But Gentleman Joe wasn't going to be taken advantage of by these "sharpies." Finally he just wore them down.

The compromise was . . . well . . . unnatural. Channel 11 could televise the eclipse for about an hour and a half.

But the audience glued to its set that night saw (to borrow a description from the *New York Times*, Wednesday, April 13): "Starting at 9:28 P.M. a shadow of the earth cast a dark gray crescent across the moon. Creeping slowly across the brightness, the shadow completely veiled the moon at 10:28 . . ." And at this moment, people saw another rare event. Superimposed on the moon, which showed up as a bright disc on the television screen, was:

CALL SUNSET NOW

FOR THE LOWEST PRICE TV'S

HICKORY 6-4000

That same day, editorials in city newspapers commented in this vein: "How nutty can that television be? All the city population had to do was to open their windows, look up and see the eclipse for themselves. And they didn't need Joe Rudnick's permission to do it, either!"

*Read All About It:*

# Tales from the Dumb Side

From coast to coast, not all the nutty things were on television. . . .

## HIS FISH ARE SUCKERS
## FOR TV COWBOYS

WAYNE, Pa., April 15 (AP)—Maj. William J. Bates, Jr., keeps a goldfish bowl near his television set.

Says the Major, commandant of Valley Forge Military Academy: "The fish swim 'round and 'round ignoring the TV vaudeville shows and news programs. But when there is a Western movie the fish stop swimming and watch the cowboys in action."

Bates insists the fish never miss the cow-boys.

*(1950)*

## CALLS TELEVISION
## A HOME-WRECKER

OKLAHOMA CITY, Okla., May 17—A father pleaded guilty here to a charge of wife and child abandonment. He admitted he didn't work because he spent all his time watching television.

Judge Jess I. Miracle gave Delbert Jones Jr., 25, a two-year suspended sentence and warned him "to get to work or go to prison."

*(1950)*

## TV MURDER IN HUNTINGTON

March 18—A metal worker was a guest at a neighbor's house celebrating the acquisition of a 20-inch TV set.

Dorothy Kirsten, sweet-voiced Metropolitan Opera singer, came on.

"I do not like her singing," said Steiner, whipping out a pistol. "Who needs it?"

Rooty toot toot three times he shot.

The TV set was dead when the police arrived.

*(New York Post, 1952)*

## RADIO AND TELEVISION

### An Irate Video Owner Has Come Up With an Unusual Solution to Your Chief TV Bête Noir

By JACK GOULD

October 22—Police of West Hempstead, L.I., have taken away the revolver of Frank P. Walsh, electrician and night industrial guard, who on Sunday evening fired a bullet into the picture tube of his receiver because he couldn't stand the noise any longer. They should give him back his gun; his work has barely started.

Mr. Walsh, who was trying to get some sleep in an upstairs bedroom, drew a bead on his console just as the Abbott and Costello program got under way on Channel 4. As anyone who saw the program can attest, Mr. Walsh is a man of discernment.

No doubt it will be only a matter of days before the Russians lay claim to Mr. Walsh: the genius who uninvented television. His public-spirited act opens new vistas for the television industry. No longer need the broadcasters worry about popularity ratings or how many receivers are tuned to a show. They can just go around and count the pieces.

According to the latest communiqué from West Hempstead, the Federal Communications Commission isn't joking about operating in the public interest, convenience and necessity, they'll move immediately to keep Mr. Walsh in a fresh supply of receivers. At least he found a use for the focus control. With just a modicum of effort there's no reason why cathode-homocide can't supplant canasta. The first step is for the newspaper to stop listing program highlights. Thanks to Mr. Walsh, they may now be identified as "targets for tonight."

Mr. Walsh has not yet detailed what other programs are scheduled to attract his fire, but there's no reason why the individual viewer can't make his own nominations. Some possibilities readily come to mind:

The announcer who insists that a cigarette is mild, milder or mildest.

All middle commercials.

English films that look as if they were taking place at midnight in a cellar.

The synthetic excitement of the masters of ceremonies on giveaway shows.

The after-midnight programs that are straight commercials occasionally interrupted by a movie.

All entertainers who close their program by saying, "Thank you for having us in your home."

Sports announcers who close their "talkathons" by saying, "We hope you enjoyed this as much as we enjoyed bringing it to you."

Comedians who blame their gag writers.

Anyone singing "Wish You Were Here."

*(New York Times, 1952)*

### *But Who Is She?*

## FACE STAYS ON TV SCREEN
## EVEN AFTER SET IS TURNED OFF

Special to the Herald Tribune

BLUE POINT, R.I., December 10—A television set that frightens children stood in exile today in a remote corner of Jerry Travers' home, its face to the wall, its speaker silent, its darkened screen haunted by the ghostly image of an unknown woman whose face shimmers eerily in the shadows and won't go away.

Not always was the set an object of fear and loathing. Only yesterday, it occupied a place of honor in the living room, respected for the entertainment it was capable of bringing to Mr. and Mrs. Travers and their three pre-school-aged children.

At 10 a.m. yesterday the children tuned the set to Channel 4 and gathered around to watch the "Ding Dong School," a show now in vogue among the nursery crowd. Suddenly six-year-old Caroline ran to her mother crying, "We can't see it. A face is in the way."

Mrs. Travers, familiar with the inventive twists of a child's imagination, accompanied Caroline to the living room with an indulgent smile. The smile disappeared. A face was in the way.

It was the face of a woman—a woman who stared fixedly from the right side of the seventeen-inch screen, oblivious to the Ding Dong School activities in progress on the left side. Fear gripped the children. They began to whimper.

Mrs. Traverse turned off the set, and then a feeling of apprehension stole over her too. The face was still there, not quite as distinct but quite distinct enough.

Turning the set to the wall so the children could no longer see the screen, she waited for her husband, an aircraft company employee, to return from work. He arrived home at 6 o'clock and they swung the set away from the wall.

They came face to face with the face. It was still there.

Efforts to find an explanation for the lingering image were fruitless at first. Engineers at several television stations not only had never heard of such an occurrence but were inclined to doubt the possibility of it.

"It can't happen," one engineer stated flatly.

A somewhat less dogmatic declaration came from the Radio Corporation of America, which offered an opinion although it is not the manufacturer of the set in question. An RCA technician said an explosion of electrons during a previous program might have burned the image of a woman into the phosphors that coat the inner surface of all television tubes.

"It could happen," he said. "Very rare though."

Neither he nor officials of two television networks questioned could disclose, from a description, the identity of the woman whose face has apparently become a permanent fixture on the Travers' screen.

When Mr. and Mrs. Travers awoke this morning, they examined the set in the hope their unwelcome visitor had departed. She was still on the screen. And the screen is still turned to the wall.

*(1953)*

## WESTCHESTER CURBS TV'S IN RELIEF HOMES

Special to The New York Times

WHITE PLAINS, N.Y., March 10—Spurred by a Nassau County investigation of television sets in possession of relief recipients, the Westchester County Family and Child Welfare Department reported today that it had found ten families in Westchester owning sets. It said most of them would have to relinquish these "luxury" items.

Mrs. Helen C. Young, director of the department, said several of the families professed to have received the sets from "marvelous friends." Two persons with television sets were dropped from relief rolls. One was a Mount Vernon woman who contended that her set had been a gift.

When a war veteran on relief was ordered to sell his set, Mrs. Young received complaints against "depriving a war hero of a little enjoyment." A doctor who had treated the man in a veterans' hospital said he needed television to improve his mental outlook. Mrs. Young said she would let the veteran keep the set.

*(1950)*

## TV A CO-RESPONDENT AS WIFE ASKS TUNEOUT

By HENRY LEE

June 25—For the first time television was named as co-respondent in a Manhattan matrimonial action yesterday, but in the family troubles of Betty Jo and Leighton J. Hill even this newest wonder science took second place to the oldest husbandly flaw known to woman—drinking with the boys.

The trouble with Leighton, Betty Jo complained in a separation action in Supreme Court, is that when he wasn't fussing over his TV set—completely ignoring her—he was away from home altogether at meetings of the LABA (Lexington Ave. Bar Association).

### They Write Notes, Too

LABA, she explained, is "a fictitious organization of drinkers who hold their meetings at the King Cole Bar (St. Regis Hotel) and other bars where liquor is dispensed." Apparently it is also a young organization because the members do something no veteran drinkers would consider for a moment—they send back funny notes to the wives they leave behind.

Thus, one sleepless night, after she had worried, worried and worried about her absent Leighton, he finally rolled home in high humor and presented her with a note which she said had been written in a napkin of the Hotel Shelton bar.

### Certify Attendance

"This is to certify that Mr. Hill was in actual attendance at the official meeting of the LABA," the note said. Wisely, the club official had limited himself in the signature to initials, S.E.C.

Leighton thought it was very funny. Betty Jo didn't. Worse, she said, when he did stop drinking for a while, he almost got posted by LABA, and she received the following communication.

"At a duly constituted meeting of the LABA, a resolution was unanimously passed to wit—ad lib—whereas and how come: Since member Leighton Hill has been conspicuous by his absence from recent meetings of the association, it was resolved that he attend a meeting forthwith or forever after surrender his right to belong to this association." That's the word LABA used; apparently the note was written late in the evening.

### They Forgive, Not She

There was a postscript, Betty Jo said, which annoyed her even more:

"P.S. Hill is now in good standing."

The deduction seemed to be that Leighton suddenly showed up at the meeting and got his foot on the rail just in time to beat the LABA rap.

Besides, Betty Jo said, Hill, being an industrial engineer, fell so madly in love with television that for hours at a time he would sit silently before the set in their apartment, 825 Lexington Ave., completely forgetting her.

### Tries Every Set

"My husband deprived me of companionship and would ignore me completely and devote himself exclusively to watching television programs," Betty Jo stated. "During the brief period of a month and a half he purchased and subsequently traded in every conceivable television model."

*(New York Daily News, 1949)*

# 3 / Low-Tech

*Unbelievable!*

**WCBS-TV SETS RECORD OF
19-DAY AIR SCHEDULE**

—headline from *Radio-TV Daily,*
January 1948

"For Chrissake, Bernie, I don't see any bullpen!" The frantic call came over the CBS sports director's headset.

"I said pan to the bullpen, shmuck. The BULLLLPENN!" Was this an impossible direction? The bullpen was where it always was at Ebbets Field.

"But, Bernie," the cameraman shouted, "I DON'T SEE ANY BULLS!"

If you have any doubts that this actually happened, you can ask Bernie London himself. He survived early television and is living practically unscarred by the experience in New York City.

That simple exchange, circa 1947, gives you nearly the lowest grade of stupidity thriving in television. From that point the only way is up—but not far, let me tell you. Between the Neanderthal technology and the innocents and incompetents working with it, it's a wonder anything got on the air. But how could things have been different? Cameramen and floormen and directors weren't born. They were made—and in a hell of a hurry. Sure, there was some element of professionalism. There were a handful of pros who had nursed TV through even more primitive stages before the war. RCA ran a training center in New Jersey. A few legitimate schools taught directing, and there were eager kids tumbling out of university radio and speech departments. At least they knew a control room when they saw one. But for the most part, crews were hastily patched together from anything available. And that meant anyone who could get out of bed in the morning. It was as if the industry nailed up a huge sign proclaiming: NO EXPERIENCE NECESSARY. WE TRAIN YOU ON THE JOB.

Literally true. One of Bernie London's aides was an intern who has since garnered fame and fortune as producer of "60 Minutes." But when we meet him, Don Hewitt is an ambitious young intern pestering Bernie for a chance to direct the camera. "Just for a commercial, Bernie, come on!" Bernie's soft. He gives in. But there was no "just" in early TV.

Directing is sort of like being an air traffic controller— split-second timing. You must watch the monitor showing what's on TV now and at the same time decide what your next shot will be. This General Motors spot begins with the camera focused on a picture of an auto. It's on a huge card that will take up the entire TV screen. The card rests on a tripod. The tripod is in front of a wall with nothing on either side of it. Time to go into next scene. It's Don's Directing Debut.

"Pan slowly . . ." Don commandingly commands.

And then he goes blank. He forgets how to instruct the cameraman to get to the next shot. Camera keeps panning . . . across picture of car, to edge of card . . .

"OOH OOH OOH!"

That's the only directorial command Don can think of. . . . Camera pans to side of tripod . . . "OOH OOH OOH" . . . to blank space . . . "OOH OOH OOH."

Bernie takes over.

Of course cameramen were no bargain either. Many a one hadn't worked anything more complex than his trusty family Brownie. In fact, when WLWT in Cincinnati flipped its "on" switch, cameras were operated by a self-taught crew of actors and musicians. And if you'd been on the assembly line at a light bulb factory—where some guys came from—your "electronics expertise" could qualify you to be a station engineer. Some of these raw recruits didn't know the difference between an "on" and "off" switch. Could be a few are now pressing pants for a living, but one of them—to this day he remains anonymous—should be honored for making possible the first live nude show on television.

It was the summer of 1947 in New York City. A station —also anonymous to this day—sent a crew to a men's swimming pool to set up cameras for a program scheduled later that afternoon. But the show went on sooner than expected. Somehow, an engineer threw the wrong switch and for fifteen glorious minutes, incredulous housewives watched naked men dive in, climb out and do imitations of female strippers in front of cameras they thought were not working.

A year later, our technical techniques were getting better. We had more equipment, with more knobs—but more airheads in front and behind the cameras, to match. And now we faced TV's biggest challenge yet: the 1948 presidential nominating conventions. Both parties decided to meet in Philadelphia not out of any affection for the city's hallowed place in American history, but because of television. AT&T had laid coaxial cables so that cities from Boston, Massachusetts, to Richmond, Virginia, could receive the convention. Stations not on the cable, and those out West, would receive films each day. (For you non-techies, coaxial cables are insulated cables put underground to send audio and video to stations on the receiving end.)

The industry trumpeted to the public: Thanks–to–the–miracle–of–modern–technology–the–drama–of–the–democratic–process–can–unfold–in–your–living–room. But since Dewey and Truman were practically assured of their nominations, and many convention bigwigs were so scared of television that they prohibited interviews, most of the intrigue and excitement took place between stations as they finagled and flamboozled to best each other. The two conventions promised a potential audience of millions of viewers. Who cared about politics? Each station wanted to be NUMBER ONE.

(A quick aside: Networks were so jealous of each other that they trained their own spy corps. A friendly invitation for drinks could be a trap. Guy from Network A says obligingly, "Hey, pal. Why don't you let me buy tonight?" He buys—but doesn't drink while guy from Network B gets drunk and starts blabbing. After some state secrets got out this way, nobody was drinking!)

NBC indicated immediately that this convention business better be show business as well. They kicked off a campaign to elect Howdy Doody as president. Radio and TV's bad-boy comic Henry Morgan added to the irreverent tone with a gigantic poster on the marquee of the Ritz-Carlton Hotel: "WELCOME TO HENRY MORGAN'S UNCONVENTIONAL HEADQUARTERS."

Because there weren't enough cables for all the stations, they agreed to take turns using them. These preconvention powwows were as relaxed as Custer's Last Stand. Now history was ready: the GOP convention began on June 21.

For weeks now, NBC had been hyping "Room 22," a joint NBC-LIFE interview program. Exclusive! Scoops!

Prominent public figures! Everything you couldn't get on the other stations. Wrong. At the stroke of 4:00 p.m. the program hit the air. And NBC execs hit the ceiling. Somehow (there was always a "somehow" in early TV) the cables got crossed and the program ended up on the Dumont network. Dumont officials, always amenable to embarrassing a rival network, were ecstatic. Then there was more merry mixup when one of famed columnist Drew Pearson's TV reports landed on a station that had refused to carry it in the first place. Could things get more snafued?

Certainly.

Channel 11 (WPIX) in New York City was the new pup in the litter, having gone on the air June 15. Owned by the nation's largest and most influential paper of the time, the *Daily News*, it was determined to show up any of the networks. So, it had packed off most of its staff, including me, to Philly. But it didn't even need us—NBC fell right into our laps. With all its brains and top names, NBC lacked enough programs to fill its time on the day it had dibs on the cable. They tried everything. They hustled their top makeup man, Dick Smith, on camera. His demonstration of how he could crayon hair on a bald head was one of the most entertaining bits to come out of the convention! They cornered one of their own top commentators, Alex Dreier, in the hotel barbershop. I was hanging around the area at the time, waiting to trap interviewees, and I saw the whole incredible thing. Dreier was getting lathered up, but that didn't stop NBC. They persuaded him to do a man-in-the-chair interview with the barber while the razor did its work.

Even after that close shave with dead air, NBC ran out of crayons and barbers and program ideas—and Channel 11 found out. We smelled a chance for major upmanship. One of our engineers happened to have a buddy on the AT&T staff, and he convinced the poor sucker to let

Channel 11 slip on the air during NBC's unused cable time. Well, General Sarnoff wanted Channel 11 bombed, but settled for getting the AT&T guy fired.

Next day, the now ex-AT&T employee ran to his buddy at Channel 11, and they appealed to *Daily News* radio and television critic Ben Gross. Ben was a nice guy and a sweet guy—but being a columnist, he could wield his pen like an executioner's ax. And he hated to see the ordinary guy in life get screwed. Ben's solution was a little civilized blackmail. He knocked out a couple of columns on the convention. One praised television's coverage and the other shot the nuts off the industry, NBC in particular. Ben sealed the columns in an envelope with a letter to the NBC honchos. It informed them that they had the power to decide which one would be printed. Ben would know their decision by the status of the man from AT&T. You can guess which one ran in the paper. As much noise as television was making, it still couldn't beat the power of the press.

During all the skullduggery, I buzzed around for interviews like a miked-up mosquito and landed on H. L. Mencken, a grand old writer and cynical oberserver of society. Mencken gave the viewers an earful on the convention, but off the air he told me his jaundiced opinion of my new profession. "Take some advice, young man," he said. "This television thing will never go. Find yourself another game." (Mencken was a hardline television trasher. Ultimately I found out from Bob Cochrane, program director of WMAR-Baltimore, that when the *Baltimore Evening Sun* wanted to open its own TV station (WMAR), there was only one dissenting vote from its board of directors. Mencken. The story goes that he snorted, "I hear television will never advertise hard liquor. So what good is it? Vote here is NO.")

I didn't believe Mencken's dour prediction about

television. It was going to be big—and I was planning to be big with it. Despite my splash in TV sports, I was itching to do more Serious Stuff. Philadelphia was crammed with name reporters and commentators for the convention. Doug Edwards was there. And John Cameron Swayze. And Ted Husing. H. V. Kaltenborn. Drew Pearson. Walter Winchell. And now . . . Guy LeBow. Fate tossed me a news report that would be picked up by other stations.

I arrive at Channel 11's convention studio—a suite in the Bellevue Stratford hotel—way ahead of time. I want to appear on camera with cool authority. I'm even more confident because Channel 11 is using Dumont TV cameras and I'm completely at ease with them, having worked at the Dumont Network for an entire year. I sit in my chair, keeping an eye on the tally light. The tally light is the little light at the lower left of the camera. When it glows red, you know the camera is taking a picture of you and you're on the air.

Right about now I get a tickle in my nose. An inner tickle, the kind that makes your nose do a St. Vitus dance if you don't take care of it right away. I don't want to be distracted while I'm on the air. So I do a little scratching outside and a little digging inside. And I see a green tally light. I think, "What a guy that Mr. Dumont is." He's the network chief and also the camera inventor. He's always making things comfortable for his crews, like putting the cameras on dollies for easier moving. "And gee," I think, "now a green standby light to warn you before the red light goes on." Goddammit, my nose won't stop tickling. I scratch a little here, pick a little there . . . And then I see the floor director lying on the floor waving a sign and, my God, it says,

YOU'RE ON THE AIR

Without warning, Dumont has changed its tally light to

green. People feel sorry for jerks. That must be why I got through this experience. But by a nose.

To survive low-tech, you had to learn how to use it in your favor. That is precisely how I did my most memorable interview in the City of Brotherly Love. All week, the Governor of New Jersey had fed me double helpings of inside information and interview leads. At a price. Since it was an election year for him as well, he wanted an exclusive one-on-one interview with me the final day of the convention.

I get to the Channel 11 suite-studio just in time to hear the director tell the camera crew, "Wrap it up."

"Hey, wait," I yell. "I've got the Governor of New Jersey on in four minutes."

"Not anymore," the director says, picking up his jacket. "We're off the air for today, LeBow."

That governor was a decent sort, but he comes in to a dead camera and I might as well lace up a pair of cement shoes. Then I remember a trick that veteran radio announcer Ted Husing taught me in my radio days. With my power of persuasion—and some stupendous groveling—I convince the director to AT LEAST leave me the cameraman. The governor will answer my questions for fifteen minutes.

Call me lucky. The governor doesn't know about tally lights. This tally light is not on. The camera is dead. What Husing had taught me was this: A microphone (or camera) plus an interviewer plus an interviewee equals an interview—whether they go on the air or not. Especially if no one's around to wise up the interviewee. (I paid that cameraman plenty to stay mum.) And anyway, since so many of the convention shows got botched up, the governor would never know for sure why nobody saw him. Yeah, it was a rotten trick and I've felt guilty for all these years. Would I do it again? Don't ask.

In spite of the fiascos at the conventions, the result augured well for what the industry was to do best: cover a happening on the spot. These programs out of the studio were called "remotes." To do a remote, you needed to transport a lot of equipment and, to do that, you needed a truck. To get a truck, you needed money. And most smaller stations were poor. In Washington, D.C., when WTTG launched itself in 1948, it had to appeal to its viewers for trucks. But KOB-TV in Albuquerque takes the cake for the most inventive remote vehicle. They used the local bakery truck. On days they needed it, the bakery driver started his daily sixty-mile run to Santa Fe at 2 a.m. instead of his usual 6 a.m. By the time he chugged back to KOB, the television crew was waiting with brooms to sweep out the crumbs.

Oddly enough, it was in the supposedly more controlled confines of studios that life went haywire. Maybe it was because the TV veterans—those of us with at least one year of experience—were often assigned to the live pickups, leaving the rookies to hold down the fort. And deplorably, even with the terrible shortage of capable TV hands, the ancient enemies of progress—favoritism and nepotism—flourished. While all stations were partial to hiring returning servicemen, NBC and Channel 11 rolled out the red (white and blue) carpet—to their own detriment. This practice extended beyond those who had served. If you were related to a veteran, specifically top brass, so much the better. It was through this painstaking screening process that Channel 11 inherited the nephew of a retired Army colonel. This guy was so dumb that his IQ was probably near his age, which was twenty-four. He loused up show after show, reaching his zenith of witlessness when he met a famed comic from Hollywood.

As its production of musicals was wheezing down, Hollywood coughed up a fine old drunk, one Cliff Edwards, known as "Ukelele Ike." Edwards had pop-eyes, a round face and stood about as high as a terrier on its hind legs. Since the 1920s, he'd been entertaining vaudeville and then movie audiences with his trademark ukelele and comfortable voice. He'd also furnished hundreds of cute voices for cartoons. When I tell you that Edwards was Jiminy Cricket in Disney's cartoon *The Adventures of Pinnochio*, you'll know his voice. Edwards migrated East in an alcoholic haze and was grabbed by Channel 11 to create another cute, squeaky voice for another make-believe character: the mechanical owl that opened and closed our late-night movie program called "Night Owl Theater."

The scenario is thus: The little dummy owl roosts at one end of the set and Edwards stands out of camera range at a mike, maybe fifteen or twenty feet away. (I'm near Edwards, as I'm the commercial announcer.) The colonel's nephew is the floor director. His job is to keep order on the set and cue the performers. So what does he do? On a command from the director in the control room, he points his finger at the little dummy owl to indicate that the owl is on the air. The owl sits, silent as the Sphinx. The Nepotitic Nephew points again.

Silence.

Point.

Silencepointsilencepoint.

Silence.

I nudge Edwards in the ribs—maybe he's been drinking too much again. "Fuck him," he fumes. "I don't speak till the jerk learns he's gotta cue ME. I got the lines. The dummy don't speak."

(As a guy who did sports, I enjoyed timing Edwards' sprints down to the De Santis Bar at the foot of the *Daily News* Building. He called it "filling the horn," but where he got that term for drinking I never found out. Edwards could get to the bar, knock down a few snorts and arrive back on the tenth floor in four and a half minutes flat—when he did come back. More than a few times I had to try to be the cute mechanical owl, and I'm not cute. "Look, Ike," I asked him one day. "Why don't you just bring a bottle to work?" He stood on tiptoe and breathed his most recent distilled spirits into my face. "Where's the challenge in that?" he asked me. "For a sports announcer, you don't have any balls.")

But we couldn't pin all the blame on nepotism and favoritism. Screwups were a fact of life. And is there anyone left from those impossible days who can honestly say he didn't forget about the camera . . . ?

With a heavy schedule of sports and human interest programs, I needed an assistant. I knew of a real livewire working over at WINS radio for fight announcer Don Dunphy, but I didn't want to steal him. Turns out the kid was anxious to break into TV, so Don released him from his contract. Irving Rudd was a red-headed munchkin with a pugnacious Irish face and the oh-golly enthusiasm of Mickey Rooney. And what a find. Rudd not only had broadcast experience, but he was smart and enthusiastic. And capable of ending my career in a flash—an ability he proved his first day on the job and on my first sports interview show.

I was winding up the program and getting close to a commercial. I had my timing down pat, but Irving was a bundle of nerves. He stood to the right of the camera and gave me the "cut" sign—finger drawn horizontally across the throat. I wasn't going to "cut." I had a razor commercial coming up and I was segueing into it, like butter. Irving jumped up and down, waved, sliced his throat. I ignored him.

"And now . . ." I began. Then the unbelievable. None of the accoutrements of the studio—the enormous cameras emblazoned with WPIX-TV, the sinister cables, the hellish lights—reminded Irving that he was no longer at a radio station. He dashed in front of me—which placed him smack in front of the camera—and continued "cutting." The producer went purple-red. The director hissed into his speaker. Still holding the razor with one hand and still talking at the camera, I lowered my other hand out of camera range and motioned for Irving to scram. Finally an AD slithered over and pulled him out of camera range. I continued the commercial, for what it was worth, by now.

As I staggered off the set, I got the news that our station manager Robert Coe had expressed a keen interest in seeing me—first thing next morning.

"Give me one good reason I shouldn't fire you," he said when I opened the door. But he was laughing. "I heard I can get a hitman to take care of Irving, but I need fifty bucks," I implored. Coe had come to us from KSD-TV, St. Louis, where he had been one of the engineers to get the station on the air in 1947. So he understood that mistakes were waiting to be made. But ruining a commercial? Cut my coaxial cable and fog my lens. Channel 11 was having such a rough time finding sponsors it was practically rifling trash cans outside ad agencies for leads. Coe wanted me to fire Rudd.

"It's only his first mistake." I mumbled.

"Yes, but it's his first day," Coe countered. "I hate to think what he'll do tomorrow."

In the end, I was able to keep Irving on. And I was right about him. He was smart, enthusiastic—and trouble. He went into PR work later on and one of his accounts was Yonkers Raceway. For its opening day, in 1956 or 1957, Rudd had the giant sign overlooking the highway adjusted to read: YONKERS RACWEAY. So many drivers looked twice to check the spelling that there was a rash of car accidents and Irving had to untangle the sign.

Irving's later PR stunts and campaigns were safer, but as memorable, and he became one of the most quoted PR men in the country. I guess everyone has to start somewhere, but Irving, why was it with me!

"Making it" on television wasn't just talent or luck or connections. You had to survive the boot camp of primitive technology. The most frequent ad-lib in early TV was "Ouch!" Before the invention of cooler lights at the close of the 1940s, we worked under 1000-watt candlelit power. This meant enduring 115 degrees or higher on the set. Just picking up a telephone was torture. During the call-in quiz shows—a staple of our early era—you answered the phone maybe thirty times. One of Channel 11's "quiz quties," Candy Jones, immersed her phone-answering hand in a bucket of ice between calls for "Your Lucky Star" (callers could win a date with a movie actor or actress!). And when she touched the receiver, it sizzled. (Later, Candy traded buckets of ice for buckets of champagne when she married model maker Harry Conover. She became one of the most famous faces of the fifties.)

The heat was so intense it turned Dumont's first musical show, "The Boys from Boise," into a sizzling success when the backdrop burst into flames. As viewers dialed the fire department, stagehands formed a bucket brigade to save the set. And now that you know just how hot these lights were, you can appreciate why this incident, which happened on a very popular kiddie show, "Small Fry Club," is branded on a Dumont cameraman forever. In those days, when we needed more brightness on a set, we used "cherry lights." These were smaller lights, mounted on a panel, which a technician would wheel as close to the set as needed. But this technician was so nervous about missing a cue from the technical director that he never took his eyes off him, and he pushed 1000 watts of candlelit power into the

*The author is in a baggy suit (far right) with movie star
Humphrey Bogart on a tour to publicize* The African Queen.
*And that's water in Bogey's cup, too!*

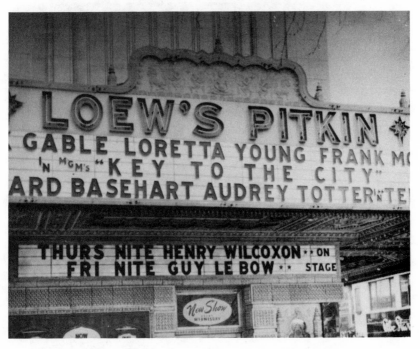

*Loew's Theaters give in, and feature a TV star
on Friday nights—please note.*

77

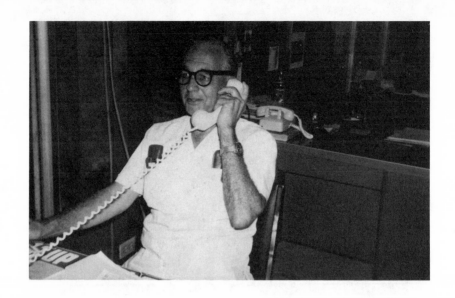

*Film expert Ed Woodruff, the guy who broke the film world's stranglehold that barred great movies from TV. (Courtesy Ed Woodruff)*

*I look cool doing this commercial on ABC, but I'm dying inside—the girl holding the cue card has just fainted.*

*Note the Spartan early-fifties set while I'm warbling commercials for "Douglas Edwards with the News," CBS.*

*Here I'm spieling for Hudson automobiles . . . before I catch the chairman of Hudson driving a Cadillac!*

79

**JOE FRANKLIN**
on his first television appearance
September 30th, 1953

*Memory-maker Joe Franklin, unchallenged King of Nostalgia,
was not even shaving when he made his first TV appearance.
Thirty-nine years later, he's still with us every day.
(Courtesy Joe Franklin)*

*Lovable Cliff Edwards ("Ukelele Ike") made the big jump from Hollywood to Channel 11, New York. (Photo courtesy Photofest)*

81

*Look to the right for television's first camerawoman. (Photo courtesy Marvin Pakula)*

82

cameraman's ass.

"Ouch! What the FUCK . . ."

All the kiddies listening at home—and their parents—heard the bloodcurdling cry, which host "Big Brother" Bob Emery hastily covered over with one of his extra big laughs. The cameraman was the first to be able to say, "I worked my ass off for TV."

The heat did strange and terrible things to the human body. There's no telling why some people could withstand it better than others. Milton J. Cross, one of radio's most eloquent announcers, was afflicted with nosebleeds the minute he sat under the lights. He had to quit television almost as soon as he began. A number of announcers who started with me had to retire because they developed skin cancer from exposure to the lights. So many people fainted—men and women—that studios looked more like hospitals on some days. Strong, healthy males, including rough-and-ready sportscaster Bill Stern, crumpled to the floor and had to be revived. And one afternoon while I was talking to fellow announcer Don Roper, his face turned red . . . and then redder . . . and then a bright, terrible red. It was as if he were bleeding from every pore. Clutching at his head, he stumbled to a chair where he sat until we got a stretcher. "I'm through," he said as they carried him out. "I can't take it." It took him six months to recover. And he didn't return. He joined the ministry, and today has a long-running religious radio show from coast to coast.

If you needed a heat-resistant constitution to last the lights, you needed an iron stamina to put up with other lesser pitfalls. There was the simple matter of space. Almost every station had humble beginnings, but I can't believe that anyone worked under the conditions they did at KTLA in Los Angeles. Stan Freberg, one of the funniest writers around, couldn't have dreamed up the situation he found himself in. As a young writer and comic, Freberg joined KTLA, where he wrote and performed for the kiddie show, "Time for Beany." Which—incredibly—turned out to be Albert Einstein's favorite show. Now, KTLA was owned by Paramount pictures, which wanted to see what TV could do, but didn't seem to want to help it succeed. They gave KTLA a garage as a studio. There was no office space for the Beany writers, but that didn't prevent the award-winning scripts from being created. Each night Freberg and his co-Beanies took to the streets, where they casually went from car to car until they found an unlocked one roomy enough for the four of them. They wrote all night and into the morning until the car's owner returned—at which moment they pretended to be in the wrong car and scrammed.

The Dumont station was so short of room in the beginning that they sent the announcers to the toilet to broadcast. Almost eight years later, the same thing happened to me when I was freelancing a sports show for WOR. To save money, the station had moved from their spacious quarters on Sixty-sixth Street to a cozy 1 rm with vu in the Empire State Building. When I reported for work, a world-weary AD gave me my script and told me to go to the bathroom, "I don't have to go," I said, understandably mystified.

"Yeah, you do if you wanna work here," he said. "We don't have room in this nutshell for a second announcer. You do your stuff in the *pissoir*, got me? And hang up this sign before you go in. Last guy didn't, he was flushed off the air."

You know something? I never sounded better than in that bathroom.

Actually, things were so bad financially for WOR that they were doing complete off-camera TV shows. Only a photo of the announcer or newsman appeared on camera. As long as the viewer can see SOMETHING, isn't it television? The FCC didn't go along. Here's their position, from the June 25, 1949, *New York Herald*:

## INSISTS TELEVISION
## MUST STRESS VISION

### *F.C.C. Warns Mere Sound Is Not Enough*

WASHINGTON, D.C., June 24 (AP)—The Federal Communications Commission said today television programs should always include something to look at as well as to listen to. . . .

Among FCC stipulations were that ". . . sound broadcasts made while still pictures or slides are broadcast visually do not meet the requirements, except for testing station equipment or when the aural and visual transmission are integral parts of a program and the visual transmission have a substantial relationship to the aural transmission."

They didn't say anything about broadcasting from the john.

The guys who made it possible for us to be heard and seen—the technical crew—held their life-or-death power over our heads. We had to stay on the right of them because if they didn't like us, they killed us. They cut off our sound, claiming "atmospheric conditions." They forgot our cues. Made sure we read from the wrong cue cards. These "mishaps" were a holdover from radio, in which practical jokes were as common as station breaks and new announcers were initiated with unofficial hazing ceremonies.

For my virgin newscast at WHN, the engineer kept imperceptibly raising the boom mike suspended over the announcer's desk. To stay near enough to the mike to be heard on the air, I had to stand up. Then climb on the table. Then stand on tiptoe. I didn't miss a syllable. So the next day, another engineer walked in while I was doing the news and calmly peed in the wastebasket.

But in the transition from radio to television, even this heavy-handed humor disappeared. Probably it was the pressure of struggling with the more complicated techniques. At one New York City station, an engineer got fed up with an announcer for missing his cues and threw a chair through the control room window. And will you believe me when I tell you that some creep filled the area under my hubcaps with rotten shrimp? Another time with rocks? It was out of hand!

And if we survived the ill-tempered technicians and hot lights and other vagaries, there was another drawback: the director. And my nomination for the Greatest Idiotic Director goes to Jack Balch. Don't be modest, Jack. You clearly deserve the award. At this time we had few special effects for regular programs like talk and variety shows. We were locked into superimposition, upside-down shots (turning people on their heads) and reverse polarity, which was seldom used. You've seen it on your photo negatives—everything dark comes out white and vice versa. On this particular evening, the premier black singing group in the country, the Four Mills Brothers, was harmonizing its signature number, "All God's Children Got Shoes." Something in the song aroused the artist in Mr. Balch. "Vic," he said to his technical director, "let's throw a little creativity in this. Reverse polarity."

A second's hesitation from Vic. But orders were orders. Everything black went white and everything white went black—and the viewers saw red. They bombarded the switchboard, wanting to know what was wrong with their sets. They complained that our stupid trick interfered with the show. And a few socially conscious viewers accused us of setting back race relations a hundred years. Turning the Mills Brothers white was an insult. Shortly thereafter, Mr. Balch was on a train to Chicago.

But even splendid talents were overwhelmed. Emmy Award winner Clark Jones, who directed some of the most seamless, professional and entertaining hours on television, including the Tony Awards, got trapped in a Byzantine maze called "Ford's 50th Anniversary Special" on NBC in 1953. This was TV's first "special." Twenty-seven locations, four cameras, umpteen cast members—and more chances than ever to screw up. At one point in the show, Wally Cox (TV's popular "Mr. Peepers") stopped, stared helplessly into a camera and admitted, "I don't know what to do." Jones didn't blame him. He didn't either.

When directors or circumstances didn't make fools of performers, we picked up the slack and did it to ourselves. (A quick intermission. There were some actors who seemed to float above the chaos and carnage. One in particular was Don Ameche. I was asking him about his early TV experiences—he played the Manager on ABC's "Holiday Hotel," in 1951. Nope. Don couldn't recall any of that turmoil. I think it's because Don was—and is—the consummate pro. Why, the guy didn't even use cue cards for his TV performances!)

To continue . . . the Nepotitic Nephew was not the dumbest person around the studio. That I will reserve for the Jimmy Jemail, who wrote (pardon the word) the "Inquiring Fotographer" column for the *Daily News*. Supposedly Jemail posed questions to people in the street or celebrities, got their answers and took their photos. A small-spirited operator, Jemail was a reporter the way I was an opera star. One day I open the paper and lo! I behold my photo and a quote from me in "Inquiring Fotographer." Interesting, when you consider that he hadn't interviewed me. I asked around the paper and was told that Jemail did go out to photograph the public but never asked them a thing. He had a file cabinet full of stock questions and answers. Like this for young males: "What's your favorite part about going to the beach?" "The parts in the bathing suits!" Of course the public didn't mind—people love seeing their pictures in the paper.

When Channel 11 went on the air, they needed programs—anything! So they turned "Inquiring Fotographer" into a TV show. Those hollow brass bells in the front office thought that anyone could be on television. Jemail was assigned to interview live celebrities live during Channel 11's opening-night ceremonies on June 15, and he was deadly. Nevertheless, the program went on the air. . . .

Then a new director rolled into town. Ted Estabrook wore glasses and tweeds, and was as earnest about television as he looked. He had a real background in television; he'd been instrumental in getting WAAM (today WJC) in Baltimore started. And he was delirious at having the chance to work in New York City until after his first day with "Inquiring Fotographer." As Jemail stood in front of the camera, speaking animatedly, Estabrook couldn't hear a thing. He signaled the engineer, who signaled back, that, yes, there was no sound. Estabrook motioned at Jemail, who, as always, interpreted any communication to mean that he was fantastic. And now Estabrook realized what he hadn't seen—Jemail wasn't holding a mike. He called for a commercial and yanked Jemail aside.

"Where is it?"

"What?"

"Your mike!"

"Oh, my MIKE," Jemail said. "Oh, I knew I forgot something. Here . . ." He reached into a jacket pocket and took it out. "But don't worry," he said. "I'm sure it picked up everything anyway."

One goof-up by himself was just that: one goof-up. But what if a whole station goofed? Then you had a disaster. And that only begins to describe the opening night of WOR-TV on October 11, 1949.

The station opened at 6:55 with a few words from the very popular WOR-radio star John Gambling. Host of the much-loved show "Rambling with Gambling," he had a huge listenership. But not tonight. The sound was not working. Audio did return for the commercial that followed, but the picture did not make the sponsor happy. They got their close-up of their bread wrapper, all right, including a housefly that had chosen that precise second to land. The sound continued to work beautifully; in fact, it was so clear now that the audience heard the crew yelling that they weren't ready for the main program to go on. And when it did, the sound faded out again. You can see this stuff done as parodies on "Saturday Night Live" or "The David Letterman Show." Everyone laughs. But this was the real thing!

And *this* was very low-tech. In the winter of 1948, Channel 11 sent an engineering crew out to Roosevelt Raceway on Long Island. Racing season didn't begin until June, when the station was due to go on the air, but by erecting a microwave antenna now, there would be plenty of time for technical adjustments. The signal would go from the Island to the antenna on the *Daily News* Building in Manhattan and from there to the various antennas on private homes and taverns. There were two requirements for the signal to make its trip: this microwave antenna had to be erected on a straight line of sight to the Channel 11 antenna and its tip had to be unobstructed. That is, no buildings, water towers or giraffes in the way. In the cold, nasty closing days of winter, the engineers and crew had to climb up the icy metal and keep raising the antenna until they got the signal that it worked.

Opening day at the racetrack. June. Announcer Jack McCarthy and I ride to Roosevelt along with the crew that includes assistant head engineer Otis Freeman. The engineers are puzzled. The picture comes in part of the time but keeps dissolving into zigzags and snow. "This is crap," one engineer growls. Otis Freeman phones Forty-second Street and gives his Southern battle cry: "We'se in trouble!"

The solution is worthy of Sherlock Holmes. Our engineers discover that in a scant four months, an apartment building had been constructed on our line of sight. (The postwar housing boom was devouring Long Island farmland.) To a non-techie, the answer would be either to tear down the building or raise the antenna. But we have no time!

Two hours before the race we haven't solved a thing. Then Engineer Otis comes up with the most absurd suggestion we've heard. "Let's ride over to that apartment," Otis says. "We'll get tenants facing the raceway on the top floors to open their windows. That way," he explains, "our signal from the track can go through the apartment house and reach our master control in Manhattan. Got it?" We tell Otis to stop fucking us around. We now have one hour and forty-five minutes to the starting gate. This is our first major remote. And we start knocking on doors? Engineer Otis is unflappable. He hauls us to the apartment house, where we explain our predicament. We offer a little pocket money—out of our own pockets. The tenants cooperate. The race goes on the air. Who needs sophisticated technology?

Three years later, on April 15, 1951, the *New York Post* reported:

## POPE NAMES GABRIEL
## PATRON OF RADIO, TV

My only question, Saint Gabriel, is where were you all those years when we really needed you?

*Station Break:*

## "Sing, Kid" . . .
## "Announce, Mister"

Before there was the early TV I'm talking about in this book, there was early-early TV. And since I'm going to be weaving in and out of things as you read, maybe you should know a little about how I got into television in the first place. TV and I made our acquaintance at a very young age, for both of us. It was not love at first sight.

## ". . . SING, KID . . ."

"I'm blind. Help. Help. I'm blind. Somebody help me."

"Wait a minute. Wait a minute, young feller," said a soft voice.

It was the soft voice of Mr. Uniform. Mr. Uniform, who had been my guide into this torture chamber. The kid is me. I'm about twelve, and a singer on the "Horn &

Hardart CBS Radio Hour," a kiddie talent show. Even at this stage, my voice is regarded as romantic—your 18KT crooner style.

I guess the "H&H Hour" was where the person got my name—the CBS man who called me at home to find out if I wanted to do what he called an "experimental television" performance for the station. I could sing anything I liked. I didn't ask if I'd get any money. I'd been on the "H&H Hour" for a year and a half with a bunch of other kids, including future comedians Robert Q. Lewis, Al Bernie and opera star Risë Stevens. Even though Horn & Hardart was making heaps and heaps of money, they never gave us anything. Not a piece of pie, not a cookie, not a slice of cake. We even did the commercials for these Simon Legrees—free! "Well, kids," the announcer would say heartily into the mike. "Tell the folks how much you love . . ." and he'd mention a cookie or a cake or a kiddie drink. That was our cue to chorus, "Yummmm-zzuk," the cute little word some copywriter had thought up for us. "Yummmm-zzuk!" But I would have sung for my supper, so crazy I was to sing. I would have paid those pennypinching creeps at H&H to let me sing.

The experimental program was on a weekday afternoon, so I had to cut school—no novelty for me. After lunch I skillfully performed a high fever and was sent "home" by the nurse. But on the way, I stopped into the subway station and rode down to Manhattan, to the CBS studios at 485 Madison Avenue. My rendezvous with destiny was on the 22nd floor, where we kids worked our little hearts out. Floor 22 was also where all the stars performed. They loved having us adoring kiddies around. I delivered sandwiches to Bing Crosby. I couldn't stop staring at fat Kate Smith—she took up two seats on the sofa. And the legendary Arthur Tracy, known as the "Street Singer," used to pinch my cheek and say, "You're doing all right, kid."

So here I am. Mr. Uniform comes over to me. That's what I'll call the thin, blond guy in the CBS uniform.

"O.K., Guy, follow me."

I forgot to tell you. The 22nd floor of CBS is actually a duplex. It has a balcony, and offices and studios are on that balcony. To reach them, you walked up a long flight of stairs. And a few months ago I had watched a terrible scene there. CBS had a great singer named Ben Alley. He must have been performing in one of those offices or studios on the balcony when a crazy-looking lady ran up the steps and started pounding on the door. "Ben," she screamed, "Ben, they're trying to keep us apart. Ben, you bastard, I love you! Come and get me." She fell to her knees, howling and clawing at the door.

Ben didn't come, but the police did—lots of them. About six ran up the stairs, and it took all six to drag her down, put cuffs on her and shove her in the elevator. At age twelve, I knew what sex was. It was what Bernadette O'Hara and I did under the porch. And I knew what love was. That was what Jeanette MacDonald felt for Nelson Eddy. But "Ben, you bastard, I love you" wasn't either of these.

"Go ahead, kid." Through a door I went . . . and I want to describe this just right.

I walked into a corridor about fifteen feet long—and there were two empty wooden benches against the wall. Mr. Uniform kept pushing me straight ahead to another door. It opened into a strange room about the size of eight telephone booths, if you glued them together. It had a low black ceiling and all-black walls. In the middle stood a little piano like I'd seen in nightclubs in the movies, with a boom mike hanging overhead and a cheery guy plunking the keys. To my right was another microphone, this one standing in front of a pane of glass. I could see another room and two people, probably engineers, busying themselves with what looked like a dark-gray camera. The camera had a four- or five-inch snout on it, with a light mounted overhead. It didn't look like any other camera I'd ever seen.

Then one of the two men came out and took my music, which he gave to the piano player. I'd brought "Auf Wiedersehen," my good-luck song. It won me my place on the "H&H Hour." The pianist warmed up and so did I. And I wondered, "What the heck comes next?"

What came next was another man putting a white clay on my face, just leaving my mouth and eyes uncovered.

"What's this?" I said. "We didn't have to wear anything on the 'H&H Hour.' "

"Makeup. You have to wear makeup for television," he explained. "We have to take out all the lines on your face."

"Lines?" I'm twelve years old!

He patted and stroked and smoothed the stuff on my face. "If we didn't put this on, you might wind up looking like a zebra. These lights make people's faces— even kids' faces—look strange unless we cover you up."

Oh, sure, I thought to myself. I don't want to look like a zebra. Better to look like a zombie.

So here I am in front of the standing microphone in front of the glass, the pianist is ready—and suddenly the place goes pitch black. Everything—the dim bulbs in this little room, the lights in the room on the other side of the window. I thought we had a power failure. But a half second later the brightest light I've ever seen points at me from the top of the camera. I blinked. "Don't blink, sonny," a voice said. "O.K., take five beats, kid, and sing."

How could anyone sing facing this contraption? The more I looked into the light, the more strange I felt. Like I was disappearing into a huge white hole. Then my eyes adjusted and I didn't even think about it as I gave CBS my best warble.

When I finished, the light went out and everything stayed dark. I heard someone walk over to me and I heard Mr. Uniform's voice. "O.K., kid, you can come with me." He led me somewhere and sat me on a wooden bench. This must be the corridor, I thought. But the lights were out here too. "Hey," I said. "When do they turn on the lights again?" "They *are* on," Mr. Uniform told me. I got the same pit in my stomach I did when I pictured the insane lady yelling at Ben. I panicked. "I'm blind. Help." I was sure that the light in the studio had blinded me. It was my punishment for lying to the nurse and skipping school. "Help, I'm blind. Somebody help me."

"No-no-no, don't worry, kid," said Mr. Uniform. "You just have eye bends. Everybody gets them. In about two or three minutes you'll be able to see fine. You'll be able to see everything."

He was right. It took about three minutes, my vision cleared up and then Mr. Uniform told me that even the big stars went through the same thing when they stood in front of that light.

But I was thinking. For crying out loud, I wanted to be in show biz. Radio and films in particular. I had seen photographs of the glamorous Hollywood studios in fan magazines. And sung on the "H&H Hour" at the beautiful, spacious CBS studios. Chrome and glass and thick carpets and swell-looking ushers. Boy, what I just came through, none of my pals would believe. I sang in a black two-by-four room. White garbage all over my face. I went practically tragically blind from the lights. . . .

Even at twelve years of age, I had smarts. This television thing will never happen, I said to myself. And if it does, it's going to have to get along without Guy LeBow.

After waving "Auf Wiedersehen" to CBS's experiment, I didn't think about a career in television until years later. And just like the first time, I was involved in radio when the phone rang . . .

## ". . . ANNOUNCE, MISTER . . ."

In 1946 I was a sports announcer and night manager at WHN Radio in New York City. One Monday in June, I get a call at the studio from a man identifying himself as Jack Murphy. He says he's a director at Channel 5, Dumont Television. Would I like to audition as their boxing announcer?

I'd heard about that outfit. But as a radio announcer on the way up—and I assumed that was my direction—I tended to put television out of my mind and hope that it wouldn't encroach too quickly on radio, which I was just beginning to earn a pretty good buck at. But I never turned down an opportunity. Especially since I'd already had a little television experience (in my H&H days). "Sure, I'll audition," I said confidently. Murphy told me to be at the Jamaica Arena out on Long Island on Thursday evening, at 6:30.

Six-thirty seemed awfully early. I'd been doing at least two fights a week for WHN for the past year and a half. And usually, I'd get to an arena at 8:30 for a bout that went on at 10 o'clock. But what the hell. This was television. Everything was bound to be different.

And it sure was, when I got there. First thing I see is a big truck. More like a bus. It says "Dumont Channel 5 Mobile Unit." (Later on I was to find out that this was used as the temporary engineering emanating point on remote shows. I understood a little about that—radio had something like that, too.)

Inside the arena, however, I understood nothing. You see, when you're doing a radio fight, there's only you, your color man—if any—and the engineer. Three guys carry the weight of the broadcast for a couple of hours or so. But this looked like a strike was in progress. At least thirty men standing around, wearing overalls with "Dumont Television" emblazoned on their backs. They turned out to be engineers, lighting men, cameramen and "cable pushers." At this stage of TV, the cables connecting the microwave antenna and the cameras, especially to the truck outside, were so heavy and thick that a cameraman couldn't move his camera around the floor. So they had to have brainy guys who did nothing but push the cables along, and I suspect for a pretty good payoff, too. Carpenters were erecting a pair of platforms above the crowd, at one end of the arena. I don't know it now, but this is where the cameras will sit during the fight—one camera and one man to a platform.

Out of all this mystery and maze to me appears an Irish leprechaun, freckles on his face, friendly hand out in greeting. He's Jack Murphy and he tells me to call him "Jack," not "Mr. Murphy."

I get right to the point, which is that I'm kicking myself for having gotten myself into this mess. "What do I do now, Jack?"

"Come on!" he says. This guy is full of enthusiasm. "Let's grab a seat over here, where'll you'll be working." He walks me over to the front row, ringside. And proceeds to indoctrinate me about being a television announcer. I hadn't thought about the television part of the audition. I knew I knew boxing. But I'd never done boxing for television. LeBow had talked his way into another impossible situation.

Flashback to 1945 . . . Welcome to radio station WSTC, Stamford, Connecticut, where a young announcer is trying to Make It in the Radio World. Every morning I get up at four a.m. in the Bronx, where I live, and catch the five-o-something at 175th Street. I'm in Stamford by six-o-something; I sleepwalk the fifteen minutes to the station. At six-thirty sharp, I put the station on the air for the day. "Goodddd morning, and welcome to another day with your friennnd, WSTC, Stammfordd." From then until one in the afternoon, I do news, sports, weather, music, commercials. Then I get a three-hour lunch break. Yeah, three hours. I've gotten to know every small-town shop window in this city. The only reason I hate it is that it isn't New York. Back to the mike from four to six, catch the something-o-something to New York and fall into bed around ten o'clock with the sinking feeling that my career is going nowhere . . .

And . . . then . . . one fine spring day the other two and a half announcers and I are meeting with the boss. (I said two and a half announcers because the third guy was a half-wit. He only had his job because his stepfather was a famous actor.) "O.K., boys," the boss says. "We're doing prize fights starting next week. Anyone here know anything about boxing?" One hand goes up. "LeBow," he says, "you got the job."

The extent of my boxing expertise was knowing Joe Louis's name, but I had to get out of this rut. For the next five days I soaked up the experts' expertise. I listened to fight announcer Don Dunphy on WHN. I read articles and books by boxing champ Barney Ross. And my first night at the ring reads like a Cinderella script from Hollywood.

Sitting next to me, although I don't know it, is middleweight champ Jake LaMotta. He's come to watch his brother Joey in the ring. When the bout's over I'm wrung dry. I want to get to sleep—I have to get up to put the station on the air tomorrow. Outside in the lobby, I meet Joey in his street clothes. How could he be dressed so fast? "Hey, Joey," I joke. "You wear your street clothes under your boxing shorts?"

"You schmuck! How the hell you gonna be my renouncer if you can't see who I am? I'm Jake. Hey," he says to his cronies, "what a schmuck, huh?" Jake gives me a heavyweight slap on the back to show me he's kidding.

"Relax, blondie," he says. "You're a hell of a renouncer. Next week, you make it your business to come to New York. You know New York? Go up to WHN. I'm gonna get you signed up as my new renouncer in my new boxing arena."

I still haven't said a word.

"Say, kid, you want to be my renouncer or not?"

Do I want to leave Stamford, Connecticut, for New York City? Do I want to be the personal announcer for one of the most famous boxers around? Will I miss getting up at four a.m.? Racing to catch the train? Working until eleven p.m. on boxing nights? And every Saturday, to earn an extra $20, coaxing my secondhand heap along the Boston Post Road to Stamford to host a music show for a funeral home? Ask me again, Jake. Yes, I want to be your renouncer.

I didn't start working for Jake at his new Park Arena in the Bronx for a few months. But I did get the job and began work at WHN. . . .

So it's forward to 1946, the Jamaica Arena. As I said, I knew I knew boxing. I also knew the boxers who were going to be in this match, because this was a club fight and I'd done a million of them for WHN. What's a club fight? Before television, there were thousands of "clubs," or small arenas, around the country. They usually sat 3,500 to 4,000—like the Jamaica Arena. Generally they featured boxers who everyone knew weren't going anywhere. But they were locally popular and drew in crowds, which was what the club owner wanted. Three or four thousand loyal fans added up to a nice gate. The Jewish fans had a Jewish favorite, the Irish had theirs, there was a German favorite and so on. Most club fights consisted of six bouts. They'd feature one new guy the club owner thought had potential, a couple of old guys who were washed up but had a following, and a few nitwits who shouldn't have been fighting at all.

So I'm trying to calm myself with positive thoughts like "You are the Number One Club Fight Announcer," but a little voice keeps horning in with, "You've really done it to yourself this time, bigmouth." And Jack Murphy is giving me a one-year announcing course, above the hammers banging and men yelling. None of it seems to bother him. "There are several things I want you to remember about television," he is saying. "Right, Jack. Right!" I respond brightly.

"When you see a guy bleeding, you never say, 'He's spilling blood.'"

"You don't? What do I say? Folks can see the blood."

"Uh-uh. We can't say 'blood' because that word denotes a color, red."

The clock is ticking down to my citywide television debut and this well-meaning simpleton is telling me what everybody knows: blood is red. "So?"

"So you say 'claret.'"

"Cla . . . What?"

"Claret. It's a shade of red but a lot of people don't know that, so they won't exactly know what you mean, yet you've covered the point. Remember: don't say 'blood' because 'blood' denotes red. That's inimical to us in television."

"Why?"

"It's because of films," Murphy tells me. "The film industry doesn't want us to grow and they're putting out a lot of color films to make us look bad. So we don't mention colors—let's not remind the folks we're only in black-and-white." At this point I am not interested in the politics between some cigar-chomping fatties in Hollywood and television. Television, in fact, is fast becoming an unwelcome word in my vocabulary. It is too much trouble. "But what about the fighters' trunks?" I ask him.

"They're in color."

"Well, just say 'light' trunks and 'dark' trunks. Look at the jeep," he tells me, pointing to a little television screen. (This was the monitor, and it looked like our ten-inch portables of today.) "It's hooked up only to our broadcast. Don't announce what you see from the ring—announce what you see on the screen, because that's the same view the folks get at home. When you see the difference in shades between the trunks, point it out. Shades, got it? Or striped. Or maybe a monogram. That way you'll denote the difference between fighters. Just stay away from color."

There was more. "Don't talk too much. Just let the action take over; you explain what's happening. Remember: you're not broadcasting to a radio audience that can't see for itself."

Wonderful. Because I had made my reputation on being a rapid-fire announcer, who gave his ravenous audiences blow-by-blow descriptions. "A-right-to-the-head-a-cross-to-the-jaw-he's-in-a-clinch-comes-out-of-it-with-two-uppercuts-to-the-chin-ducks-a-right-to-the-head-ducks-a-left-to-the-head-comes-pounding-in-with-two-hands-to-the-body." Now what?

Murphy finishes off with a few hundred more hints in his patient, encouraging manner. Then he takes off for other duties, leaving me time to visit the fighters' dressing room. I always did this before a radio bout. I talk to these fighters and make some notes, but I'm already familiar with some of the fighters on this card. A good thing, too. I'm  so tied up about the problems of television that I'm only half concentrating on what they say.

For the first two rounds, I forget almost everything Jack told me and fire off blow-by-blow announcing. Stationed in the mobile truck in front of the arena, Jack keeps hollering at me through my earphones. Say this.

Say that. Say this, no, now that. Say the other. Don't say that!

I'm going to murder this maniac when the fight is over. Can you imagine trying to concentrate on machine-gun action while someone else is interrupting you every second? By the third round, Jack's repeated blows to my ear have the desired effect: as confident as I am in my accuracy of reporting, I realize I'm doing something stupid. Maybe I should stand back and give details of how the fighter was taking the blow. Whether he's hitting strongly. Whether he's using his best punch. So I begin to do that. And something more. I stop trying to second-guess the bosses at Dumont and the audience at home and in the bars. I'd been so worried about saying something a viewer might not agree with that I lost my confidence. Instead of a blunt "He's deeply cut!" I'd been mealymouthing with "He's cut. . . . It may be deep . . . It may not be so deep . . . We don't know at this point . . . We do know he's cut." Screw this, I tell myself. I'm the announcer, that's why I'm here. If I say he's cut deep, that bastard is cut deep.

And I also do this: I reach into my grab bag of boxing knowledge and pull out all the stuff I couldn't use doing blow-by-blow because there wasn't time. I override Murphy's directions when I think I've got something more interesting to say than what shows on my jeep. Murphy's hollering in my ear, "Go to the right-hand corner!" and I give the audience little-known facts about tricks of the trade. That all rings aren't the same size. That size can help determine the outcome of a match if a manager gets the one his fighter needs. If he's fast, he can dance around a lot and befuddle his opponent in a larger ring. If he's slower, and a hard-hitter, he has a better chance to nail his opponent in a smaller ring. I point out that the ring has padding on it. And that sometimes a sneaky manager with a fighter who can't move very well can outfox a quick, graceful fighter. All he has to do is make sure there's very little ring padding for less buoyancy. The twinkle-toes is then at a disadvantage.

Murphy is still yelling at me, but I'm unstoppable. In between punches and clinches and commercials, I'm on to the medicines trainers used between rounds. Some are forbidden by the Board of Health and the Boxing Commission. Like vaseline. If you put it on your fighter's face or body, the opposing fighter's punches glide off their mark. And, since I know most of the trainers, I explain how they affect their fighters. Suddenly I realize that even with the noise in the arena, the sounds of the fighters blasting each other and my talking, it is very quiet. No more barking from Murphy. A clear indication he's washed his hands of me, I think, but so what? If I've ruined my chances, I can at least give the audience an evening of great entertainment.

Then, as at most club fights, something happens in the third bout. When you're not dealing with real pros, something's always happening. But dealing with it on radio and on television are two different things. As Murphy warned me: "The audience at home sees everything. Everything."

It's round three, and this kid—a strapping ex-Navy-looking type, about five-foot-five, hair shorn to the scalp —gets popped on the chin by a skinnier guy. Down he goes on his face. The referee begins to toll right over my microphone. He gets to "ten." The kid's still as death. I'm getting worried that he's hurt when the referee bends over him. Nobody else can hear him, but the camera closes in for an easy read of his lips. "It's O.K. now, kid. It's safe to get up now." I didn't want to let the public know that this kid was scared—it might ruin his chances of ever fighting again. On radio I could have said simply that the kid was down for the count. But television was cruel.

And slapstick. The next bout begins with the very elegantly dressed announcer Mr. Harry Balogh in the center of the ring intoning, "This . . . bout . . . will . . . be . . . for . . . six . . . rounds. Six rounds." Hearing that, one of the fighters yells in a heavy Spanish accent, "Me no fight. Me no fight six rounds. Me fight four rounds." The managers and seconds jump into the ring. The crowd is unhappy. "No fight, we want our money back!" The Spanish guy's manager is pleading with him. Murphy's voice blurts into my headphones. "What the hell is happening?"

When I sort it all out, it comes to this: The fighter had asked for a certain amount of money for six rounds. When the manager couldn't get it, he signed his stooge for six rounds anyway. Then he told him he'd be fighting only four, thinking that once the guy was in the ring, it would be too late for him to complain. Not for this cookie.

He wouldn't budge. So they renegotiated right then in the corner. This two-bit cauliflower ears was making history. The fight itself was anti-climactic.

The last bell of the last bout.

I've sweated out five pounds in nerves and I've bungled the job. Through my earphones I get the message of doom: "Guy, we want you to come to a little anteroom just to the left of the exit." Inside this tiny room, the size of a bathroom, maybe, two massive lights shining on a couple of empty chairs, a television camera, a cameraman and a pretty blonde. They've set up an interview for me with Ruby Goldstein, the famous fighter and referee. The discomfort quotient hadn't changed much since I had sung "Auf Wiedersehen" for CBS. This time, instead of being blinded, I was melted. It was so hot I felt as if I was in a sauna, fully dressed and wearing an overcoat.

Jack Murphy squeezes his way into our interview

closet, smiling his Irish eyes. "LeBow, you did great. A great show. You're going to be terrific."

Did that mean that I was going to see another bout? Was I going to be hired again? I wasn't absolutely sure, but I was praying. And then the girl pushes in and says, "Mr. LeBow, you looked great. You were handsome."

She talking to me? I'd never thought of myself as handsome or even good-looking. I'd never had to think about it in radio. Just get the voice in there and the expertise, bathe regularly and shave regularly. And what you wear, wear it pressed. But this television has a new wrinkle. Sounding good is great. But looking good is greater? For the next week I contemplated myself in every mirror, in every store window, and I even preened before the shiny pots and pans in our kitchen.

Murphy gives me a ride into Manhattan—and the news. I'm official. Hired. He liked the way I handled my expertise—my grab bag of facts. That's what made him stop shouting directions. Later events in my career proved out the discovery I'd accidentally made this night and which Murphy learned as well. The public really didn't object to the quantity of talk. It was the quality of talk. And this realization led to jobs in baseball, wrestling and other sports, and to work as a variety show host, interviewer and newsman.

Murphy drops me off at a subway stop. I'd left home that morning as a radio announcer and I arrive back a "handsome" television star who annoys his wife by spending so much time in front of the bathroom mirror.

And also eventually annoys his boss, Bert Lee, Sr., at WHN, after he spends so much time with the Dumont television station. "LeBow," says Lee testily. "Make up your mind. You're either on radio or television. You can't be both." I wasn't smart enough to realize that seeing as how prophets were spelling out radio's doom with the word t-e-l-e-v-i-s-i-o-n, a radio station might not want me shifting my allegiance to the enemy. Especially a radio station owned by a film company—WHN was owned by Loews M-G-M.

If you were called "handsome," you were recognized on the street and mobbed for autographs. If your ego was fed daily doses of flattery, which would you chose—radio or television? I'd originally wanted to try for Hollywood anyway, and television was a good runner-up. So on a Friday in the early fall, I told Lee I'd like to leave WHN in a couple of weeks. No hard feelings—so I thought. But pique works in mysterious ways.

One of the alleged perks of working for WHN was free movie passes to our parent company, Loews. Like all employee passes, this one had restrictions that made it difficult for employees to get the most pleasure out of it: You couldn't use it on Saturdays, Sundays, holidays (you know, when you normally wouldn't be working and would be able to go to the movies) or very special previews. And it wasn't really free. You had to pay tax and a service charge. But my wife and I went to the movies every Friday night and saved about fifty cents between us. On this particular Friday night it was five-thirty when I gave Lee my notice, six o'clock when I left the WHN studios, six-thirty when Toby and I ate at a restaurant near our favorite Loews theater and eight-oh-five when my formerly friendly ticket taker—a distinguished-looking former actor—said, "Sorry, Le-Bow, your pass isn't good here anymore."

I couldn't believe it. In my head I'm seeing a fantastic scenario: When I left Lee's office he started the phones ringing, typewriters clanging, communications buzzing throughout the vast kingdom of Loews theaters with a final message carried by two armed ushers: "Head off LeBow at the pass." If Lee had gone this far for vengeance, was he going to make me turn in my badge as well? I put my hand over the "I love the movies" button on my lapel. I myself had given them out the last time I was host at a Loews theater quiz show.

No turning back now. I was truly committed to television.

*Read All About It:*

# Rancid Camera?

The TV Disease—it can even kill you . . .

## DAD TURNS OFF VIDEO
## THRILLER; SON KILLS HIM

MOUNT CLEMENS, Mich., January 23 (UPI)—Television brought tragedy to the home of a former minister today.

A 15-year-old boy shot and killed his father who had turned off a mystery story because "children shouldn't see that type of picture."

John Sikon, 45, Macomb County Deputy Sheriff and former minister, died in St. Joseph's Hospital today, 10 hours after his son, Gerald, shot him in the back with a shotgun, authorities said.

112

**Family Was Watching It**

Gerald, remorseful after the shooting, said his father had walked into the living room last night and turned off the television set which the family were watching.

An argument followed and Gerald, cleaning his gun in the kitchen, stepped into the living room and shot his father.

Sikon told authorities before he died that he objected to the program for "religious reasons." He said, "Children shouldn't see that type of picture."

Gerald said his father and mother argued frequently and that his father often struck her. Mrs. Sikon's face was bruised and she had a black eye.

*(1952)*

## TV BECOMING PAIN IN NECK

CHICAGO, July 31 (AP)—A physician reported today that a new malady has arisen to plague mankind—television neck.

Dr. William Kaufman of Bridgeport, Conn., who has a special interest in such disorders, said he has observed the symptom in several persons recently.

He said the condition can be caused by strained posture over a long period of time. The faulty posture comes from attempting to keep the face roughly parallel with a low TV screen or, when the room is crowded with viewers, from holding the neck sideways.

*(1952)*

## TV WILL GET YOU IF YOU DON'T WATCH OUT

### Impact on Family Life Grows— How to Handle Children Is a Problem

By CAMERON DAY, Special Writer

September 9—"Television has become a menace in our household. Our 9-year-old son refuses to leave the set at mealtime. When he does, he bolts his food in order to get back to it. He stays glued to the set when he should be outdoors. Something just must be done about television!"

That and similar reactions have turned up repeatedly in recent surveys on video's effect upon children. The situation leading to such comments is becoming more acute as television steadily moves ahead, as schools resume, as the days grow shorter . . .

*(New York World-Telegram and The Sun, 1950)*

## EDUCATOR SAYS TELEVISION MAKES NATION OF MORONS

Special to The New York Times

BOSTON, June 4—Dr. Daniel L. Marsh, president of Boston University, today warned in a baccalaureate sermon to the university's graduating class that "if the television craze continues with the present level of programs, we are destined to have a nation of morons."

He declared that television could never

substitute for books as a medium of learning.

"I deplore," he said, "the intrusion of lazy short-cuts which fool a student into thinking he is learning something when he is not. I refer particularly to television. The habit of reading is a sine qua non of intelligence and television will make impossible the formation of such a habit on the part of young people."

*(New York Times, 1950)*

## TV MAKE YOU THIRSTY?

February 15—TV programs can affect water consumption, according to Water Commissioner Albert Annunziate of Mount Vernon, who claims he has proof they do.

He says a study of his meter charts reveals that water consumption drops when certain TV shows are on. When they're over, however, his meters indicate folks dash to the kitchen for a drink or to the bathroom for a bath or shower.

And he concludes, therefore, that "some shows make people thirsty and give others the feeling they need a bath."

*(New York Daily News, 1953)*

## TELEVISION CAN BE BAD FOR FEET, EXPERT ON LATTER SAYS

February 16—Long Islanders, who, in addition to the ordinary eyestrain hazard that may accompany overzealous televiewing, have already seen one of the neighbors fire a pistol pointblank at a video comedian who disturbed his nap, and were given further cause for caution in their parlor peering last week.

Dr. George C. Horn, Hempstead chiropodist, addressing the Nassau County Podiatry Society, declared that television was fast becoming a prime cause of sprained ankles and other assorted foot troubles.

Dr. Horn pointed out that thousands of people view TV with their feet curled beneath them in a most unnatural fashion. This causes cramped feet, which leads to the feet falling asleep. In this condition, when the program they've just been enjoying ends, and they have to adjust the set to another channel, the viewers' feet cannot hold their weight. "Then," Horn warned, "fractures, sprains and other troubles for the foot and ankle bones occur."

So, Horn urges, assume a good sitting position before the television screen, with your feet flat on the floor, Then you will be ready for a quick, safe sprain-free lunge toward the dial. It is also wise, in the semi-darkness that attends most viewing sessions, to have sundry objects such as children, hassocks, toys (especially those with wheels) and slippery floor mats clear of the path between you and the set, fellow podiatrists suggested.

*(New York Daily News, 1952)*

## SOCIOLOGIST LOOKS AT TV; FINDS IT CUTS TALK 50%

By The Associated Press

LOS ANGELES, July 12—Conversation is off 50 percent and reading all but forgotten among Southern California families that own television sets.

So says a University of Southern California survey conducted by a sociologist, Edward C. McDonagh. Checking through a group of 80 families, he and his interviewers also found:

Ninety percent are listening less to the radio; three-fourths are going to fewer movies; almost half are attending fewer sports events and all are doing less pleasure driving.

Housewives were unanimous in complaining they never went anywhere any more.

*(1950)*

## TV BREEDS ILLITERACY, SAYS HOOTON

CAMBRIDGE, Mass., June 2 (UP—Harvard anthropologist Ernest A. Hooton predicted today that television would "reduce mankind to complete illiteracy.

"It will also ruin our eyes and our nervous systems," he said.

The world-famed scientist said radio and the movies already have delivered a severe blow to human literacy and that television would provide the final stroke.

"People can't read now," he complained. "Our ability to read has deteriorated just as our legs have shrunk from using mechanical transport.

"Already, institutions of higher education have to give special courses in order to teach their students how to read."

Hooton said he had no quarrel with television itself, as a "mechanical gadget."

"It is simply that television offers, for the most part, foolish and harmful material which stultifies its audiences," he said.

### Stultifies Audiences

TV crime shows, he said, present "a correspondence course in crime—a sort of visual education in criminal procedure."

He claimed that such shows "only inspire more people to do the same sort of thing.

"These vicious programs result from the ignorance and venality of movie, radio and television producers," Hooten said.

"Thinking is in danger as well as reading, Hooton said.

"Of course, the majority of mankind doesn't think and never has," he said. But now, he said, modern methods of communication have given more impetus and greater uniformity to the "mouthings of propaganda slogans."

*(1951)*

## TV BLAMED AGAIN

LINCOLN, Neb., October 4 (UP)—J.H. Schleckman, manager of Lincoln City Lines, a bus company, has a theory that transportation lines have financial troubles these days because of television and suburban shopping centers. TV keeps people home nights and daytime travel is curtailed because shopping can be done near homes.

*(1952)*

## TV IS ACCUSED OF TEACHING DIRTY SPORTS

DETROIT, December 8 (AP)—Television wrestlers and roller skaters are teaching children to "play dirty," the head of the Detroit Department of Parks and Recreation complained today.

Superintendent John J. Considine told his staff to rule out in supervised play periods the tactics used by "alleged wrestling and skating stars" on TV programs.

Considine told of a schoolgirl who he said sent her playmate sprawling on a roller skate rink because she had seen such tactics on television.

"And one young wrestler rammed his knee into his opponent's chin, shouting 'This is the way they did it on TV last night,'" Considine said.

He said youngsters have started "to look upon these ridiculous second-rate ham actors as heroes," and added: "The things these clowns pass off as sport do more to teach children dirty playing than we can do to teach them good, clean sportsmanship."

*(1950)*

## SAYS VIDEO
## MAKING U.S. IMMATURE

February 15—Dr. George N. Shuster, president of Hunter College, says television is making American culture "more and more immature and silly."

Shuster yesterday told students at New Jersey College for Women, New Brunswick, that "potentially television could be one of the greatest education forces," but it will prove a failure unless American mothers start wielding their influence.

*(New York Post, 1950)*

## BLAMES TV, RADIO FOR
## SEX ATTACKS

September 17—Dr. Frederic Wertham, nationally famed psychiatrist, today foresaw a possible increase in the city's wave of sex crimes despite the efforts of Police Commissioner Monaghan's new anti-crime patrol.

Dr. Wertham, former director of psychiatric services at Queens General Hospital and one of the nation's leading authorities on sexual misbehavior, blamed TV crime shows, sexy radio programs and lurid comic books for inspiring sexual abuses.

"What good does it do putting 100 extra cops on the street to protect women," he asked, "when the public has helped encourage these attacks?''

Dr. Wertham said the wonder was that there were ''so few rape cases.''

There is no doubt that for the past few years young people are committing violent acts against women and more ruthlessly than ever before.

''Look at our entertainment media. The average young boy is shown, or told, that it's proper and glamorous to hang, punch, rip clothes off, kick or spank a woman. He gets it from all sides, TV, radio and comics.''

The psychiatrist charged that New York's ''real trouble'' was the lack of adequate clinical care in the mental hygiene field. He cited cases of potential sex offenders, who sought treatment and were told they would have to wait long for consultations.

*(New York Post, 1952)*

# 4 / Watch That Zipper, Check That Cleavage

Excerpt from contract of Batten, Barton, Durstine & Osborn, Inc., with Guy LeBow for his services as narrator and commercial announcer for the New York Ranger Hockey Games, 1948:

*Paragraph 10.* "The Artist represents and warrants that the Artist will conduct himself at all times conventionally and with due regard to public morals and decency and will not do anything that will tend to degrade the Artist . . . or will tend to shock, insult or offend the community or reflect unfavorably upon the reputation of the Principal and/or its Advertising Agency, forthwith by giving to the Artist written notice of the Principal's desire so to do if the Principal determines, in its sole discretion, that the Artist has violated any provisions of this paragraph."

—Comment from the "Artist": Baloney!

Don't let nostalgia fool you. Television wasn't the sweet, innocent kid it pretended to be in "Kukla, Fran and Ollie." It was a troublemaker from the start, wearing low-cut dresses, smoking, drinking and telling dirty jokes. But you don't have to take my word for things. The record is down in black-and-white in national headlines:

## THE SINKING VIDEO STANDARDS

### Recent Lapses in Taste and Judgment Underscore Need for Watchfulness

*(1949)*

## THE LOWDOWN ON FAYE'S NECKLINE ROW

*(1950)*

## F.C.C. CALLS ON TV
## TO CLEAN UP ITS PROGRAMS

### Tells Station Operators of Complaints
### of Nudity, Crime Shows and Ads

*(1951)*

## TV MAKES SEX, DRINK SEEM FUN,
## DRYS' PLAINT

*(1952)*

## REP. GATHINGS' SHIMMY
## BRINGS DOWN THE HOUSE

### Says TV Is Too "Lewd"

*(1952)*

Hey, you think television gets raunchy *these days?* With few restrictions on itself, TV *started out* pretty risqué. Sex lurked in every picture tube. Tune in a variety show and you got a good dose of the ripe comedy that had flourished in vaudeville and nightclubs. (Not surprising, since that's the genesis of so many early TV performers.) You know the stuff. Blue jokes, busty girls and sight gags that concentrate on breasts, buttocks and legs. Double entendres: A well-stacked girl passes by. The comic leers, rolls his eyes and says, "Hey, you're the kind of dame that stands out anywhere." There was was lots of lap-sitting, ass-pinching, tit-touching. Bosoms galore in plunging necklines. Stations themselves threw in sex any way they could. Sex had sold Hollywood. Why not TV? The Dumont channel hired girls to work cameras and outfitted them in shorts. At least once during a show, a camera cutie showed up on screen, even if it was a serious program. And when Dumont dressed its models in red for a fashion show, I knew they had to be up to something. (Red didn't show up on TV, remember?)

Sex wasn't just for the men, though. Directors of wrestling matches ordered crotch shots for female fans —who numbered in the hundreds of thousands. (This lesson wasn't lost. Today, when football players go into a huddle, the camera goes into a rearview close-up to please the ladies.)

Compared to what's on TV now, these transgressions may seem tame. But they were serious matters then. Arthur Godfrey caused a national scandal by holding up a miniature toilet and describing it as his "office." (Over a decade later, Jack Paar's bathroom humor led to another scandal.) But TV was so new that what should—and shouldn't—be seen was continually a hot issue. Even a woman in pregnancy was a cause for high anxiety. At WCAU-TV in Philadelphia, station executives' blood pressure rose when half of their husband–wife talk show became pregnant. Should they keep her on the air? Should they let her go? How would the public react? Uniquely inspired, they decided to keep her . . . hidden. The crew built a special chin-high desk where the mother-to-be could be entertaining without shocking. Shocking was NOT what television was supposed to be. Because it came into the home, it was supposed to be wholesome, family entertainment.

But television's women uncovered their talents by dressing in plunging gowns, dubbed the "TV neckline." (Some people called this "nudity.") Even songbird Dinah Shore wore them, and you have to ask why. She had one of the most gorgeous voices for pop songs America has listened to. But in 1950 a bleached-blond phenomenon called Dagmar wore them—and everyone knew why. Teamed with comedian Jerry Lester on "Broadway Tonight," the forerunner of late-night shows, the five-foot-eleven-inch Dagmar cavorted the biggest bust America had ever seen, every midnight, Monday through Friday. The Dagmar Bust was so large one reporter said,

"If she got into an elevator alone, it was crowded!"

(A note on the TV bosom: While there was a boom in busts, there was also a bust in busts. Pulchritude was welcome on the stars, but not on the showgirls. Producer-director John Wray revealed that bosomy girls need not apply. "I would say a 34-inch bust would be the absolute maximum we could stand," he said. Larger breasts moved too much and he didn't want anything distracting from his dance numbers. Distracting for whom, fella? The killjoy even required that his modest-sized girlies wear tight bras to avoid a jiggle.)

Busts, by the way, leads me naturally to another problem: blondes. In early TV, blond hair wasn't sexy, it was a pain in the neck. Technicians called blondes "blizzard heads" because under the intense lighting that color appeared as a shimmery blur. Makeup man Bob Kelly (one of the major innovators of makeup for TV) had to rub carbon paper in blond hair to tone it down. With technical improvements, television was able to prefer blondes by 1950, but Hollywood TV actress Sybil Chism claimed that although it was fine for TV's luminaries, like Faye Emerson, to be blond, less important performers—such as herself—were pressured to change their color. To fight this hair discrimination, Sybil formed the "Benevolent and Protective Order of TV Blondes" (better known as BPOTVB). "I refuse to dye for dear old TV!" she announced dramatically.

Blond hair aside, the dame who milked the most mileage out of her cleavage was Faye Emerson. She became affectionately known as the girl who put the "V" in TV. Faye's road to television read like a "B" picture, and as a matter of fact, Faye had had a so-so film career, appearing in such pictures as *Lady Gangster* and *Manpower*. Then in 1944, divorced and with a young son, she married Elliott Roosevelt. She chucked acting for life as FDR's daughter-in-law and moved to Hyde Park.

Elliott was like early television, totally unpredictable and still trying to find himself. One month he had Faye in Russia, meeting Joseph Stalin, and the next he was selling Christmas trees in Hyde Park. What with one thing and another, the marriage wound down right about the time Faye was discovered by TV. The minute they met, Faye knew she'd found her niche—and she figured out instantly how to fill it.

In case you are misfortunate enough to have missed Faye in her day, she was a dimpled, ample blonde, who could have qualified for *Playboy*'s first centerfold. I always believed it was Faye who started the run on bigger picture tubes for TV. Each night, she appeared on her show with her dress just covering her nipples. At the commercial break, the director raced over to her and yanked her gown UP. Funny how most of us managed to be around the set then. Faye stood demurely watching him with her enoromous brown eyes. But as she walked back onto the set, she pulled her gown DOWN, where she knew it would do her the most good.

Let me not misinform you about Faysie, as famed show-biz columnist Earl Wilson called her. She was not a scheming bimbo. She was one of the nicest people any of us ever met. She was talented, smart, entertaining and if she was around today, she'd be riding the ratings to well-deserved success. All the same, Faysie was a shrewd publicity woman. She could have made a fortune doing PR for others, if she hadn't been in the business for herself. So when John Crosby, radio-TV columnist of the *New York Herald-Tribune*, discussed Faye's neckline, Faye saw gold. She read Crosby's column on the air, inviting her viewers to write in with their opinions. Almost every fan letter said, "Yaay, Faye." "I purchased my television receiver for the purpose of enjoying the football games" wrote in a Harvard grad, "but thanks to you and the other lovely young ladies, I find that I now enjoy watching a plunging neckine as much as a plunging fullback." There were a few complaints, like this one: "You still haven't worn a gown as low as some of our friends do, but I wish you would. Why do you think I turned in our 10-inch set for a 16?" protested another man.

Women adored Faye. One spirited group formed the "Faye Emerson Plunging Neckline Club of Brooklyn" And a housewife said: "I cannot stress too strongly our need to see glamour on television. We have enough cooking and other responsibilities, and when we relax we want to see beauty. So by all means wear your beautiful low-cut gowns. We enjoy them, and that goes for my husband too."

But by 1951, the naysayers in the land were defeating the Fayesayers. In less than three months, the Federal Communications Commission tallied up one thousand negative letters about everything from alcohol ads to violence to indecency. (NBC was the first to go puritan. Even Dagmar passed her neckline exam.) Faysie had seen which way the bodice was moving. Apparently reformed by now, she said huffily, "Some of the girls on television think all they have to do to get ahead is lower their necklines. It's this sort of thing," she warned, "that is going to bring censorship." Naturally the photo of Faye accompanying the article showed her cleavage down to her bellybutton, and that edition sold out. Alas, the reason for buying a sixteen-inch set was soon gone.

If TV couldn't clean up its act—and that included violence, nudity, weak moral fiber—the government threatened to step in. That was all TV needed to hear. The National Association of Radio and Television Broadcasters (NARTB, now the NAB) drew up a code of ethics that took the "V" right out of TV. And a lot of other stuff, too. It's intriguing to see what we're still complaining about, so I've included highlights of the code adopted by the NAB. If all points had been followed, it's even more fascinating to contemplate what television might have become. . . .

*LANGUAGE*: Profanity, obscenity, smut and vulgarity are forbidden. (Say goodbye to cable TV . . . and certain talk shows.)

*ATTITUDES*: Divorce must be treated seriously. Illicit sex must be presented in an unfavorable light. No references to sexual perversion. Sex crimes and abnormalities cannot be considered for programming ideas. Illegal use of drugs cannot be shown. No liquor in American life except for plot or proper characterization. Gambling may not be displayed in a manner to excite interest or foster betting. (Scratch most cop shows, soaps, lottery drawings and more than half the made-for TV movies.)

*CRIME*: May not be condoned or presented in a frivolous, cynical or callous manner. (Kill all the buddy-buddy-lovable-guys-jewel-heist-and-bank-job plots.) No presentation of techniques of crime in such detail as to invite imitation. (Eliminate over thirty percent of scenes in detective shows where we get boring detail of cracking a safe, picking a lock, making a bomb.) No shocking or alarming visual or audio effects. No detailed presentation of brutality or physical agony. (Say bye-bye to "based on a true story" docudramas of serial killers, sex maniacs.)

*ADS*: No hard liquor, firearms and fireworks, intimate personal products, advertising and other organizations promoting betting or lotteries. (No intimate personal products? Scratch off a whopping chunk of sponsors.)

*POLICE*: To be portrayed with respect and dignity. (More cop shows out the window.)

*SUICIDE*: Not to be depicted as an acceptable solution for problems. (That might keep certain classics off the air. "Dear Mr. Shakespeare: Your story line about two teens who fall in love is interesting but not the type of program we find acceptable for our audience. We are returning your script for *Romeo and Juliet*.")

*CHILDREN*: No excessive violence or morbid suspense; no reference to kidnappers or threats of kidnapping. (Scratch more docudramas.)

*DRESS*: Costuming of all performers must be "within the bounds of modesty." (No more Cher?)

*ANATOMY*: Forbidden—lewd movements, indecent dances and camera angles that emphasize anatomical details indecently. Also, "exposure or emphasis on any anatomical details that could offend home viewers." (While some eyes  concentrated on bosoms, another section of the torso slipped into camera view at Channel 11. A stunning young thing later known as Nightbird the DJ, a.k.a. Allison Steele, wriggled into a leotard to do an exercise show. But she wouldn't wear tights and there was the crux of the problem. As she stretched her thighs, she revealed pubic hairs. And the camera, which was lovingly following every stretch and pull of her thighs, showed them clearly. Director Ted Estabrook and the all-male crew were too embarrassed to tell Nightbird. But after an indignant female called the station, it couldn't be put off. The AD with the least seniority, a kid named Herb Holmes, was ordered to talk to her. "I gotta tell her WHAT?" he sputtered. He tentatively broached his subject. "What's it to you?" Allison spat. "I never wear tights, get it?" The cameraman had to focus on another section of anatomy and, single-handedly, Allison the Nightbird fought "emphasis on any anatomical details that could offend home viewers"—and won.)


The code was ratified in 1952. It didn't solve a thing, and by now, the government was involved up to its . . . er . . . neck. TV's morals became the subject of a House subcommittee investigation. Witnesses included a high percentage of temperance members, rabid conservatives and eccentrics. One nut actually testified that television could spread tuberculosis if you talked about the disease over the air.

But the show-stopper of the probe was a sensational belly dance performed by a United States Congressman. Rep. E.C. Gathings of Arkansas had seen the dance on the program "You Asked for It" and was convinced that words alone couldn't convey its "lewdness." His shimmying and shaking brought down the House (subcommittee), got his photo in the papers and no doubt another ballot box of votes in the next election. My question is that if the dance was so disgusting, why didn't Gathings just turn off the TV? Rep. Arthur Klein of New York asked the same question. Gathings' answer, "My children wouldn't let me," also brought down the House.

Yet another bugaboo were alcohol and cigarette commercials. "No!" Rep. Harris of Arkansas thundered. He had witnessed beer commercials in which "people were drinking beer and smacking their lips. This is not something people want coming into their home!" he roared.

But TV was infinitely more evil than this, according to one C.S. Longacre of the American Temperance Society. He described the dreadful situation of church members who could not buy a TV for "fear the liquor interest will present the attractive side of the barrooms and their brothels right in our homes and church programs." (I haven't been able to figure out where the "brothels" come in yet.) Worse, lamented other temperance members, sex and drink were becoming too "alluring" for children. (They weren't all wet, those temperance people. We're finally doing public service commercials cautioning people not to drink too much. As for making sex alluring, I have to tell you that you never know what turns an audience on. I remember a letter received by the popular book-review radio show "Author Meets the Critic" when I worked as its announcer. "The show is wonderful," a woman wrote. "My husband and I listen every night and we have improved our sex life by having sex on the sofa while it's on.")

Luckily for us free souls in the studios, no one thought to investigate what was going on behind the camera—or TV would have been shut down for good. We already had our own code anyway: the straitjacket contracts we signed with advertisers. (You've read the morals clause from one of mine at the beginning of this chapter.) Were they kidding? From the beginning, life was half Hollywood, half fraternity and one-hundred-percent crazy. And none of us wanted to miss out. How else can you explain this note tacked up on the bulletin board at WJZ-TV (now ABC, Channel 7 in New York City)? "Found in bottom drawer of my desk, one pair of slightly used ladies' stockings. Owner please call—preferably after hours—no questions asked."

Across town at Channel 11 that same hot summer of '48, we were somewhat less subtle. On this Saturday afternoon, a young thing ran out of the models' dressing room and along the corridor between the elevator bank and the main studio. She was clad in only her panties. "I can't take it anymore!" she howled. "What fucker stole my bra?" Jiggling with fury, she stopped in front of a bunch of us guys (including the bra burglar) stationed there for that very purpose. "It's brand new and it cost me twenty dollars." She delivered her ultimate threat. "I'm not moving til I get it back!"

O.K., maybe our latest brassiere raid was ill-timed. It came only one week after the models had been victimized by a girl-crazy crazy director. He'd ordered huge mirrors placed on the floor area where models and showgirls changed costumes between numbers, when there wasn't enough time to use the dressing room.

I don't know how the women stood it. But, let's be truthful. Les Girls were no babes in les woods. It was open season on what they call today "interpersonal intraoffice relationships." We called it sex. And there was no lack of equal opportunity. If you were a woman, you got pursued by a man; if you were a man, you got chased by a fantastically and memorably aggressive woman. But we never knew whether the girls were attracted to us or just using us for their own ends. Actresses enticed cameramen, aiming for more and better shots in future TV appearances. Models turned on for directors, trying to reserve a job on the next show. (We guys didn't grouse —there's nothing like knowing you've been of use to someone, right?)

Married or single, women used used every device to meet men. I couldn't go on location for a wrestling match without a couple of Channel 11 secretaries squeezing themsleves into the car along with the director and the camera crew. "We LOVE wrestling!" they shrieked as they squirmed on our laps. Female fans? Not a shrinking violet among them. They called us at the studio and got right to business. "Hi, I watch you all the time. Would you like to come over to my house after your show tonight?" They picked us up in restaurants if we dared to eat there alone. And we caved in like fallen soufflés. Most of the announcers I knew had an extra-curricular affair going in which they'd been the hare, not the hound.

Occasionally a vision of purity and sanity floated into this circus. Like Edie Adams. This lovely, virginal, sweet young girl had been studying to be an opera singer when television leered her way. Edie had answered an ad inviting young talent to vie for Channel 11's entry in the Miss Television World of 1949 contest. She entered and won. On her merits. Then she went to Chicago and won the national title. On her merits, even though the contest director had the hots for her. Returning in glory to Channel 11, Edie came to work with her beautiful, sincere smile and demure, schoolgirl dresses. Which I found out when I talked to Edie recently were no accident. "My mother," Edie said. "She deliberately bought me the most unalluring clothes she could so I wouldn't tempt anyone." All that work from Edie's mama couldn't save her daughter from meeting and falling in love with the craziest, wackiest guy of us all, Ernie Kovacs.

Edie's mama probably would have been happier if Edie had been working way up north in station WBEN, Buffalo. One of the two original engineers there, Neil O'Donnell, filled me in with the details of this family-owned, family-operated station that wouldn't have put up with any of us for a day. WBEN was owned by the Butlers, who also ran the *Buffalo Evening News*. To say that the Butlers were conservative is being conservative. They ran WBEN like it was a finishing school. There was a dress code. Men, even engineers, says Neil, were required to wear a jacket and tie to work at all times. They got off easy, though. Radio announcers had to dress in tuxedos. But that was only the cosmetics.

The Butlers treated their employees like family. In other words, employees had to live the way the Butlers wanted them to. First off, the Butlers believed that a married woman's place was in the home. So they didn't employ married women. When a WBEN couple did marry, the woman had to resign from her job. And once a couple walked down the aisle, the Butlers just about moved in. If they heard rumors of problems, they tried anything to keep the couple hitched. If, God forbid, the divorce went through, there was a penalty: the ex-husband could kiss any promotions goodbye. But, shucks, even the best intentions fail. The Butlers missed a humdinger right under their noses. A husband–wife team on their station turned out to have lived separately for years and admitted that each was gay.

What the hell did they do for fun up there? At Channel 11 we kept a community "first aid" locker stuffed with condoms and liquor in case we got lucky. And one of our engineers was inspired by gossip that Errol Flynn had put peepholes in the women's changing room at his house. The engineer did Errol one better. He installed a hidden camera and hooked it up to monitor in the announcer's lounge for our unlimited viewing pleasure. The only danger to our paradise was Bishop Fulton J. Sheen. Once a week he came to Channel 11 to do his inspirational show. On his stately procession from the elevator to his dressing room, the Bishop passed the announcer's lounge. Although we regarded him as pretty much of a regular guy, we knew he was a man of the cloth and subject to a higher law. If he ever caught on to us, we wouldn't have a prayer.

So we worked out a human alarm system. The bell was comic Danny Webb, imported from Hollywood by Channel 11 to do a kiddie show. Just before the Bishop arrived (like clockwork), Danny stationed his almost five-foot self by the elevator and defogged his glasses. When the doors parted, the sight was enough to convert you, even if you already were Catholic. Six feet plus of purple robe and a flowing cape—a cross between saint and Superman. As soon as the Bishop floated out of the elevator, little chubby-faced Webb—who barely reached the Bishop's crucifix—scampered ahead, shouting, "Jews, run for your lives. Jews run for your lives!"

The Bishop, who had a wicked sense of humor, got a big kick out of this little scenario. And we got the signal to turn off the monitors. No, Les Girls never discovered that they were playing live to a studio audience. P.S.: A few months down the road, the Bishop left Channel 11 to do his show at Dumont's Channel 5. He and Danny, a Jew, had become such a hit performance in the halls that the Bishop presented him with a gift on his last day. It was a bishop's cap, which happens to look like the Jewish yarmulke. "After all," he told Danny, "the Jews invented the yarmulke. We Catholics just changed its religion!"

As I've explained, "Look but don't touch" was not our motto at Channel 11. Watching girls from afar was only a rest stop on our road to conquest. I made unofficial station history in the sponsor's booth—an incident that almost wrecked us with the Federal Communications Commission.

Let me explain. Hoping to impress its sparse sponsors, Channel 11 constructed a special booth with a window that looked down on the main studio. From here sponsors could view their programs and commercials in luxury. The setup had several monitors, wall-to-wall carpeting, a seductive sofa and a bar. The opposite of the knocked-together, bare-bones sets we announcers toiled on. Was this fair? So an announcer devised this bet as a private joke on the sponsors: The first guy to lay a girl in the booth, won. There wasn't any money involved. What do you think we were, crass? The prize would be the respect and envy of fellow announcers, engineers and film men. Eligible for participation were pretty models, female announcers (we had a few, only a few), station secretaries, jr. girl executives and any innocent visitors on the premises.

For weeks now, no one had won the bet. I thought that the girls had caught on and made a counterbet among themselves to see how long they could frustrate us. During this same time, though, a ravishing actress had been sending me meaningful glances. But the day our glances—and schedules—finally meshed was the same day that Frieda Hennock, the first female commissioner on the FCC was visiting Channel 11. (In the journalistic spirit of the day, Frieda's nomination to the FCC was announced in *Newsweek*, June 7, 1948, as "GOVERN-MENT GLAMOUR." And in case anyone doubted her femininity, she was referred to in the article as a "comely New York lawyer.")

Frieda Hennock had charged into the TV industry with the zeal and blunderbuss of the 1920s temperance ladies. She had high hopes for television. She described it as a "living blackboard" or a school without walls—a technological blessing to use for enlightenment, education and world peace.

In preparation for Frieda's visit, the staff had received daily memos on dress code and suitable decorum (as if we needed any reminders). But let's get back to my ravishing-actress pursuer. Miss Ravish and I were at last in the sponsor's booth and now there she was, Frieda, being fawningly ushered into the main studio by program manager Warren Wade. But I wasn't going to be fucked out of making it with Miss Ravish just because the FCC was on the premises. Besides, having to spend so much time on location at wrestling bouts, I was missing out on the opportunities enjoyed by studio-bound announcers. I locked the door to the sponsor's booth. Clothes peeled away . . . and I noticed Miss Ravish wasn't wearing underwear. Was it possible that she had planned to seduce me in the booth all along?

Quick as a newscast, the bet was won. Skirt down. Trousers up. We dared a look to the studio below. Frieda was still observing TV-in-the-making, but I was worried about Wade. He had a sixth sense about sex. If he felt someone else was getting some and he wasn't, he got mean. Wade glanced up, saw me and my gal and glowered. We left the booth . . . fast.

I hated Wade. Everyone—men and women—hated Wade. And everyone had a good reason. For one thing,

Wade was giving sex a bad name at Channel 11. It was understood that we all had our own seduction schtick. Jerry Jerome, bandleader for "The Ted Steele Show," a musical hour very popular with the ladies, cunningly fixed the auditions for female singers. If he thought a girl was a potential score, but she wasn't a strong singer, Jerome arranged for one of the horns to drown her out during the difficult passages. She got the job and he got the girl. But Wade had no couth.

His first day on the job, we saw workmen change the glass wall of his office from clear to opaque. His intentions became crystal clear a day later, when I witnessed a willowy model slam the door and stand outside buttoning her blouse. "That cocksucking shit," she muttered.

Being program manager, Wade had the influence to fire any girl who refused his horny advances. That steamed most of us guys. We didn't hold jobs hostage for sex. But Wade must have have had fantasies about being a Hollywood producer because he turned his office into a casting couch. It didn't take long for word to get around. You could always tell when a girl had received a summons: she scurried down the hall, muttering to herself and fixing her hair at the same time. Leering in wait for her was the prototype of the office satyr: a fat, squat body connected to an ugly oversize head. And for a movie mogul touch: a wet cigar between moist, rubbery lips. Every now and then, Wade met with a stunning defeat, which called for drinks all around. Gail Meredith, a vibrant blond singer on Ving Merlin's "Enchanted Strings" (a show with an orchestra of all "girls," called "violin Venuses"), emerged from her ordeal with every hair in place and not a wrinkle in her dress.

"What happened?" I asked.

"I looked him right in the balls and said 'No!'"

You think only females had their Wades to run from?

We men got the business from males, too. But it was conducted more subtly because homosexuality was still in the closet. It happened to almost all of us at one time or another. And you'd think it would make us more empathetic with the girls' plight, but it didn't. You could be in a meeting with an ad agency account executive and find a too friendly hand persistently slapping your thigh. The kind of gesture that was open to interpretation by the slappee. Even more arcane was a code I bumped into, after winning a commercial audition. The account executive invited me up to his office. Full of enthusiasm. "Guy, I really like your work. Very impressed." Etc. and etc. When I got up to leave, he said, "Looking forward to working with you, alrighty?" "Great!" I said. He frowned slightly. "Really looking forward to it," he repeated. "Alrighty?" "Great!" I replied. And left.

I never got the contract for that job. I never heard from the agency or the sponsor. It was as if I'd never won the audition. And I should explain that winning an audition was, in essence, clinching the job. The contract was a formality. I replayed that scene in my head a dozen times. I was sure I hadn't said anything offensive. So I asked a friend of mine in the ad business what went wrong. I told him word for word what was said in the office. At "Alrighty," he stopped me. "That's it," he said. "You were supposed to answer with 'Alrighty.' That's how he'd know you were willing to play pants down. Otherwise, he wasn't going to hire you. There's a network out there and if you come up against it, good luck!"

If you don't believe me, take the word of one of the country's most respected media critics, *Daily News* columnist Ben Gross. An old-timer by 1952, Gross never wrote for sensationalism and always checked out his sources carefully. So when a television writer of high standing came to Ben with the situation below, you know Ben spent weeks going back over the man's tracks. I have to warn you. The following excerpt contains language that might be offensive to some readers. Nineteen hundred and fifty-two was a different climate. Homosexuality was regarded as a sickness that could be cured. Newspapers thought nothing of printing stories about cops rounding up—and I quote: "hoodlums, homosexuals and other undesirables" in Times Square. Nonetheless, the writer's problem must have been a very real one of the time, for the reason that Ben enunciates in his piece. Gross's column was called "Looking and Listening with Ben Gross." This one was dated April 20, 1952.

### VIDEO PIONEER BLAMES
### INCOMPETENTS & 'QUEERS'
### FOR POOR PLAYS ON TV

Said Ben, "The chief obstacles to better plays on television, according to this informant, are the lack of qualifications on the part of those who pass on the scripts —the so-called editors—and the alarming influx of queers on TV.

"These are sensational charges," he continued, ". . . but are of national interest because they affect the quality of the entertainment seen on millions of home screens throughout the country."

The TV writer had told Ben, "Writers today are 'frustrated and insulted' in trying to 'deal with these people who set themselves up as the alpha and omega of what is TV drama.'" He had also pointed out, "What is even more incredible is the ever-increasing number of homosexuals who are placed in these positions. . . . I have been in radio for more than twenty years and in television for seven. My personal observation is that the rate of influx of the 'queers' in TV in the past three years is truly alarming. Where did these phonies come from?

What gives them their power? What makes them geniuses? I can't find any satisfactory answers. My friends and associates—many of them fine writers and actors—lead normal lives, stay married and have families. They want to work and stay that way. But that is becoming quite a problem in television!"

The other day, I was sitting around talking over the early-girly days with some of my old crazy colleagues. We all grew up into responsible adults. I even reformed and eventually was one of the first ten men asked to join the American Women in Radio and TV. I also became a member of NOW. (I hope they don't make me turn in my pins after reading this!)

We had families and dogs and station wagons, even the bra-snitching engineer and the mirror-mad director. It was he who shook his head and said, "I can't believe I really did all those things!" (The same could be said by the announcer who came from CBS with a reputation for scoring regularly with a girl in a CBS phone booth. (Remember when phone booths still had little seats in them?) Or the famous adorable kiddie show puppeteer who couldn't wait to leave the set to start playing kiss-and-don't-tell with her director. Or the now legendary and avuncular CBS news commentator who did twice-weekly in-depth "interviews" with a charming Miss of a rival station. And, my God, I almost forgot the weather-man who stayed around after the station went off the air for the night. He'd found that sex in the ladies room—with ladies—kept his temperature at heat wave levels.)

So being serious for a minute, we began to seriously analyze why serious professionals—because we were serious—had been so insane. For that matter, why the whole business had been. We think it was combination of factors. Most of us were young guys, coming into a brand-new business with zilch tradition and fewer rules. Unlike radio, TV had no hallowed performers of twenty or thirty years to make us feel like the upstarts we were.

Well, one. That paragon of TV success, Arthur Godfrey. He hadn't been on TV as long as some of us, but he beat us all to the punch when it came to girls. During his halcyon days, he was forced to keep his New York City home phone number secret because he was constantly harassed by his fans. The FBI, CIA and KGB combined couldn't have cracked this one. But on a slow afternoon, a showy actress-model boasted that SHE had Godfrey's phone number. The bet was on. She dialed and we listened breathlessly on the extensions.

"Hello, Arthur?" she said.

"Helloww darlin. This is Ahthuh," crooned the unmistakable voice. "How ahh ya? How ahh ya?"

Doris smiled victoriously. Then Godfrey said, "And what's your name, darlin?"

We found out that he'd given scores of models his private number and never knew which one was on the line. The way Godfrey was going, we were glad he wasn't at Channel 11. We couldn't compete with Ahthuh —we could only stand and applaud. What a man. . . .

And, as I was explaining, a lot of us were returning servicemen, still hyped up with risk and adventure and used to the ripe atmosphere of all-male life. Then too we were happy victims of circumstances. The war had caused a man shortage and women were just as glad to see men as the other way around. And the women, who had so long fantasized about Hollywood screen stars, were discovering that they could live out their fantasies with us, the smaller fry on the smaller screen. Add to this the fact that everyone was constantly keyed up because live TV was so frenetic. Throw in our egos; introduce a constant stream of photogenic, luscious females . . . and you have high-voltage sexual current that never shuts off. Whoever said "Youth is wasted on the young" never worked in early TV.

*Station Break:*

# Who's Laughing?

I've been warned by friends not to include this chapter —but what the hell! If as a journalist I saw evidences of rabid discrimination around the broadcast industry during the times I'm writing about, would you respect me if I said nothing . . . while plying safe waters only?

Anyway, I give myself the right to speak. Like many people, I naively thought that things would be different when peace came in 1945. Since 1941, America had been united in a single effort to repel an enemy so evil that it was not merely countries or men but a force of darkness. The Allied triumph was the victory of freedom and brotherhood and humanity—so some of us liked to believe. But these were just words to the heinous bums who brought to the new magic called TV the same old wearied venality that had putrified the world for so long.

I got a sour dose of the status quo after winning an

audition as baseball announcer in Baltimore.

"Do you happen to be Jewish?" asked the owner of the team.

"What kind of question is that, especially since *you're* Jewish!"

"That's true," he said. "But in your case it could be a problem."

"Problem?"

"They don't let us into the country clubs around here," he explained. "You wouldn't be able to mix with the social set and the high rollers, so you won't be any good to our beer sponsors as a spokesman. That's the way it is." And for several years, that's the way it was.

In at least four New York City stations, anti-black, anti-Semitic and anti-Italian sentiment flourished in the late forties and early fifties. (Perhaps the lice that polluted TV came well prepared by the conduct of the major ad agencies of the time. No blacks. No Jews. No Italians. In fact, no one out of the three-button suit, polyester jacket, khaki jeans mold. Your car'd better be a Ford. And drinkie-winkies at "21.") A chief announcer of NBC, Pat Kelly, was known to be rabid in his dislike of Jews, and blocked their employment with his special filing system. It was very simple: after your interview he shoved your application in the back of his drawer. That way, no one leafing through the file drawer of applicants could ever find yours.

Philadelphia had a notorious bigot at WCAU-TV, G. Bennett Larson. You met Larson in "And Now a Word from Our Sponsor . . . We Hope," when he reneged on promises to advertising companies. He got his practice for that in Philly where it was alleged he embezzled announcers' commercial fees. Larson was a Mormon who tolerated no Jews unless absolutely necessary. Occasionally he hired them as salesmen, because they "made good peddlers"—as he didn't hesitate to tell them.

But G.B., an equal-opportunity bigot, was prejudiced against women too. When he moved to Channel 11 in New York City, he fired one of our most versatile directors, Peggy Gannon, telling her to "go home and have babies. Television is not woman's work. Women, my dear, belong in the kitchen." Peggy took part of G.B.'s fatherly advice. She switched to an ad agency, where she became their premier director of TV ads featuring kitchen and home equipment. I would like to have been around when G.B. was informed that the latest commercial on his station was done by one Miss Gannon.

You never knew *who* held *what* hatred, but I was shocked when Alan B. Dumont's cousin, Ed Woodruff, revealed that Dumont had once told him: "This station is going to remain lily-white. I'm not going to hire Negroes. And I don't want Jews around unless it's necessary." Maybe that explains the predicament of a young fellow named Marvin Pakula, who worked at Dumont as a floor manager. This was a relatively low-grade job, normally a stepping-stone to director. But in more than ten years Pakula never made it, though he was ultra-creative: an artist, photographer, writer, sculptor. He was also Jewish. He received myriad letters from producers and sponsors lauding his work, which he turned over to management for its files. Later, when he asked to see them in a salary dispute, he was told that they were "missing."

The arch-architect of this and other inquities was an executive named Tom Gallery. But Tom's special distinction was being married to the only screen actress actually barred by President Roosevelt from visiting Veterans' Hospitals during the war. This was Zasu Pitts. Before she was stopped, she had already traumatized injured veterans, lying blinded, maimed and forever emotionally scarred, by telling them that their injuries had been for nothing, that the United States shouldn't be fighting the Germans.

The television campaign against blacks—an immense and painful subject—deserves its own book. Who can say how much further television would have come if it had opened its doors more widely to this pool of talent? Even by 1956, Nat King Cole couldn't find a sponsor for his show. And much earlier, Channel 11 tried to force white and black performers to use separate dressing rooms. Those of us opposed to this went to New York Senator Jake Javits, who threatened to challenge the station's license at the FCC—and it backed off. Good people fought discrimination in their own territory. At the same station, an ordinary good guy—announcer Joe Bolton—refused to show any movies Channel 11 programmed on his popular shows if they denigrated blacks, which they often did. Bolton was easily one of the best local TV talents developed.

For every story I give you there are hundreds upon hundreds of others, most of which have never been printed in a newspaper or magazine. Only the Commie scare got big press—probably because it wasn't color . . . or religion . . . or ethnic. When certain congressmen went berserk about the Commie threat, things got even crazier at television stations. I witnessed stars like Zero Mostel fired unceremoniously after Channel 11 executives were told he was a Communist. (No proof needed.) I saw the great singing group The Weavers dropped after a dress rehearsal. The charge: "Commies." No proof wanted. And that station also barred all Charlie Chaplin movies on complaint from Cardinal Spellman that Chaplin was a pinko.

But time and trouble in the USofA march on. The point of this chapter is that yes, these things happened—but yes, they're happening less and less (we can hope). The insidious bastards who tried to perpetuate the society of privilege and hate in their TV reign are mostly on file in the obituaries by now. If they'd had their way, we wouldn't have Bill Cosby or Lorne Greene or Arsenio Hall or Joan Rivers or Lesley Stahl or Judy Woodruff or Ed Bradley. But hey, man, this is a hell of a country! This morning I woke up, watched Bryant Gumble, parlayed that with Geraldo Rivera and Oprah Winfrey (switching back and forth with Donohue, of course), caught Barbara Walters, then Ted Koppel and went to bed with Johnny Carson and big Ed McMahon. Tomorrow morning I'll catch my *paisan* buddy Pat Cooper on radio. I'll laugh a lot with Pat, but I'll be thinking back to the days I've been writing about. The troubles were no laughing matter.

I've been thinking too about the friends who warned me not to write about this stuff. Ya know, who needs them? I could never borrow a cent.

# 5 / "It's a Helmet Bout, Men!"

"Who likes wrestling? Nobody. Only the people."

—comment of the day
from a critic

It stopped a sensational murder trial cold, captured a world-famous conductor and drove women into a frenzy. It was . . . TV WRESTLING!

I see some of your lips curling up in a sneer, but stand by, please. This wasn't the lily-livered parody foisted on audiences in the last twenty years. This was wrestling with a capital "W," the sport that starred the one and only Gorgeous George, that won an Emmy in 1949, that played a starring role in making TV. Maybe it wasn't the sport of kings, but for a time wrestling was the king of sports—and its announcers were royalty too.

Let me take you back to a spring day in 1950, to that murder trial I mentioned above. There's this fifty-year-old guy, Camilo Leyra, Jr. He's accused of the most heinous crime: murdering his elderly mother and father. New Yorkers have been eagerly following every detail of

152

the gruesome evidence during the trial. Presiding is Judge Samuel S. Leibowitz, one of the most respected and feared justices of the day and the greatest criminal attorney of all time.

It happens that Leibowitz is also one of the great wrestling nuts of all time. Two weeks earlier, I had found him next to my seat at the Eastern Parkway Arena in Brooklyn, when I arrived to do my regular Tuesday-night television match. All evening I kept one eye on him and one on the ring. This internationally famous lawyer —so revered that he became the first judge invited by the Russians to sit at their criminal trials—was up and down like a gavel at a messy court case. He screamed at the bad guys, egged on the good. It was unbelievable. I'd been reading about the career of Sam Leibowitz ever since I was in kneepants. How he risked his life to defend nine Alabama blacks in the landmark Scottsboro Case in 1933. How he refused to defend the Lindbergh baby kidnapper, Bruno Hauptmann. And now he's going nuts.

After the match, Leibowitz took me for bagels and coffee at his favorite cafeteria a few blocks away. He explained that wrestling relaxed him. "It's gratifying to be able to boo the villain!" he tells me. I give him a copy of the book I've just written, *The Wrestling Scene*, which covered the whole business from coast to coast, across the seas and back centuries to the ancient Egyptians, who thought it was a great way to break bones. And Leibowitz gives me an invitation to be his guest at the Leyra trial.

So now it's two weeks later. I'm in Leibowitz's courtroom. It's eleven a.m.; lunch is scheduled for about one p.m. The judge spots me and what happens next I wouldn't believe if I hadn't been there. Leibowitz stops the trial. From under his desk he brings out his copy of *The Wrestling Scene,* shows it to the spectators, introduces me. The crowd cheers and applauds. I'm waving like I'm playing the Palace Theater. The prisoner beams.

# TV'S EARLY HEROES

*Gorgeous George.*

*Baron Michele Leone.*

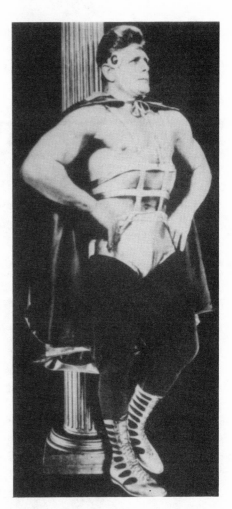

*Golden Superman.*

155

*Nature Boy Buddy Rogers.*

*Iron Mike Mazurki.*

156

*The French Angel.*

*The famous Rocca–Stanlee match, Rocca performing his flying dropkick.*

157

"Ladies and gentlemen, we're taking a short recess," Judge Leibowitz announces, glaring at Leyra. "The accused will be taken from the court." As the guards lead Leyra past me to get to the anteroom, he winks. "Hi, Guy. Good to see ya." Icicles form on my gut. The prosecution alleges that after this cool character hammered his parents into the Great Beyond, he changed out of his bloody clothes and gave them to a derelict on the street. Then he bought his wife a box of candy for her birthday and went home. I still get that frozen feeling forty years later when I think of Leyra being chummy with me. (The Leyra case had a believe-it-or-not ending which you've got to read. It's the end of this chapter, along with a note about another crazy side of Leibowitz's character. What a guy!)

Was Leibowitz the number-one wrestling fan in the country? If not, he was certainly in a dead tie with the world-renowned conductor Arturo Toscanini. My publishers ran TV ads just before the book came out—and a check signed by the maestro himself came in with a note asking for the first copy. Toscanini's adoring public would have been shocked to see the white-haired maestro leaping around and yelling himself hoarse as he watched bouts on his television set. His home in New York City's exclusive Riverdale section was crammed with almost as much wrestling memorabilia as music.

Send me up for perjury if the above isn't true. From 1947 to 1950 this country was in the grip of a wrestling mania. It crossed all age, sex and occupation boundaries. Lawyers, milkmen, children, housewives—you name it. When I was digging into wrestling for my book, I interviewed New England's prime wrestling historian and promoter, "Papa" Bowser. "We get a lot of high-class people," he said. "Judges, big doctors and some of the best citizens in Massachusetts go to matches."

The grunt-and-groan game was just reviving from a

fifteen-year slump when television came along. It was perfect timing. You could get cross-eyed trying to follow team sports on seven-inch or ten-inch TV screens, but it was easy to concentrate on a pair of opponents confined to a ring. For stations scrambling to fill program slots, wrestling was ideal. All they had to provide was a technical crew and an announcer. The stars (wrestlers) and supporting cast (spectators) were taken care of. By 1948, you could tune in a wrestling match every day of the week. Wrestling got a bigger audience than boxing, and in some areas of the country, better ratings than "Uncle Miltie" on Tuesday nights.

Kids became as familiar with the latest wrestling holds as they were with the call, "It's Howdy Doody time!" Walk by a schoolyard and you'd hear the shrill voices of young boys challenging each other to a match: "I'm Rocca." "I'm Stanlee." In fact, TV announcers like myself were begged by parents to discourage their kids from imitating the pros because there were so many injuries.

But the real fanatics were the females—teenagers, grandmas, mothers, wives, delicate maiden aunts. They baked cakes for their favorites. Knit them sweaters. Even sewed wrestling trunks, especially for Gene Stanlee, Mr. America. One girl stitched "I love you, Gene" inside the crotch of the trunks. When she presented them to him at a wrestling bout, he turned the trunks inside out to show the crowd. Scream! Gasp! A woman in the audience fainted and had to be carried out. Mr. America, a blond twenty-six-year-old Adonis with a picture-perfect phy-sique, was called "Wrestling's Heartthrob." (And was he dumb! During an interview he told me that he had studied "injineerin' at 'Tchicago Collitch.'") Other women just lost contact with reality. Like the one who shaved her head to imitate her hero, "Chief Little Wolf." Irate husbands wrote me about their wives' crushes on wrestlers. "All I'm entitled to now is leftovers, especially when it comes to affection," complained a lonely guy. "By the time a Mr. America match is through, she's too tired for anything."

With the enormous amount of publicity it was getting, wrestling attracted the acting world. It became the "in" thing, like buying season's passes to basketball games is now. Marlon Brando and vaudeville star Bennie Fields dropped by to sit ringside with me; established movie actresses like Arlene Judge and newcomer Edie Adams made appearances. Or was it that they wanted to see the competition? Because wrestlers were siphoning off glory from Hollywood. While movie houses sobbed over sagging sales in 1949, wrestling walked off with 36 million dollars. Even the distinguished *New York Herald-Tribune* admitted there might be something going on when its sports editor, Bob Cooke, reported from Hollywood, "Celebrities like Sheik Lawrence of Arabia, Antonino Rocca and the famous wrestling team of Garibaldi, father and son, are destroying the prominence of names like Gable and Turner."

There had to be something to all these fireworks, and trust me—there was. Wrestling could be corny and overdramatic, but by and large the wrestlers were great athletes and knew how to fake it. And wrestling wasn't all costume and corn. The main star of the night might be a faker with costume and corn, but the other bouts would feature genuinely skilled athletes who put on breathtaking exhibitions. There was Marvin Mercer, known for his atomic drop-kick maneuver; Abe Cohen; Tony Martinelli (I nicknamed him the "Clifton Cutie"); Lou Thesz (considered the "champ" by most wrestlers); and George Becker. Every time Becker was in the ring, I knew I'd have to sharpen my tempo and use all my skills in calling holds. Becker got in and out of holds with a smooth guile that kept a match at a suspense-filled pace.

Wrestling had a far more sophisticated past than you'd imagine from seeing its commercial fate. It was a civilized form of competition in the Greco-Roman times, and later. As the nineteenth century came to a close, most wrestling around the world was either under collegiate rules or Greco-Roman rules: Athletes fought very slowly and one wrestler might hold another in a lock for as long as two or three hours. You had to be obsessed to sit through one of these matches. In the early 1900s, when professional entrepreneurs tried to commercialize wrestling just like boxing, audiences yawned and stayed away. Can you blame them? So they turned wrestling into a show of "flying mares" and somersaults, which they called "catch-as-catch-can" wrestling. It caught on big. To fill the demand for more wrestlers, promoters recruited tough guys from the infamous barnstorming days of wrestling. This was when a so-called "Strongest Man in the World" would troop from town to town—like the old traveling medicine shows—and challenge anyone to wrestle for $100. From this bunch came such behemoths as the ogreish Dusek family and the wiley Garibaldis, who augmented the ranks of genuine stars like "Strangler" Lewis and Jim Londos.

By the time I got to wrestling after the war, it was a three-ring circus of sex, comedy and skill that added up to a spectacular show. And what a cast! Recently, one television station presented what they called a "history" of wrestling. "Let's go all the way back twenty years," some squeaky-voiced announcer said. (That far back? I thought. Gosh!) No mention of the glorious, notorious fellows forty years ago who filled TV screens night after night with their talent, skill and great PR.

There was California's Gorgeous George. He flaunted a wardrobe bigger than Joan Crawford's and turned every match into a fashion show. Anglophiles cheered for Lord Leslie Carlton, a British aristocrat (so he said) every bit as suave as David Niven. He swept in with a top hat, cape, monocle and valet—all of which accompanied him into the ring. For freakishness, there was the French Angel. His grotesque face was the opposite of his name: it looked as if he'd been hit by a train and then run over by a tractor. Actually, it was the result of a glandular disorder. Trained in law, the French Angel decided his looks would do clients more harm than good, so he turned to his second love, wrestling.

Many of the wrestlers I encountered had been collegiate wrestlers, or strongman acts in vaudeville or nightclubs, or were physical culture enthusiasts. The public was drawn to personalities, but they demanded skill along with eccentricities. Clothes or gimmicks didn't make the man. If you couldn't cut the mustard in the ring, you were booed out of the circuit. People wouldn't come to see you. The Big Daddy Promoters lost money. And this made them very unhappy.

In 1947, the country was already carved into wrestling fiefdoms, or circuits, each ruled by a powerful overlord. And just as in the Mafia, one kingpin didn't invade the other's territory. I mean never. An old grizzled grappler, Joe "Toots" Mondt, controlled the East. He allowed another former wrestling star, Ed Don George, to hold court over Buffalo and Canada. Vince McMahon, father of the now prominent Vince Jr. headed Washington, D.C., and parts of the South. The remainder of the country—Midwest, Southwest and Far West—were parceled out to lesser figures:

With the coming of television, each entrepreneur cannily developed his own gang of stars. But there was no national "champ." A guy could win in New York and his promoter could claim he was undefeated—when in truth he might have lost ten consecutive times in Pennsylvania, Maryland and Delaware. Who would know? Television still had no network and the newspapers didn't cover much wrestling, insisting they were above such phoniness. But by 1952, when television networks were formed, it became embarrassing for a promoter to advertise a guy as undefeated when the TV audience had seen the guy get his ass kicked on some other station the night before. I checked with my wrestling colleagues, Dick Lane in Los Angeles, Wayne Griffin in Chicago, the indomitable Sam Taub in New York, among others. We were all having the same problems of having to cover obvious promotion lies. The scene was getting out of hand. We didn't know it, but the erosion of wrestling as a top TV drawing card had begun.

But I want you to know how it was in the glory days when the wrestlers and we announcers couldn't walk five feet without being surrounded by autograph hungers. When we couldn't have a bowl of soup in a restaurant without people shoving papers in our faces for signatures. When we couldn't have a family outing in privacy. Wrestling fans adopted us like we were their family. Years later I, was still receiving Christmas cards from diehard wrestling fans.

It was during this time that Dumont Television assigned me to pinch-hit for their regular grunt-and-groan caller, Dennis James, the most popular early-TV personality. James, a dark-haired, photogenic fellow in his late twenties, was a transplanted radio DJ and game show host with a smoooth manner that wowed the ladies. (He had supposedly lost his job at WNEW Radio for wolfing one ardent fan right on his boss's desk.) James had no real sports background, but Dumont used him anyway. At least until he hit football and allegedly sabotaged his sportscasting future by announcing "the ball is down on the 55-yard line." A goof like that could laugh you into oblivion.

Dumont figured they'd better have a genuine sportscaster at the mike, so they sent me in as relief. When I went over to Channel 11 in 1948, I was tapped as the wrestling announcer. And given the Herculean task of luring audiences away from James—and Dumont. If I was going to beat James, I'd have to dope out something better in order to beat him at his own game.

All this time, I'd been methodically studying James's ringside technique. He was glib and funny, and he had a great gimmick he'd brought from his radio days: sound effects. During certain holds he ran his fingers over a balloon for an unearthly screech. He played a harmonica. He cracked bones near the mike for bone crushers. Beautiful accompaniment for the drama in the ring— because all the world's a stage for wrestlers. They play shamelessly to the audience: wince and grimace when they're hurt, cry and beg for mercy when they see defeat stalking them. I took my cue from their overblown acting and prepared a slew of sounds even more ridiculous than James's. The engineers back at the studio got explict instructions: "Put on the babies crying sound track if they show pain! Play the sheep bleating if they strut arrogantly. Use the wolf howling, dishes breaking, cars screeching to a halt, women sobbing—I did it all. Sound hokey? Of course. Hokum is what my audiences came for.

We announcers were definitely part of the entertainment—if that's what the fans demanded. Out in Los Angeles, though, where you'd expect the zaniest antics, things were much different. The top wrestling announcer there was Dick Lane on KTLA. (As a matter of fact, KTLA's wrestling coverage copped an Emmy in 1949 for best sports reporting.) Lane was an established supporting movie actor (familiar as a reporter, cop, explosive businessman), and he could have souped up his narration with the worst of us. But he told me that his audiences liked good clean wrestling with no gimmicks. That, I insisted to him, was real talent—doing wrestling and keeping a straight face! New York audiences liked their wrestling with a side of hammy announcer. And I was only too happy to oblige. . . .

Like the one and only time I called a match starring Gorgeous George. My sponsor, Ripley Clothes, helped me carry out a reception for Gorgeous that almost uncurled his peroxide ringlets. This night, Gorgeous makes his usual modest entrance. He's preceded by his valet, Jeffrys, who spritzes George's perfume into the ring. I feint a faint and spray my own bottle of Parfum d'Amour. Then . . . HE appears in the aisle, scattering golden hairpins among the ladies. Pandemonium, as they knock each other over clawing to retrieve the cherished souvenirs. Gorgeous doesn't even glance at them. He stands in the spotlight, ringlets glowing, chest expanded, brocade robe glimmering. I let him have this round.

He climbs into the ring, unwraps his golden hairnet and throws it into the crowd. Major hysteria, with piercing shrieks of "I got it! It's mine!" from the fourth row. Now I fling out a rose to the audience—more yelling. You could always count on wrestling fans to play along. Georgeous's eyebrow is raising. His valet elaborately helps him off with the robe, revealing—shriek! sigh!—spangled trunks. I turn to the audience—making sure the camera is on me—and reveal my Gorgeous Guy garb: Ripley has made for me a gold lamé tux, with matching cummerbund and tie. My assistant is in a sober black tux for contrast. Now, mass hysteria.

Gorgeous shakes the ropes like a bleached gorilla. "You stupid bum, get out of my act! I'm the great Gorgeous George!"

"You call this an act?" I shoot back. "Start wrestling, you creep!" (Boos and cheers from the spectators.)

He leans over the ropes and snarls, "You're dead. I'll take care of you later, chump."

As insurance, I repeat what Gorgeous said to the

crowd. "If I'm not back here next week," I yell dramatically, "you know who to blame!"

Gorgeous was an ugly sport. That night he kicked resin in my face. I retaliated with a rose, throwing him off balance. He shook his fist, I called him a coward. There's something to hearing all that cheering and clapping for yourself. Maybe there's a little Gorgeous George in all of us. . . .

Gorgeous never returned to that arena. I retired, champion of Ridgewood Grove.

My penchant for performing almost did me in with Ripley Clothes. As a publicity stunt, I was made an official member of the Apache tribe. I had been hoping for a heroic name, like "Chief Stout Heart." Or romantic: "Chief Swell-Looking." But the Indians put my moniker where my mouth was and named me "Chief Talking Eagle." At intermission, a full-blooded Indian and his wife showed up in native dress to do my honors. To keep the pace jaunty, I did some light ad-libbing. "I hope there are no dues in this organization," I said. The real Chief came back with: "For you, Chief Talking Eagle, it's free." "Good," I said, "because if there were any dues, I wouldn't join."

The next day, the president of Ripley, Moe Newman, summoned me from my office at Channel 11 to lunch with the Ripley boys. Thanks to my wrestling following, Ripley Clothes had grown into a lucrative chain. Fans wrote me that after seeing the show, they'd go to Ripley to buy their clothes. I passed all these letters along to Moe. Each week, I wore a different Ripley suit to call a match—and after each night I returned it to them. The tight sons of bitches had never let me keep a handkerchief. But after my performance last night they were going to bite the bullet and give me a suit, I thought. Instead, I was burned at the stake.

"LeBow, we're very disappointed in you." Moe

began. The other Ripley persons nodded in agreement with "tsks" and "tssks." "We trusted you and you've let us down."

I'm thinking—how? How? Did I wear the suit inside out last night? Did I put on another brand by mistake, God help me? Did I murder the commercial?

Moe is still shaking his head with a few "nuus." "We didn't realize you were anti-Semitic," he told me.

You could have knocked me over with a feather headdress. I told Moe *et al.* that I was Jewish. It didn't cut any matzoh with them. "You said," Moe continued, "that you would not join the tribe if there were any Jews. We heard you."

"Dues," I said. "I said, 'Dues.'" I turned somersaults trying to convince them, but they didn't believe me. "We'll be watching you, every word, Guy, every word."

Back at the mike, I had several techniques for doing broadcasts straight when the match called for it. I used all the techniques I had developed for my other sports broadcasts. The combination worked so well with the audience that by 1949 my Channel 11 wrestling casts were rated one of the "Top Ten" telecasts in TV. To be truthful, James and I both got star ratings for our wrestling shows. And though we wanted to get into other kinds of television—how long can you keep your sanity doing wrestling!—neither of us was going to give the other an inch. We battled on all fronts. If James made a personal appearance at a movie theater, I hosted the opening of a shopping mall. If he toastmastered a dinner, I'd do a political banquet. Then I hit a grand slam when *TeleVision Guide* featured me on its cover. (Not for my boxing or my baseball or my football—but for wrestling! I told you it was hot!) And what did James do? He hit me with a haymaker. The lights nearly went out for me when Hollywood announced it was featuring him in a movie, *Mr. Universe.*

I nearly turned in all my sound effects. How do you top a Hollywood movie?

My viewers had a voracious appetite for information. Each week, my fan mail bags were bulging with letters asking for facts about the wrestlers, their holds, the great wrestlers of the past. I boned up on history at the library, interviewed wrestlers and stayed up till the wee hours to answer each letter. It finally dawned on me. Cover the questions in one book. Write a book! The result was *The Wrestling Scene*, which sold just under 300,000 copies that year. (I was told that it outdid the Bible, which, as a wrestling announcer, I could understand. That book had only one paltry wrestling scene, the one between Jacob and the angel.) Boy, take THAT, Dennis, I thought every time I saw a pile of LeBow books in a window next to a big poster of me. What could be better? This: James quit calling wrestling for good and went into game shows. Now I was King of New York and the Eastern Seaboard.

A lot I knew. My reputation as a wrestling announcer is something I've never lived down. Forty years have passed. I've gone legit and been a newscaster. (Even won awards for it.) The World Series. Been an anchorman for ABC. Done a few movies. Radio talk shows. But no, to a former wrestling fan, there is no such thing as rehabilitation. They still see me on the street today and say, "I know you . . . you used to do . . . wrestling!"

On the cover of that *TeleVision Guide* I was wearing my World War II air raid warden's helmet. That wasn't just for the picture. Some of the wrestlers got sore at me for my entertaining sound effects. They retaliated with the only weapon they had—their bodies. They threw each other's 180, 250, 300 pounds at my head or my lap. I could get hurt! Or laugh them out of it. I retrieved my air raid warden's helmet from the back of our hall closet, found a few extras for my crew, and when I sensed some crusher was going to come flying out of the ring, I donned my helmet and sounded the warning: "It's a helmet bout, men!" That became my trademark.

For variety, I stayed bareheaded and ran up to the third or fourth row of seats to get away. But the audience could be just as deadly as the wrestlers. We needed extra insurance for this sport! For their five bucks admission, fans threw themselves wholeheartedly into every match. Each zealously supported a favorite—and if we offended one—which we were bound to do—we were the target for a popcorn carton or a beer can (once the beer was gone, of course). And occcasionally, an umbrella up our behind.

The most aggressive, unpredictable and deadly of the species was the female. Men booed and threw beer cans, but at least they stayed put. The women were uncontrollable. Some psychologists said this was because wrestling gave them a chance to let loose with suppressed hostilities and sexual feelings. What I know is what I saw. Policeman prying hysterical females from the ropes as they tried to climb in to be with their heroes. Down South, so we heard, one housewife was watching a match at home when she saw a wrestler try a dirty trick. She drove to the arena, leaped into the ring and attacked the culprit with a hammer. Another woman tried to drive a nail through the television set when the referee made a call she disagreed with. (She missed.)

The femme fatale of them all was Hatpin Mary. She looked like somebody's harmless grandma with her gray bun, rimless specs and sexless laceups. Don't be fooled. Mary was deadly as a snake and shifty as a fox. This was years before metal detectors, so Mary and her murderous hatpin had no trouble getting into the arena. During the match, she circled the ring. If her favorite was in a jam, she stuck his opponent in the rump until he bled. It got so that the "villains" in the matches boasted about their Hatpin scars. Mary could get stuck on announcers, too, if we insulted the wrong person or didn't seem serious enough. Between ducking airborne wrestlers and beer cans and guarding my flank against Mary, some nights I could barely concentrate on the game. "Get away from me, you nut," I yelled (fully aware that I would be heard on the air). "Go stick fat Dennis James." (Dennis—if you're reading this—I'm sorry!)

What was going on here? What was unbalancing the hormones of millions of women? It was something that poured out of the wrestlers, and it wasn't sweat. It was sex. All those near-naked bodies crammed into scanty shorts. Massive thighs. Tarzan chests. The ladies didn't suspect a thing, but some wrestlers helped Mother Nature. In the dressing room before a match one night I saw a notoriously well-built specimen stuffing a sock into his jock strap. "What the hell," he said. "Dames wear padded bras, don't they?" Cagey directors zeroed in on this, early on. When I first started doing bouts, it bugged me when I wanted to describe a fantastic hold and the camera was ogling a guy's crotch. I complained to the cameraman. "Orders," he said. "The more crotch shots, the more the girls keep watching."

Think I'm making all this up? How about the time Warren Wade saddled me with Lola Montez as my co-announcer. (Warren must have had plans for her behind his opaque glass.) Lola was a Grade B movie actress with C-cup sex appeal. Dusky and dangerous, she generally went through scenes with her eyes closed, mouth open and breasts swelling. Lola showed up true to form, looking exactly as she did on movie posters. There were more prolonged holds in the announcer's corner of the ring than I'd ever seen. Lola was properly appreciative. "Oh, Guyyy," she breathed. "The men they are so beeeeg."

Came intermission and Lola vanished. I found her on her back in the dressing room with the beeeegest wrestler, in what I guess you could call the missionary hold. Word of Lola's interview method found its way back to Wade because that was her last bout.

Now the sticky part of this chapter. Everybody always asks me the same question: Wasn't wrestling fixed? I have to say it was. A phony, a fakeroo and a lie. But the public believed in it, wanted to believe in it passionately. The promoters billed it as an "exhibition," not a sport. They made no bones about it. It was the public that insisted on creating the myth. No matter how much they were told that wrestling was a fraud, they refused to abandon it. And you can bet we guys doing the TV stuff were not going to screw up our good deal. We learned our lesson from the print boys. Every single time one of the prominent newspaper like the *Daily News* or the *New York Journal American* did a so-called exposé on wrestling, their circulation plummeted.

When an irate wrestling fan complained to *TeleVision Guide* that the referee seemed to know in advance which holds the wrestlers would use, the editor answered loftily: "Wrestling in New York is an exhibition, not a sport. There is no real competition because everything is planned." (Recently, the State of New Jersey, which lists wrestling as a sport, was implored by entrepreneurs to change its category to "exhibition." Why? To keep from trying to fool the fans? No way. To save the money they had to spend hiring doctors to be on the premises. A "sport" requires them, an "exhibition" wouldn't. Request denied. I say good for New Jersey. Because wrestling, exhibition or no, was dangerous.)

Did that angry fan stop watching wrestling? Probably not. There's a sucker born every minute, but in wrestling it was every second. If you had eyes and a sense of logic, and you watched your screen closely, you could see the wrestlers' holds were done loosely. You could see the four-arm smashes were phony. And when two wrestlers who have sworn death upon the other could be spotted walking out of the arena buddy-buddy, you have to figure that something was rotten. But has the audience learned anything in forty or fifty years? Nah. There are more people attending wrestling matches, there are more televised matches than ever before.

Don't get me wrong. I'm not denying that the outcome of the matches was fixed. It's what happened before that was up to the wrestlers. Broken legs, sprained backs, torn ligaments, busted noses—these were real. In doing research for this book, I learned that star wrestler Billy Graham (no relation to the Evangelist B.G., although he has often reported "wrestling with his conscience") needed intricate knee operations and replacements after his career was over. That bad guy Red Bastein had to have hip replacements and that some of the greatest have to use canes for walking. Some were paralyzed. And in a match with Bruno Sammartino at Sunnyside Arena, Chick Garibaldi died in the ring. A heart attack? Nobody knows. The point wasn't to injure your opponent. Wrestling was a club and everyone was in it to make money. Which you couldn't do if you were in the hospital. To satisfy the crowd's thirst for blood, wrestlers hid capsules with red dye in their mouths so they could "bleed" after a vicious slam to the mat. But things could get out of control, especially if a wrestler wasn't a good athlete. A mistimed kick could send someone crashing to the cement floor outside the ring, or headfirst into a post. I saw plenty of veterans tone down their act when a rookie was matched against them.

As fixed as the outcome was, the holds themselves were 100-percent authentic. To make the match seem real, they had to be well executed and planned from moment to moment. The wrestlers used signals to clue each other about their next hold. This way the wrestler who was about to be twirled around and slammed to the ground would be ready for it. Otherwise, he could easily break his neck. (If you've ever seen the movies *Farewell My Lovely, Blood Alley, Cheyenne Autumn*, you'd recognize the battered face of Iron Mike Mazurki in an instant. Iron Mike was also a wrestler. When he was in the ring he protected his body like it was the Hope Diamond. A broken arm could lose him his next role in Hollywood. But his face? "It's so bad already," Mike said, "whatever anyone does, it can only look better.")

Such fine planning required that the wrestlers be superb athletes. If they didn't know how to get out of a hold, they could get hurt. Or look foolish. During a match between Tony Martinelli (the Clifton Cutie) and the Golden Superman, I heard the following: The Clifton Cutie was a crack grappler but the Golden Superman couldn't wrestle his way out of a candy wrapper. He was all show, no go, with a cloak and crazy gold headpiece that made him look like an extra from a Wagner opera. The Clifton Cutie had the Golden Superman in a leg lock. The Golden Superman was whining, "Let me outta this. Hey, Tony, leave go. You're hurting me."

The Clifton Cutie hung on, and as the crowd yelled, hissed and rang cowbells, he whispered: "Fuck you! You're staying until you figure out how to get loose. I ain't lookin' like no snow job." I can tell you that after the Golden Superman figured out that defense, it's one he never forgot.

So for all this sweat and struggle, what was in it for the performers? Run-of-the-mill grapplers earned between $200 and $300 a week, doing maybe five or six nights a week. But those like Gene Stanlee, Mr. America, or Antonino Rocca or Gorgeous George earned a piece of the gate. And if their fame spread across the country and they made it to national TV or a syndicated film show, their salaries flew up to six figures. The whole process ran smooth as butter. All wrestlers trained and rehearsed in appointed gymnasiums. Often they knew several days in advance who they were going to wrestle. Opponents got together at their training sessions and discussed the kinds of holds they would use. Just before the match, one of the entrepreneurs' aides would come into the dressing room and inform the contestants of each match how long it should be and who would win.

The front office didn't care which minor contestants won or lost. Their big concern was for the big drawing cards. Win, lose or draw, Toots Mondt, Don George and the others pulled the strings and made the real gold. The big heroes had to keep winning. Their myths had to continue. But some of the losers could be great drawing cards too. Like the long, greasy-haired Italian lover, Baron Michele Leone. Or the Teutonic titan, Hans Kaempfer. Audiences lined up for hours to get in and see them lose. But before they finally got smashed to the ground, they would seemingly knock the hell out of their big-hero opponent. It was a perfect sport for an audience that had almost seen the forces of Nazism defeat the world. Wrestling acted out the belief in absolute good, absolute evil, the struggle between light and darkness, hero and villain.

But even the Overlords' well-oiled assembly line could run into difficulties. The owners couldn't regulate egos. And these wrestlers had them to match their girths. Sometimes it happened that an established wrestler was told he had to lose. "Hey," he protested. "I'm the big earner here; this guy don't do nothin'. And you want me to go under for him? Shit, not me." This was the signal for the Front Office to call in their Enforcers. These big, deadly gallooks literally wrestled sense into the stubbornest of guys. The holdout would suddenly find himself in a match with a stranger. Next thing he knew, he'd wake up in the hospital with a get-well card and a friendlier attitude toward his boss. The general dirt I got was that a Midwestern wrestler named Ruffy Silverstein was Chief of the Enforcers. Silverstein had been in World War II and was as decorated as a Christmas tree. The only fear Ruffy knew was the panic he saw in the eyes of his terrified victims. They say Ruffy caused more damage than the Battle of Iwo Jima.

Ruffy never got a shot at the biggest ego of them all—and why I don't know. This was the Italian-born Argentinian, Antonino Rocca. Rocca was a soccer player in his twenties, when a famous wrestling scout named Kola Kwariani spotted him. Kwariani's first attempt to train Rocca, in Texas, failed. Rocca returned to Argentina. But Kwariani was relentless. He knew Rocca could earn millions. Not for Rocca, of course. For the Overlords. He coaxed Rocca back here, and the Overlords got out their deposit slips. Here was a young guy, Mr. Perfect Body, gallant Roman head, a fantastic athlete, extraordinarily durable. Also, glossy black hair, white-white teeth and big hairy chest—a shoo-in for a female following. Could Rocca wrestle? No. But who cared? He stunned audiences with his sweeping style using cartwheels, somersaults, flying kicks—and his bare feet. His signature hold, the Argentine Backbreaker, actually appeared to have broken his opponent's back. The Overlords arranged for him to win against most other big-time heroes immediately.

When Rocca finally traveled to New York, he was already as famous as the reigning star of the East: Mr. America. All anyone could think about was a match between these two. This was going to be the War Between the Worlds, the Clash of the Titans, the Showdown at the OK Corral.

One sunny weekend, I was relaxing out at Lake Ronkonkoma on Long Island. Lying on the beach, I heard a mammoth buzzing, like the sound track for the kind of movie that's called *Killer Flies*. A stranger ran up breathlessly. "Have you heard?" It had just come over someone's radio—the Rocca–Stanlee match was set up. You could actually hear the waves of sound as the message was passed from group to group, all around the lake. Only the World Series had caused that much commotion before.

The wrestling mafia knew if they orchestrated a draw between Stanlee and Rocca, there would have to be a rematch. Double the money. Match Number One at Yankee Stadium was a sellout and Number Two filled the place to the rafters. The order was for Mr. America's red-white-and-blue trunks, lovingly stitched by some fantastic-looking blonde, to fly at half-mast. It was curtains for his career. He'd brought in a fortune for the Overlords but the star of Argentina was in its ascendancy. Mr. America, with his golden capes, multi-colored trunks, luminous shoes and bevy of devoted females sank below the horizon. When last heard from, he was frying his own eggs in a one-room apartment somewhere in Florida.

And Rocca? In spite of his weak wrestling technique, he rose higher than any other man—ever—on the circuits. The promoters worked him every night, usually in major cities in top arenas. He became one of the hottest public figures of the day. Everyone had to have Rocca. David Brinkley interviewed him on his national network show, usually reserved for politicians and world celebrities. Rocca guested with Johnny Carson. *Life* and countless major newspapers around the country featured him in glowing stories. And in the ring, opponents fell before him like toy soldiers, even if he barely touched them. Even Rocca's gargantuan ego must have been a little suspicious.

During Rocca's halcyon years, he and I became great

friends. Our respective careers were booming. Why not team up? More than anything, Rocca wanted to be a leader. He was sure he had the ability to change people's lives. And he had an inherent compassion for the underclass. Although he was Italian-born, the Latin Americans, rich and poor, worshiped him. I found Rocca a pulpit: a daily radio show from New York City, sponsored by Schaefer Beer. They were as quick to sense a sure thing as the wrestling promoters had been. Rocca's dark good looks smiled down from billboards all along the East Coast. At night his glistening body flew through the air and his flying kicks moved thousands to frenzy. By day he conducted his radio program, talking philosophy, giving advice to the troubled poor and playing music. It was the Rocca Personality Cult.

Rack your brain all you want. I was in the thick of sports for thirty years. No DiMaggio, no Mantle, no Joe Louis even came close to receiving the idolatry that Rocca did. Anything he wanted, he got. Rocca loved music. I persuaded M-G-M to sign him to conduct an orchestra for an album series of his favorite pieces. He had unofficial music lessons with Toscanini, who adopted him like a brother. The famous football broadcaster Harry Wismer offered him a contract with the New York Titans (which later became the Jets). And when news got around that Rocca had a private pilot's license, commercial pilots sometimes kicked the navigator out of the cockpit and invited Rocca in.

When Rocca got back to his seat in the passenger section, he'd almost always have to get rid of a relentless fan who had slid into the seat next to him. Rocca loved his fans—their adulation was like oxygen to him. He had to have it to live. But he had to relax sometimes, too. So he dreamed up a subtle trick with his travel companion and bodyguard, former junior heavyweight wrestling champ Angelo Savoldi. As he smiled and beamed with the adoring fan, Rocca would light one of his mammoth Cuban special stogies. This was the signal for Savoldi to come sit on the other side of the visitor, puffing his Cuban special. It wasn't too long before the fan apologized and reeled back to his own seat through the haze and smoke of two foot-long stogies.

On one of these flights, Rocca met the one true love of his life, a stewardess named Joyce, who married him. The whole world belonged to Antonino Rocca. But it was a shaky world built on sands of deception supported by greedy, conscienceless men. To his television followers, Rocca had become virtually an Elmer Gantry. You would have had to come under his spell to know the strange power he had. He often visited terminally ill patients—strangers—and they'd swear they felt better afterwards. But there was a dark, spy-novel part of Rocca. He was always calling to tell me that he'd be "out of town" for a while. "Where to?" I'd ask. His answers were always vague and evasive, the same way he was about his background. In 1952 or so, Rocca made one of his strange visits to Argentina. The Perón government wouldn't let him leave the country. It took frantic calls to the State Department, Embassy (and who knows, maybe the White house) before they released him. There were rumors that Rocca had been hired by the CIA, and he boasted that FBI men on assignment visited his apartment on Fifty-seventh Street in New York City.

Wherever he went he was King: toasted, celebrated, worshiped. And then, like every conquerer, finis! Rocca was getting older and knew his star days were limited. He wanted to become an entrepreneur himself so he'd have some security. But the big boys wouldn't share. They froze Rocca out.

Rocca's story ends suddenly with his mysterious death. He had just returned from a match in Puerto Rico, where a number of people had died of food poisoning.

He developed a sudden poisoning of the kidneys. An autopsy was ordered. But to this very day, his widow, Joyce, alleges to her closest friends that he was deliberately poisoned. She will say that Rocca, who suffered lapses of consciousness before death, muttered that he was being murdered.

What *is* known is that Rocca earned hundreds of thousands a year in his time, and he was active for many years. He wasn't a big spender. He lived simply, in a three-room apartment. And after he got paid, he went right to the bank across the street from the front office and deposited his money. Yet when he died his wife and three children were nearly penniless. To the disgrace of the wrestling profession, only one wrestler, Angelo Savoldi, helped Joyce in her struggle to survive. But then perhaps the full truth of Rocca's life and death is not yet known. And the match is not yet over.

To me, the picture of Rocca will always be one of the boy-man I saw at Coney Island. Rocca was publicizing the opening of the summer season there. Mobs of fans trailed after him as he enjoyed the rides with his flamboyant good nature and zest. Ultimately we arrived at the roller coaster. Rocca looked upupup at the tallest amusement in the United States. He hesitated. I poked him. "Let's go, Tony." "No," he said. "I can't do this." First time I ever heard that from him. "It's bad for the oxygenation of the hemoglobin." He was full of scientific double-talk. Then I got the drift. The mighty Rocca was scared. He was not going to loop-the-loop this day or any other. Still, he finished the day on a high note, devouring five franks and three cotton candies like any kid.

Wrestling has come back, as most valuable things do, but it may yet need another Antonino Rocca to attain the character it had. No greater proof of TV wrestling's overwhelming popularity in the past exists than this incident at station WTTG in Washington, D.C. Les Arries, Jr., the general manager, ordered an announcement made that an evening wrestling show that week would be preempted by the Washington Senators baseball team. When Arries drove up to his house that night, he was greeted by hundreds of angry wrestling fans brandishing placards. "We want wrestling." "Don't rob us of wrestling." "Down with baseball." Arries was no hero. He gave them wrestling.

And my final word about wrestling? Well, I can tell you this. In the eight consecutive years I was before the mike, I never saw or heard of the grapplers being drunk or drugged. Only one scandal erupted—a wrestler called the "Lion Man" was arrested for allegedly exposing himself to young girls. My theory about these galoots' living pretty straight is that they knew they had to have all their senses in the ring. Being out of control could mean that they could get their neck broken on a ringpost. Or their back broken on the mat. And it seems sad—for all their TV fame, most would end up poor, futureless and frustrated. TV historians only accord them passing reference, but I'll bet Dennis James and I can still hear the noise and clamor and still feel the pressing crowds as these actually docile beasts in trunks carried early TV on their backs to greater heights, while they themselves hurtled into nothingness like so many comets before them.

*Afterword on the Camilo Leyra Case:*

Leyra was convicted of the murders of both parents. The day of his sentencing, his attorney presented an unusual plea to Judge Leibowitz. Leyra wanted Leibowitz to pronounce judgment on Leyra's murder of his father first. Thus, he would be executed for his father's death, and his mother (in Heaven) would never realize that he was also sentenced for her death since he would not have died for that heinous crime. Leyra spent over four years on Death Row in Sing Sing prison—during which time one of his former wives sued him for $30 a week alimony. (How did she figure on collecting?) Then, in 1956, after his convictions had been overturned, he was freed, still protesting his innocence.

And on Judge Leibowitz . . . In the early sixties, Leibowitz gave me the rights to do a movie on his life. Only he wanted to chose the actor who would play him. His first pick was Jeff Chandler, a tall, green-eyed, handsome and rugged-looking man. His second choice was Rod Steiger. Even a judge can dream! Leibowitz was tall—true—but was still much shorter than Chandler. And he was imposing physically—a large, dramatic head, brawny build. But nowhere near the box-office looks of Chandler. Closer to the Judge would have been Steiger. But Chandler died on an operating table in 1961 and the project fell apart. Still, you can read the story of Leibowitz's career in *Courtroom* by best-selling author Quentin Reynolds. If it's out of print, run—do not walk —to your nearest secondhand bookstore or library. It's a real-life thriller you won't be able to put down.

*It's Dagmar busting out all over—the first queen*
*of late-night television.*
*(Photo courtesy Photofest)*

182

*Bishop Fulton J. Sheen, the most popular cleric in TV history.*
*(Photo courtesy Photofest)*

183

*Faye Emerson TV-hosting "Faye Emerson's Wonderful Town." Looks as if her old problem is showing up. (Photo courtesy Photofest)*

*The guy on the left was a guest on TV shows such as mine, but surreptitiously was gathering evidence for Senator Joe McCarthy's Communist accusations. The U.S. government later accused him of perjury and threw him in jail.*

184

*Two of television's most talented people: Hollywood comic Danny Webb and one of TV's early directors, Peggy Gannon. She was later fired and told that women didn't belong in television.*

185

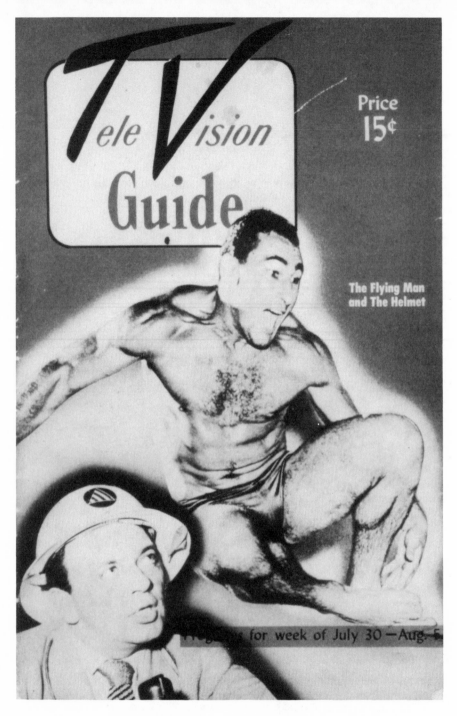

TeleVision Guide *cover, 1949, when wrestling was one of the top shows and Antonino Rocca was king of the hill.*

186

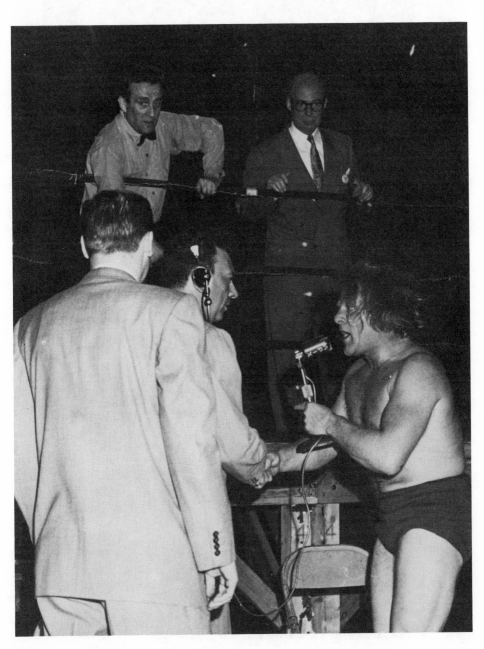

*You had to be in top condition to be a TV wrestling announcer. Anybody could drop down and take your mike away.*

187

*TeleVision Guide executives anoint me "Best Wrestling Announcer" in the country. Don't ask me what the guy on the left is doing with a flower horseshoe. Did he miss the horse show?*

*Apache Chief Lion Heart and his wife make me honorary Apache tribe member during a wrestling show. New name: "Chief Talking Eagle."*

188

Top: *Former heavyweight champion Primo Carnera on debut night as a wrestling referee, 1949—but he can't resist showing off some muscle.* Bottom: *Top Hollywood actor Dick Lane (right) became top TV announcer on the West Coast at KTLA. (Photo courtesy KTLA)*

189

*Read All About It:*

# Odd Hominem

Thank you, no comment . . .

## TALMADGE HITS TV 'OFFENSE' TO SOUTH ON RACE

ATLANTA, Ga., January 5 (UP)—Georgia Gov. Herman Talmadge today attacked television shows in which white and Negro performers are shown together and said that unless the practice is stopped southerners should boycott sponsors of nonsegregated programs.

Talmadge, a vigorous champion of racial segregation, said some of TV's biggest shows are disregarding southern segregation laws.

He singled out the Mariners quartet, composed of two white and two Negro singers, which appears on Arthur Godgrey's show; Ken Murray's Christmas program, in which white and Negro children danced together; and a Clifton Fadiman show in which a Negro and a white woman were shown talking together.

Talmadge's blast was made in a signed statement appearing in his weekly political newspaper, *The Statesman.*

He said in some of the Mariners' productions "there is a mixing and mingling of the races among both sexes" and that "Negro men frequently are seen mixed up in the dancing ensembles in juxtaposition to scantily clad white females."

Talmadge said television programs should not be permitted to offend large groups of people in any section of the nation. He said television "is just about equivalent to visiting somebody in his home."

*(1952)*

## CHURCH WILL OPEN
## TELEVISION CENTER

### *First Presbyterian Devises Plan, Hoping to Keep Young Members Out of Bars*

January 12—The First Presbyterian Church, Fifth Avenue between Eleventh and Twelfth Streets, announced yesterday that it was opening its own "television center" for children in hope of keeping the youngsters out of Greenwich Village bars and grills.

With the approval of the church's pastor, the Rev. Clarence Boyer, the parents' class of the church school has bought a television receiver and set aside a room for a weekday schedule of video shows for teen-agers and younger groups.

Mrs. Kenneth Chamberlain, who is in charge of the television project for the parents' class, explained that the modern mother had found that the advent of the electronic era had added to her chores.

"When a mother goes to look for her children she finds them down at the bar," she said. "Instead of youngsters going to the bar to see a picture, we thought it was something that the church could do."

"We want our teenagers to continue to look to the church for their good times as well as for their spiritual guidance. We hope it will inspire a pattern for many communities."

Mrs. Chamberlain noted that many taverns in the Village now had television sets and that they had proved a strong attraction for the younger generation.

The church's television center will be open from 5 to 9 p.m., Monday through Thursday, and from 5 to 10 p.m. on Friday and Saturday.

The center will be formally opened Wednesday, with the festivities starting at 6:30 p.m. There will be games, including a cakewalk; an auction of quilts; good food and television of the concert celebrating the inauguration of President Truman.

Mrs. Chamberlain acknowledged that

there would be a door charge for the opening ceremonies—50 cents for children and $1 for adults.

"To finish paying for the television center," she explained.

*(New York Times, 1949)*

## NO HALF TV'S

PROVIDENCE, R.I., September 28 (AP) —The nine wise men of the Domestic Relations Court daily face a problem that never bothered Solomon: Who gets the television set in a marital break-up?

All nine judges agree that when a divorced couple confers on division of property, all goes well until it comes to the TV, and that invariably is cause for a wrangle. Frequently, according to the judges, it is the only piece of furniture specifically mentioned.

*(1951)*

## UP POPPED THE DEVIL

September 8—The devil popped up as a keynoter for the 1948 GOP convention in a TV program last night over the Columbia Broadcasting System.

While newscaster Douglas Edwards was commenting on the selection of Gen. MacArthur as 1952 keynoter, a series of pictures of other keynoters since 1932 was shown. All went well through 1944, when Gov. Warren of California was shown. But when 1948 was reached, the devil jumped on the screen. Former Gov.

Green, the keynoter that year, was not shown.

An embarrassed Don Hewitt, producer of the show, explained that the picture of the devil was an advertisement for a record company's new album of "Faust" and got on by mistake. The operator hastily jumped back to Warren while Edwards talked about Green.

*(New York Post, 1952)*

## MD vs TV
## AND DOCTOR'S GOTTA GO!

April 4—A doctor's home diathermy unit is interfering with neighbors' television sets, Steve Johnson told the Clifton, N.J., City Council last night in seeking a law limiting the hours in which the doctor may operate his machine.

Councilman Koribanics called Johnson's request "idiotic," but it was referred to City Council Bluhy for possible action.

Johnson was advised to consult the Federal Communications Commission to see if it has jurisdiction in the matter.

*(New York Post, 1951)*

## BOSS' VIDEO SPOTS
## WORKERS LOAFING
## WHILE HE'S LAID UP

CLEVELAND, February 12 (AP)—If employees at the Cuyahoga County Auditor's Office want to do any loafing while their boss is sick, they'll do it well out of range of television cameras.

The Auditor, John A. Zangerle, 82, is recuperating from a severe illness. To help while away the convalescence, he bought a television set.

He was delighted the other night when his beloved Lakeside Av. Courthouse came on the screen. The newsreel was covering a contempt of court proceedings there, against the Cleveland Press.

But Zangerle's pleasure turned to indignation when he spotted among the spectators several of his office employees who should have been at their desks.

When the reel finished, he grabbed a telephone and gave this advice to the startled offenders:

"Such goings-on wouldn't take place if I were there, and I won't have them happening now."

*(1949)*

## RED KIDS BUST BERLIN LINE FOR U.S. TV DEBUT

BERLIN, August 13 (UPI)—Hundreds of Communist youths from the "World Peace Festival" evaded East Berlin police patrols tonight to watch the debut of American television in West Berlin sponsored by ECA.

The youths mingled with crowds watching a show on a hundred sets erected in show windows along the fashionable Kurfürstendamm—Berlin's Fifth Avenue—and in other strategic spots in the city.

The Radio Corp. of America flew nearly

40 tons of equipment to Berlin and erected a transmitter in record time of 24 hours. The Columbia Broadcasting System demonstrated its color TV over a closed circuit in the Funkturm exhibition grounds.

*(New York Daily News, August 14, 1951)*

## TV THEFT BACKFIRES: SET SHORT-CIRCUITS

August 8—A television set that was literally too hot to handle was the subject of a proceeding yesterday in Bronx Magistrates' court.

Detective Nicholas Cotter of the Morrisania station told the court that Joseph Cofer, 25 years old, of 301 Noble Avenue, the Bronx, entered the home of Hopie Davis on 586 East 165th Street, the Bronx, some time Wednesday afternoon and left with a $222 television set. "I bought it four days ago," Mr. Davis told Magistrate Joseph A. Martinis. "I just paid the first installment."

Cofer, according to Detective Cotter, took the set to the home of a girl friend. Unfortunately, when he plugged it in, the set short-circuited and caught fire. Enraged, he picked up the set, carried it to the roof of the five-story building and threw it to the courtyard, the detective testified.

Meanwhile Mr. Davis, who had rushed home from work to watch a prizefight on his television set, discovered his loss and reported it to the police.

Neighbors told the police they had seen Cofer around the Davis apartment. Somehow, word got back to Cofer within a few hours that detectives were looking for him.

He went to Mr. Davis, who was listening to the fight on the radio.

"What do you mean by going around telling people I stole your television set?" he was quoted as asking Mr. Davis. "And furthermore that set was no darn good!"

Cofer was held in $500 bail for a hearing in Special Sessions.

*(New York Post, 1952)*

## HOODS LEARN TV LEGALINGO

NEW HAVEN, Conn., March 24 (UPI)— Television has provided local underworld characters with a new out when quizzed by police. About 100 persons were questioned by detectives about a gangland-style slaying here this week. Many refused to meet questions with:

"I refuse to answer that question on the grounds that it might incriminate me."

They said that they picked up the phrase by watching [the] televised interrogation by Senate crime probers.

*(1951)*

## THANK YOU, MR. BOOKER

MANCHESTER, England, April 13 (Reuters)—A Cornell engineering student has devised a gadget to blot out the talk in TV commercials.

Henry G. Booker, in a letter to the *Manchester Guardian* today, told how he silenced them:

"Contact one end of a lamp cord across the loudspeaker and attach to the other end of an ordinary bell-push," Booker wrote. "It is possible, without getting up, to push the button during 'commercials' and eliminate the spoken part."

Britain has been considering commercial television. Booker said cutting out the sound made American television quite "acceptable."

*(1953)*

# 6 / "And Now, for Your Viewing Pleasure . . ."

**THE SHOW MUST STUMBLE ON**

October 22— . . . The score so far this week:

Talent scout Garry Moore, sitting in for Arthur Godfrey Monday night, announced the wrong winner on the show, screamed, "I could kill myself!" as he went off the air. On top of that, one of his acts had to quit midway—accordion busted down, first time that's happened in many years.

Last night Red Buttons fainted just before he went on. Show canceled. Tonight? Ellery Queen may solve problem—of maybe Herbert Marshall and his program "The Unexpected."

*(New York Post, 1952)*

Those of us working in TV were so nervous about screwing up (see the foregoing news item) that we didn't realize how fascinating we really were (see the following):

### VIDEO SO INTERESTS
### SUSPECTED BURGLAR
### THAT HE WATCHES UNTIL
### POLICE ARRIVE

February 3—A burglar made himself so much at home yesterday in a Brooklyn house he was ransacking—sitting down to a bottle of whiskey and a television show—that he could not bear to leave even to escape capture by the police.

The prisoner said he was Joseph Motyka, 46 years old. He told the police he had passed most of Tuesday night in his favorite Bowery taverns watching wrestling matches and other sports programs on the television screens in the bars. How he got to Brooklyn Motyka did not recall.

According to the complaint, Motyka wandered through the first floor, examining fountain pens, a cigaret lighter, some religious medals and other trinkets. But a bottle of rye found in a cupboard was what really interested him. Motyka sat down in the living room to enjoy the whiskey and turned on the television set.

At that hour Johnny Olsen was appearing in his "Rumpus Room" in which he plays quiz games with housewives he summons to the stage from the audience. Motyka found this fascinating; he had never seen a daytime women's program before.

The women's shrieks aroused Mr. Magalino, who managed to get downstairs and demand: "What are you doing here?"

"Watching the television, pop," Motyka said.

"Well, you better get out of here, quick," Mr. Magalino said.

"Wait'll the program's over, pop," the visitor replied.

Mr. Magalino telephoned the Vanderveer Park Police Station. Motyka politely waited for Detective Albert Timms and Patrolman George Spitz to arrive and remove him. They found the missing articles in his pockets, they said, and they later discovered that Motyka previously had served three prison sentences for burglary.

"Boy, that was a swell show," Motyka said.

*(New York Times, 1949)*

As it turned out, we could have run a cartoon backwards and people would have watched. But all we knew was that we had to get something in front of the camera, fast. At some stations that meant: "Open the damn window and shoot!" Viewers seeing familiar sights of their own cities asked themselves, "Is this television— or home movies?" Man-on-the-street interviews were another quick fix. "LeBow, we got five minutes to fill. Get downstairs and stop the next jokers who come along." "About what?" "Who the hell cares? If they're alive, use 'em."

The easiest way to fill time was with films, and TV audiences suffered through more of those than regular programs in the early years. Suffered? And how! These weren't the full-length, theater motion pictures you get on your TV today. They were punishment: documentaries, industrial films, silent pictures, old newsreels, travelogues, short subjects, short silents, and some of Hollywood's oldest and worst films (almost all the studios refused to sell TV any movies less than ten years old, remember). "Was this what we bought a television for?" viewers grumbled.

Then TV got a little help from a crafty TV hand, Ed Woodruff, a veteran of the Dumont network and cousin of Allen B. Dumont. Woodruff made fantastic deals with Alex Korda and with J. Arthur Rank Productions, one of England's major film companies. Now TV stations could show some of the finest English movies—and many of the same ones currently outselling Hollywood's films at American box offices. But TV viewers still grumbled. "Was this what we bought a television for? We can't understand those funny English accents!"

(Woodruff continued shafting Hollywood. He rounded up a herd of Westerns from a small studio not in on the Hollywood embargo and sold these to TV. Then he formed an international distribution company with Anne Budyens, a German-born Belgian who had been in the Underground in World War II. She later married Kirk Douglas. Ed retired to the Bahamas, where he enjoys watching Hollywood movies on his television set via his VCR.)

I go into this Hollywood–TV struggle because it's an intriguing irony in the whole history of early television. At the same time Hollywood was trying to screw TV, its own performers were shoring us up with the very talent it had abandoned—or had abandoned it. Without these plucky movie veterans, television probably wouldn't have developed as quickly as it did. Among the former child stars who flocked to TV studios were Freddie Bartholomew, Jackie Cooper, Jackie Coogan. We also got Don Ameche, Cliff Edwards, Boris Karloff, Bela Lugosi, Buster Crabbe, William (Hopalong Cassidy) Boyd, Roscoe Karns, Neil Hamilton, Lois Wilson, George (Superman) Reeves, Dick Lane, Helen Twelvetrees, Betty Furness (a veteran performer before she ever opened a Westinghouse refrigerator), William Bendix—to name a few. All recast themselves in a smaller image—but what the heck. It was work!

CUE: Enter Gloria Swanson, 1948.

The silent-screen queen, ex-lover of Joseph Kennedy, former countess and once the most glamorous woman in the world, needs television. She's fifty years old. And in 1948 that puts her—as one writer did—in the "oldster" category. (Hey, would you call Jane Fonda an "oldster"?!) Marriage number four or five is kaputt; number one, to actor Wallace Beery, ended after he tricked her into an abortion. She hasn't made a film for seven years. That movie, by the way, included another silent-film star who migrated to TV—and will co-host Gloria's program! This is Neil Hamilton, whose film career reportedly fizzled from too many popped corks. His television run, though, extended for decades and included the role of Police Commissioner Gordon in the 1966–68 series "Batman." One more coincidence, please: featured in this movie was another future TV performer—a young Latin American singer named Desi Arnaz.

Gloria needed television and Channel 11 needed Gloria. With its on-air date just months away, the station was feverishly putting programs together. One of the execs called Gloria's Manhattan apartment to ask her what she thought about having her own program. Gloria responded graciously with, "I'LL BE RIGHT OVER!" and in no time the astonished execs were greeting the intimidating screen presence herself! She stood no bigger than a pin, but she mesmerized everyone with her stagey ways. Thrusting her long chin up, actress-style, she peered at them through thickets of mascara, speaking with all 500 teeth bared. The deal was done. Gloria graciously agreed to help for a gracious sum of money.

You don't get talk shows like hers anymore! Her show was a combination of glamour and grit, just like Gloria. "The Gloria Swanson Hour" took you into her Manhattan abode (reproduced on the set), with a portrait of Herself hanging humbly over the sofa. There was even a butler, played by stage, screen and now television actor Erik Rhodes. But Gloria got down to brass tacks: she told you how to buy clothes on a budget. Demonstrated the newest household gadgets. Even cooked a Thanksgiving dinner on the air. And she didn't *pretend* to know her subjects. This lady knew something about everything. She designed clothes, had owned a film production company and a patent business and was a health food nut. (She eventually developed her own line of health foods, which she took to Russia—pre-glasnost.) I think it was this health food that gave Gloria her one imperfection—a breath like a bowl of onion dip. On some days I got the nod as Gloria's announcer, and one afternoon she breathed me an invitation to have lunch with her at Sardi's.

Sardi's restaurant was—and is—on West 44th Street, in what guidebooks call the "heart of the theater district." Colorful caricatures of its celebrated customers—actors, producers, directors, writers—line the walls. This is where the crème de la crème, the top of the heap and the proof of the pudding all come to see and be seen. And this is where, believe it or not, Gloria decides to brown-bag it.

When the waiter appears, Gloria produces a dingy paper bag. She removes a head of something wilted and dankly green. Hands it to the waiter. Next, a jar of what looks like burned crickets. God, is everyone watching? I look around furtively. But there's nothing clandestine about Gloria. She gives precise instructions in a voice that would carry to the balcony of the Belasco Theater. "And," she finishes, "you may bring me a glass of milk."

Gloria's health diet didn't keep her out of the hospital in December. I heard that a kid challenged her to do a somersault. But the flip flopped, and the next day Gloria was watching TV from a hospital bed. What she saw was what we knew already: The script could be professional. The actors and directors could be professional. But somewhere between the script and the screen—amateur night. In her gut, Gloria begged to be delivered from this primitive art, and just like in some of the nail-biters she'd starred in on the silver screen, along came the gallant hero. This time it was a little leprechaun director named Billy Wilder and a big picture named *Sunset Boulevard.* Sic transit Gloria.

About the time when Gloria turned into a movie star again, a British actress was in a head-on collision with the

TV talkshowbiz. You can't compare Wendy Barrie to anyone, but if you mix Ernie Kovac's off-the-wall spontaneity with Lenny Bruce's off-color sensibility, you're on the right track. Wendy's movie career hadn't revealed her wackiness. Her dewy British beauty and considerable talent had rocketed her to stardom in the 1933 international hit *The Private Life of Henry VIII*, with Charles Laughton. (Wendy was wife number three of six.) A broken heart brought her to Hollywood, where she drowned her sorrows in films with Tracy, Stewart and others. But somehow she ended up on the floor of a TV studio in New York.

It's not as bad as it sounds. You see, Wendy did her talk show sitting on the floor. As a matter of fact, Wendy did a talk show the way nobody else did then . . . or since. Can you see Oprah hosting from the floor?! Now, during this period, talk shows were generally considered "women's work." Run by the "gals," they featured "girltalk," like fashions and cooking and gossip. Everyone was always SO nice to everyone else. And some shows had an idiotic artifice. The hostess would hear a knock on the door to her "living room," she'd open it and there—surprise!—is her next guest! "Why, what a wonderful surprise!" she'd chirp.

"Screw that," Wendy snorted, and came up with a unique format: the anti-talk show. I don't know why people appeared on Wendy's show—they weren't guests, they were sitting ducks. Something about getting down on the floor knocked the stuffing out of Important Personages and Eminent Authors—and Wendy took it from there. She played the wacko that cowers in most people and her fans loved seeing her act it out. When one gentleman was sweating buckets under the lights, Wendy lifted up her skirt and wiped his forehead with it. "Is that better, bunny?" she asked him. (She called everyone "sweetie" or "bunny." In later years, on other shows, she had a menagerie of stuffed bunnies.) But if you bored Wendy—goodbye! She stopped one poor sap cold, asking incredulously, "Did I invite you here?" The next person wasn't so lucky. She walked him off the set.

She also turned a lot of viewers off. These poor sports accused her of coming on her show doped up or drunk. Nobody's that nutty, they said. Oh no? The associate producer of one of Wendy's later shows, a few years later when Wendy was supposedly more sedate, says, "Oh yes!" Among Wally Reed's duties as AD was to pick Wendy up at her East Side apartment. Here's the scene: Wendy dashes out of her building, waving "Bye, bunny" to a slightly familiar figure in a window. (She always eats breakfast with her neighbor, Greta Garbo, she tells Wally.) Ready at the curb, Wally has a low-slung red MG. Wendy has long legs.

"Christ, sweetie," she says. "I feel like a giraffe squeezing into a sardine can. Can't you get a bigger car? Everyone can see my moneymaker when I get in." She pats her crotch and eyes Wally. Wally plays it cool. He knows Wendy's reputation. Just the other day he'd had a call from a young singer, Theodore Bikel, a victim scheduled for Wendy's next show. As Wally hears it, Wendy had invited Bikel to her apartment, stripped to her bare bunny bones and . . . "And then? And then?" Wally can't wait. And then Wendy had Bikel brush her hair for two hours. That was it.

Which brings us back to the Hollywood–TV tangle. One British film shown during Wendy's early talk show days was none other than the film that had made her a star—lo, those many years ago. It's a fascinating and strange time warp for the public—seeing old movies on TV and also seeing stars of these films appearing as themselves on live shows. Sometimes a former Hollywood actor hosted a film program featuring one of his own films. The first night Freddie Bartholomew worked on Channel 11's "Night Owl Theater," he did the intro for his 1932 film *Tom Brown's School Days.* Showing these old movies, TV was creating a new generation of fans—and often a new career—on TV.

Buster Crabbe told his comeback story when I interviewed him on one of the many film shows I hosted. Crabbe had been every kid's fantasy hero in the 1930s serials. He swung through the jungle as Tarzan, fought space villains as Buck Rogers and rescued beautiful maidens as Flash Gordon. Hollywood had discovered him at the 1932 Olympics, where he'd won the gold medal for swimming. A talent scout hauled Crabbe and other beefcakes to a studio and executives sagely asked the secretaries to choose the body they wanted to see more of. No contest. Crabbe had a perfect physique, blond-Adonis features and something else—he was bright and engaging. But although he made over 150 movies, many of them proving he could go far beyond Hollywood's script choices, Crabbe was on the movie shelf in his early forties. A hell of a young age to be out of your profession. He did what numerous actors have done before and since—he went to Europe to work, around 1946 or 1947.

In the year or so that Crabbe was away, WOR (Channel 9) ran his old adventure serials. Instant success! Fan letters! Phone calls! Where is this Buster Crabbe, viewers demanded. We love this guy! They found out that he was returning from Europe, and when he stepped off the plane it was into a cheering crowd of two thousand official Buster Crabbe Fans. Only he didn't know who they were there for. "I thought there had been a famous person on the plane," he admitted to the TV audience. "But the people rushed toward me. Then I heard, 'Say, Buster Crabbe! Can I have your autograph?' It was a little boy holding out one of my Flash Gordon pictures. 'I watch you on television every week,' he told me.

"I had no way of knowing that my movies had been on television," Crabbe said. "And that so many of you had been seeing them. It's all like a dream." Goddam if old Flash didn't have tears in his eyes. Like the Hollywood studio in 1932, WOR knew a good thing when the public saw it. They signed Crabbe.

Crabbe's warmth and talent came across splendidly in the intimacy of people's homes. He even became one of TV's earliest fitness gurus. The setting was Spartan: a bare studio and a record playing "A Pretty Girl Is Like a Melody." But Crabbe gave the women a magnificent view of his powerful torso bulging out of his undershirt as he led them in calisthenics. Afternoons, he buttoned up a cowboy shirt for a kiddie program. And in 1956, his derring-do and kid appeal combined in a hit series for NBC, "Captain Gallant of the Foreign Legion." Crabbe was the first actor to do a TV series with his own son, Cuffy, age ten. Television has many stories of comebacks by "forgotten" stars. For me, the Buster Crabbe saga is the best.

Unlike Crabbe, some stars merely passed before our lens on their downward spiral. Our film shows were a chance for them to earn a little much-needed money as "guest hosts." They introduced the movie with inside stories and were interviewed during "intermission." And since a Hollywood name was tasty bait for sponsors, there was a steady parade of them. It was painful watching these once-massive stars attempting to hang on to their dignity. Appearing as an insignificant host on television was, for some of them, admitting publicly that they were washed up.

One of our saddest visitors was Count Dracula. Note that I didn't say Bela Lugosi. Dracula had literally sucked the blood out of Lugosi's career. He'd made that movie in 1931 and almost twenty years later he was still identified with the evil vampire. Never taken as seriously as his talent deserved, Lugosi had degenerated into a parody. His latest movie when he got to us was—I hate to tell you —*Abbott and Costello Meet Frankenstein* in 1948.

Parody maybe . . . but each of us who'd shivered through *Dracula* as a kid anticipated the blood-sucking count, not the sentimental Hungarian Jew who tells us that his favorite role had been as Santa Claus. One Christmas, he recounts, he put on a Santa suit and held his son on his knee. His glittering Dracula-ish eyes are misty with memory. "I vass so convincing dot da keet didn't recognize hiss own Papa," he says, reaching for his handkerchief. This is Dracula? But when we ask him about *The Body Snatchers*, one of the films he'd made with Boris Karloff, Lugosi bares his fangs. The two are locked in a feud that won't be settled in this world. "Dot anti-Semite!" he rages. "He rooeen me at studioss. He tell liess. I haate heem!"

After the program, as Lugosi is leaving, one of our models works up the courage to ask for his autograph. I swear, it's the silky Count Dracula who lifts her hand to his lips. The old fox!

In his Count Dracula heyday, Lugosi had received as many love notes from fans as the romantic leads of the time. And the letters kept coming, even when Lugosi was hospitalized for drug addiction in the mid-fifties. An anonymous letter from a fan led to a marriage between the forty-year-old woman and Lugosi, seventy-three. (But Dracula got the last bite. Lugosi was buried in his nemesis's cape, at his own request. Poor Lugosi died too soon. Today there's a Count Dracula Fan Club. And wasn't there a "Count Chokula" cereal? Lugosi would have had an automatic sponsor for his own film program!)

Sponsor. The word made hefty TV execs shiver like wet kittens. Sponsors spooned out the dough that kept TV going. But what if there was no sponsor for a program? Hell, we went on without one. Every station did this. If we'd waited until we had a sponsor for every show, TV wouldn't have happened. "The Wendy Barrie Show" on Dumont had no sponsor. But you know Wendy. She hustled for one right on the air. Sitting on the floor, she patted the carpet and alerted all listening carpet manufacturers to the possibilities. No takers.

In the search for sponsors we were shameless. And it affected the kinds of programs offered. "Quality?" "Meaningful content?" When you're strapped for cash, you can't be choosy. So we conceived shows that no sponsor could refuse—continuous commercials made to look like programs.

There were two types of sludge shows. One was the blatant pitch for anything from vitamins to hair restorer. I call these the first made-for-TV horror films. You got thirty minutes of relentless pounding, coaxing, shouting, insinuating, promising. The guys NEVER SHUT UP. And because these were filmed "programs," stations replayed them over and over and over. In one defenseless town with only one channel, a commercial program aired three hundred times in fourteen months. The nearest mental asylum had to start a waiting list. (You feel a familiar queasiness? Again, today, on the reckless hunt for sponsors, TV is throwing on the same garbage, slightly refined, with names like Robert Vaughan, John Ritter and Ali McGraw.)

The other phony-baloney was a sponsor vehicle that wore a thin veil of "entertainment." Like a program called "Auctionaire." You bid by phone for products, but instead of money, you used the labels from canned foods —as long as they were Libby's canned foods. And here's one for the record: A father–son competition to blow the biggest bubble—with "Bub" bubble gum. Some marketing wizard in Philadelphia thought that one up. How low could we stoop? I can't take discredit for this idea, but I'll admit I went along with "The Carnival of Values." Here's the gimmick: A chain of discount stores, unassumingly named "Dynamic," put up a bunch of tents and filled them with appliances at "daring reductions." On a muggy July afternoon a cameraman and I drove out to the leafy suburb of Forest Hills for our sideshow. We stationed ourselves inside a 200-degree tent and I did man-in-the-tent interviews:

"Say, what great DYNAMIC values have you found out here at DYNAMIC'S CARNIVAL OF VALUES conveniently located at Woodhaven Boulevard and Metropolitan Avenue?" I inquired.

That was the program. Genial TV critic John Crosby said, "Embarrassing."

Television was like a furnace—we shoveled the money in and watched it burn. Here's one of the sad stories. Channel 11, the hapless "Carnival of Values" station, lost something like $8½ million its first year and a half. (That's close to the national debt in today's terms.) The station couldn't get enough sponsors. Who paid for the unsponsored time? The station. And when a station has to fund itself, things get cheap!

Viewers never knew how cheap. When they watched "Concert Previews" on Channel 11, they enjoyed foremost musical talents, including Metropolitan Opera stars. Did they guess that Lou Ames, the station's musical director, persuaded these people to appear for free? "Of course," recalls Ames, "they wanted to be on television so badly, they probably would have paid *us* if we'd been smart enough to ask."

Cheap? Channel 11 fired a director because he bought a gift for a major star making a guest appearance. The director was Fred Kelly, Gene Kelly's brother and himself a gift to TV. Kelly knew the problems of performing and had the skills of directing, a rare combination in early TV.

He and Gene started out as the singing, dancing Kelly Brothers in their hometown of Pittsburgh in the 1930s. When Gene headed out on his own, Fred went solo too. Was there anything he couldn't do? He sang. He danced. He did magic tricks. He was a ventriloquist. He danced on roller skates. He directed the the first Ice Capades. But he couldn't squeeze forty-two piddly bucks from Channel 11.

The program in question was "Hollywood in New York," a review of the biggest films and stage shows, with silent-screen star Lois Wilson. (Channel 11 was turning into an émigré movie colony! Lois and Gloria S. had been buddies in the Old Days. It's possible that Lois had unwittingly been used as a decoy by Kennedy when he began his pursuit of Gloria. Lois was as down-to-earth as a star could get. The first time I met her she was on her hands and knees scrubbing the floor at a friend's house, helping them get ready for a party.) Anyway, when there were no new films or plays, Lois interviewed actors in town. With their connections, Lois and Fred had no trouble getting top names to impress the viewers. But one afternoon as showtime got closer, Lois and Fred had nothing. No film. No play. No guest. Then, at the eleventh hour, Lois got Joan Bennett. Fred ran out himself and bought Joan a bottle of perfume as a thank-you, using $42 of station money. He couldn't get to Wade, who was locked in his opaque-glass office, no doubt "interviewing" a quivering model. Then Fred called downstairs to the *Daily News* to give Ed Sullivan the scoop on Joan's visit for his column, "Little Old New York." (Yeah, Sullivan wrote for Channel 11's owners, did TV programs for Channel 11 and did his Sunday-night program for CBS. He was one busy and very powerful guy.)

Joan appeared on the show, the news appeared in Sullivan's column and everyone was happy. Except for program manager Warren Wade. The jerk wasn't aware that Joan Bennett had been at his station until he read about it in the paper. So you'd think Wade would be delirious that once again Fred and Lois have pulled off a miracle that makes him, Wade, look good. You should live so long. For spending station money without asking him, Wade, for permission, Kelly is O-U-T. However, sometimes—just sometimes—talent won out. Next day, the switchboard operators went nuts taking calls from viewers who were still palpitating over having yet another star in their living rooms. "We're going to watch the show every week!" they promised. Fred was back I-N.

You want a big money-saver? Try kid shows. Every station cultivated its own crop of uncles and aunties and shrill-voiced puppets. There was "Big Brother" Bob Emery's "Small Fry Club" on Dumont. Channel 13 boasted Uncle Hal Tunis and Uncle Fred Sayles. And Uncle Danny Webb, known as "The Man with a Thousand Voices." (You haven't forgotten Danny, have you—our watchdog for the arrival of Bishop Sheen?) Every one of Uncle Danny's shows started with his reading the comics from the pages of—of course—the *Daily News*. And we got plenty of free talent from the moppet contestants on talent shows or kiddie per-formers on other programs.

There was one kid I noticed who was extraordinarily shy among these miniature Ethel Mermans and minus-cule Milton Berles. But he was a real good little performer. Forty years later, I'm doing research for this book. My path crosses movie star Elliott Gould's. I introduce myself. But Gould says, "I know you! You used to do the commercials when my mother brought me to the studios for the show. How ya doin', Guy?" I can't get over it. I love Gould in the movies, but I never put together this wisecracking, loud-mouthed, funny guy with little Elliott of 1949.

Gould got into the kiddie talent mill by chance when he was around eight or so. His mother thought he was too uptight and that maybe some elocution lessons would loosen him up. So she took him to the Charles Lowe school of dance, etc., which turned out a regular supply of kiddie performers. But Lowe didn't stop once he taught Gould to say "Mary had a little lamb." He served Gould the full menu—tap, voice lessons, acting, endearing little charms—and soon Gould was being trotted around with the rest of the Lowe lambkins. They sang and danced and did cute little numbers at benefits and hospitals, and in their spare time they did the kidvid shows. One of these had the impossible title of "Bonny Maid Versatile Varieties, Jr. Edition." The Bonnie Maids, young pretty girls in plaid kilts, were played by later-to-be-stars Anne Francis and Edie Adams.

But where did the hosts for these kiddie shows come from? You didn't need a degree in KidVid—anyone could do it. Suddenly I'm fitted for a holster, a cowboy hat and a pair of boots—and before I know it, I'm "Cowboy Guy." They bring in a bunch of boys and girls, I serve a little milk and cake, I bring a moppet or two in front of the camera, I show a short Western movie—and it's the Gold Seal "Six-Gun Playhouse."

Even wacko Wendy Barrie did the kiddie shtick. She was the happy hostess for "Oky Doky Ranch," on Dumont. Which tells you that what the PR peddled about kid show hosts could be crap. Basically, you had to be able to act. I began thinking about this after a revelation from director Ted Estabrook at Channel 11.

"Have you seen that Howdy Doody?" asks Estabrook.

The freckle-faced puppet and his human sidekick Bob Smith are creaming the competition, including us. But most of us haven't seen it because we're all on the air at the same time.

"You know I used to work with Smith at Dumont," Estabrook says. "Strange guy. When he'd see me on the street, he'd cross to the other side and yell, 'Ted Estabrook eats shit!' Now a bunch of kids think he never says anything stronger than 'goshdarn.' That lucky s.o.b."

The kids never heard that side of Smith. Like they never knew about Howdy Doody's secret life. Howdy's own father had to sue him for support. (You didn't know Howdy had a father? Of course, not—he never talked about him . . . or about his brother. That's showbiz: guy makes it big and forgets about his family!) Frank Paris was the genius who had created Howdy Doody. But he left Smith and NBC over "differences" and sued for a portion of the dough they were raking in from Howdy's promotion deals. Paris was hired by Channel 11, where he brought a puppet he named Peter PIXie to life. (Channel 11's call letters are WPIX. PIX . . . PIXie . . . get it?) Paris, a much gentler person than Smith, appeared with the whimsical Pete on "Pixie Playtime." But without a network behind him, Pete never made it as big as Howdy, and is probably living from hand to mouth in a shabby retirement home.

Still, these were innocent times for programs. We didn't have to cover drugs or kidnapping or child abuse. And look at "Captain Video," TV's first space explorer. Every kid who watched it wanted a Cosmic Vibrator. Yeah, today that sounds like something you get in a plain brown wrapper from a sexual mail order house. The Cosmic Vibrator was one of Captain Video's most potent weapons. It could make an enemy alien vibrate until he was dead.

But with live kids on a show, anything could turn out to be a weapon—against adults. Here's the "Uncle Hal" show on Channel 13. This afternoon his darlings are ferociously competing in a drawing contest. Hal leans over avuncularly as a wee one holds up her masterpiece —and pokes her pencil in his eye.

Inside, Hal yells, "You little creep!" He's ready to vomit with pain. He can't see. But he can't stop a live show in progress. And he doesn't want to frighten the kids. He might lose viewers. So on the outside, Hal is as chuckly and wuckly as ever, with the exception that he's squinting, the injured eye is streaming tears, and he's a little hunched over in agony. The doctor warns him that he almost lost the eye and fits him with an eyepatch. But the show goes on! A few years later, George Reeves is forced to wear protective padding under his Superman costume when he makes publicity appearances. Kids are innocently throwing objects at him, believing that they'll bounce harmlessly off his body, just the way they do on the television show.

One rung above child labor on the exploitation ladder were staff announcers. Young, ambitious, and with no union, we were a station's dream. The deal was equal pay for equal work: you work like a slave and we'll pay you slave wages. But we didn't care, we wanted to be in TV. As an example of broadcast-mania, here's Ed McMahon, known in the late forties as the hardest worker at WCAU-TV, Philadelphia . . . and points east. Determined to break into the bigtime, New York City, Ed drew up what I call

### THE McMAHON MASOCHISTIC
### PLAN FOR SUCCESS

1. Request all evening/night programs at station.
2. Get rolls of nickels from bank.
3. As soon as last program of night is over, catch train for New York City.
4. Grab 4 winks.
5. When train arrives in the morning, run for a

phone booth.

6. Take out rolls of nickels. Get out 3x5 cards with contacts (i.e., anyone remotely connected to TV or who might know anyone remotely connected).

7. Start dialing! But don't let on that you're in a phone booth. You must give the impression that this is an office and that you are based in New York.

8. Make appointments for auditions—if you're lucky.

9. Catch train back to Philadelphia.

10. Do shows at WCAU.

We all needed Ed's insane energy to survive. Staff announcers were hired for voice, talent and extra batteries. Like Ted Knight, who worked at WJAR in Providence, Rhode Island, in 1949. Twenty-five years later he was famous as the untalented newsman on "The Mary Tyler Moore Show"—but no portrayal was further from the truth. At WJAR, Ted is still recalled as the guy who could do any voice, any program, anything. In fact, the station brought in a ventriloquist to teach him the art for a kiddie show—and Ted mastered this difficult art in one day! . . .

And we had to change gears in a second. At Channel 11, Joe Bolton was changing out of his kiddie-show costume when he was called to do the news. The regular guy had broken a tooth. So far, so good. But at the end of the newscast, the camera pulled away for a long shot. Viewers got a great view of Joe's boxer shorts and bare legs. He hadn't had time to put on his trousers!

I put on my World War II air-raid warden helmet to call wrestling matches, changed to a cowboy hat for "Six-Gun Theater," went hatless for the news, pitched everything from aftershave cream to storm windows, interviewed movie actors, hosted quiz shows, did baseball pre- and post-game shows, emceed talent shows and moderated public affairs panels. The audience had no trouble accepting our multiple personalities. The same men and women who watched me as part of a major murder investigation team on "Crime Panel" had been blasted out of their chairs by my "Call Now" commercials on another evening. I think it's in large part because we were *believable*. And heaven knows what other reasons they had.

The public treated us like treasured family. They baked us cookies and knit us sweaters. They sent us presents at the drop of a hat. I introduced my niece Sondra at one show, and casually mentioned that she was in the city to buy a blanket. It was like rubbing the genie's lamp! A few weeks later, hand-embroidered blankets, handmade afghans, magnificent quilts are pouring into the station. At KTLA in Los Angeles, Stan Chambers appeared on the news with a sniffle. Next day, the viewers dropped off their personal cold remedies. Then he started doing a noontime man-on-the-street show, "Meet Me in Hollywood." Stan's concerned viewers disapproved of their young man going hungry. So they fixed him lunch themselves and met him in Hollywood. Suddenly this kid was the only one at his station getting catering service! Triple-layer frosted devil's food cakes (home-baked, of course), overstuffed sandwiches, buttery cookies. Stan had to consume it under the watchful eyes of his satisfied lunch brigade and he started gaining weight. But what was he going to say—"No thank you?!" What puzzles me is that with all this largesse making the rounds, Wendy Barrie got a chain-saw as a gift. "Poor bunny must want me to cut my wrists," she said. "But a fucking razor would have done it!"

The genuine affection for us is perhaps best noted with this favor: fans photographed us off their TV screens and sent us the pictures. Why? Because our shows were live, and there was no tape, they knew we had no way of seeing ourselves. To take the pictures, get the film to the developer, pay for the prints and mail them to us—this was trouble and expense for them, but touching evidence for us that SOMEONE WAS WATCHING. I have one of me with a funny little guest who made funny little animals out of pipe cleaners. That wasn't his only talent, it turned out. He was also a spy for the Joe McCarthy goons. He became "pals" with TV performers, all the while collecting evidence of their so-called Communist sympathies. The fink was eventually tried for perjury and served time, but not before murdering a number of careers. I escaped his venom, and who can say why? It could have been something as simple as the fact that I never laughed at his pipe-cleaner creatures.

But when you talk about performer–audience relationships, the ultimate one must be Ruth Lyons at WLWT-TV in Cincinnati. "Ruth Lyons 50/50 Club" was so popular that fans could wait five years for tickets. And if they couldn't use them, they left them in their wills. Many consider Ruth the best-loved and most respected person television has produced. During her last years on the air, she appeared with two assistants at her side because she'd suffered a stroke. Did that hurt the ratings? Fie on you for asking about "ratings." Ruth's audience loved her and that was that. Ruth died in 1988, but the feeling for her is so strong that when I was doing research for this book, people at the station broke down and cried as they talked about her. (Incidentally, the title for Ruth's show is very "Ruth." She'd started it in a hotel tearoom, where fifty guests came for lunch and the program. When Ruth moved into the station studio, there was room for another fifty people—hence the 50/50.)

Ruth had a secret chemistry that seemed to dissolve

the screen between the viewer and herself. Her show was a visit to a best friend. (It must have been for that reason that Arthur Godfrey himself dubbed her the "female Arthur Godfrey.") If she had a personal family setback and cried on the air, her audience cried with her. If she brought up a problem, her viewers responded. One day, for instance, she appeared quite upset. She'd bought a new fur coat and reprimanded herself for not giving the money to charity instead. Even before the show was over, people were phoning the studio, insisting that she keep the coat. "You deserve it," they said. "You work for it!"

I should tell you that Ruth was very active in charities in her area. Her audience knew she wasn't putting on an act about the coat; Ruth didn't "act" about anything. She was honest, direct, and her audience trusted her. They knew that she didn't allow a sponsor on her show until she'd tested and passed the product herself. She also did her own commercials in her own low-key style. The best way I have of describing Ruth's delivery is to present this response. One day, Ruth interviewed a small boy on her show.

"And what is your favorite television show?" she asked him.

"Oh, I like the '50/50 Club' better than anything," he said. "It doesn't have commercials."

Truth is, Ruth's hour-and-a-half live show had over a dozen commercials—the day before, she had done eighteen. But obviously they didn't offend anyone!

Naturally, with Ruth's constant success, she was wooed by the networks and she did go national for one year. But she was uncomfortable with such a large and anonymous audience. And she hated losing her control over sponsors. Ruth returned to local television, ending her career happier—and certainly more honest—than most of us.

Ruth's was one of the few long-running programs. No matter how likeable we were, we needed a twenty-four-hour psychic to predict how long a program would last. How good it was didn't matter. Sponsors were so cautious that the standard contract with the TV station included a cancellation clause—often put into effect Day One of the contract. I became known as "King of the Four-Week Series" because I started dozens of shows that lasted from one day to a whole month. "Sign here, Guy and you're on the air" (for today). But it didn't have to be the sponsor who did us in. It could be an exec's wife. She sees a pretty female on the show and . . . uh-oh. Does she want her hubby working around THAT . . . ? O-F-F with the show. (No joke. It really happened.) And I'm dead certain that some execs asked their dogs, "Bark once if you liked it." That's how ridiculous it was.

Stations were losing money and, in their panic, owners acted like a losing ball team. They tried out any kind of heads, from ex-Hollywood directors to the chief of a gas company. They constantly changed management to find a solution to their doldrums, but they didn't give anyone time to succeed. Even brilliant minds were replaced by incompetents who undid the good groundwork. And if the station owners themselves had poor judgment? If comic Soupy Sales is a little wacky, it's because he was knocked in the head so often by so-called station experts.

Soupy began his TV career in 1948 in Cincinnati at WKRC-TV, which was owned by the Taft family (as in Senator Robert and the Taft-Hartley Act). Brother Hub Taft didn't seem to have the astuteness of the other Tafts. Soupy had a dance program for teenagers, called "Soupy's Soda Shop." Kids came from all over to dance to the latest releases. They loved it! But when Hub wandered into the studio and saw it, he snarled, "I don't want to see a lot of kids dancing, and nobody else in his right mind wants to either! O-U-T." Along with Soupy, Hub fired a young writer he called "weird." "He's always turning in scripts about people from other planets," complained Hub. "Who's interested in that?" O-U-T went Rod Serling.

(Hub didn't live long enough to see "American Bandstand" go on the air in Philadelphia a few months later. And he never caught "The Twilight Zone." His demise is so "weird," it sounds as if Serling wrote it on special order. Hub had bought the Cold War scare hook, line and bunker, and had built a formidable bomb shelter. One story goes that it was armed and dangerous against invaders, and one night Hub stumbled in drunk, pressed the wrong button and bombed himself to Kingdom Come.)

Soupy's engaging goofiness won him a place on TV in Cleveland. There his record-pantomime show was voted "Best New Show of the Year" by the *Cleveland Plain Dealer*," a hard paper to impress. What happens to the "Best Show of the Year?" O-U-T. The station canceled it the next day. "Being fired turned out to be very positive," Soupy told me recently. "It forced me to keep thinking and changing and staying fresh." You didn't have a chance to get stale in this business!

As you've noticed, I haven't attempted the standard rundown of shows in this chapter. To try to recount the myriad programs that came on TV from coast to coast and left in the blink of an eye would be like trying to count the stars on a clear night. And whole galaxies of programs have simply vanished. Like the "Sylvie St. Clair Show." In 1947 this French singer was promoted as "television's new look," and the press conveyed her every charm to their readers. Sylvie sang reclining on a couch, snacked on grapes and blew kisses to men she addressed by first name. Talented enough to be hired to sing at the wedding banquet of Rita Hayworth and Aly

Khan a few years later, she nonetheless faded from the TV screen.

Still, I want to give you a few of my favorites. Some I was actually part of, others I observed and others I heard about. They've all gone to that Great Program Roundup in the Sky . . . but some seem to have been reincarnated. For better or for worse? You tell me.

## LeBOW'S LISTINGS

1. "WHAT'LL I WEAR?": A striptease in reverse. Beauteous models put on the latest fashions, from dresses to bathing suits. Never got the gist of this one. What would the girls be wearing before they got into the bathing suits? It was one of the shows that never made it to the air then, but would get a humongous rating today. I would have paid to be its announcer, but instead I got . . .

2. "CLAIRE MANN'S PERSONALS": The first video dating service! You called Claire and she tried to match you up with one of her "interesting" people. Claire claimed phenomenal successes, but to me she looked old enough to claim Adam and Eve as her first customers. Anyway, the show didn't last long enough for a couple to finish their first date. Claire moved fast. She dropped about 400 pounds and turned up as the host of something called "Figure Magic," where she advised women how to have great figures.

3. "R.F.D. AMERICA": Would you believe that NBC was dumb enough to run a "down home" farm quiz show in New York City? This came with live sheep, but as New Yorkers are only familiar with wolves in sheep's clothing, it went off the air.

4. "THE AMAZING POLGAR": An amazing hypnotist, said to have hypnotized his wife into a

painless childbirth. He put the studio audience into a trance, but he didn't have to bother with the home viewers—they went under, the minute the set went on.

5. "KNOW YOUR BODY": High school students answered questions about the organs and functions of the human body, using mannequins as examples. The rule was that questions were to be "of a nature to maintain interest." Show didn't work. (Mannequins didn't have the parts that would "maintain interest" for high school kids.)

6. "AUCTION-AIRE": This beat the Home Shopping Network by decades. You saved the labels from your canned foods and used them to bid by phone for a Shetland pony, a diamond ring and other "fabulous" items. (One lucky viewer got a refrigerator for only—only?—225 labels.) Show ran Friday nights during prime time, during which it was mandatory to have one girl, one sweater and two big boobs.

7. "RUTHIE ON THE TELEPHONE": On CBS from 7:55 to 8:00 p.m. Same format for every show. Ruthie talked to a man she was crazy for, but he was not interested. The End. Show was disconnected, but modern-day cable has brought it back with careful budgeting. Now the girl wears no clothes and you make the call to her at $10 a pop. (A five-minute show was not unusual. Stations were willing to sell any amount of time to sponsors. Time was so chopped up that you could see seven programs in one hour on the same channel.)

8. "BOSS IN THE SKY": Dramatic series about a "boy who came to live in the wide-open spaces to find that a man's soul is his own but a pretty girl usually holds first mortgage." (Program synopsis

warned: "Almost anything can happen in this humorous serial drama." To those who knew television, it really meant, "We haven't written the next script yet.")

9. "FUN AT THE PIANO": Genial Ed McGinley fingered the ivories. One of the many pleasant little musical programs at the beginning of television. (Things weren't always harmonious between music and TV. The musicians' union went out on strike in '47 into '48, and we couldn't use live musicians. And folks didn't take to lip-synching.)

10. "HOLLYWOOD SCREEN TEST": Your chance to do a scene with an actor and win a part in a play or movie. So good, why isn't it on television today? Are networks afraid if people see good acting, they'll turn off the lousy sitcoms?

11. "OKAY, MOTHER": A rollicking audience participation show for women. Hijinks galore as audience yelled, "OKAY, MOTHER" back at the announcer, announcer got spanked, announcer ran into audience and got kissed. (Show seemed pointedly designed for Dennis James, who loved getting kissed and spanked.)

12. "TEN HAIRDOS THAT SHOOK THE WORLD": I won't bother you with the explanation for this one. I just want it out of my hair.

13. "KEY TO THE MISSING": Helped find lost persons. One of most dramatic segments: A Polish teenager, the only one of her family to survive Nazi concentration camps, was united with her sole living relative, a seventy-nine-year-old from Florida. (TV's public-spirited side.)

14. "OPERATION SUCCESS": First video employment service. Job opportunities for veterans, hosted by movie star Joe E. Brown. First show

brought in a wealth of offers from employees in the area. (One of many public service programs that couldn't survive the race for sponsors, then ratings.)

15. "NICKELODEON": The 1897 inauguration of President McKinley, the 1900 Easter Parade and other up-to-the-minute newsreels and films.

16. "TO BE ANNOUNCED": One of the most popular shows, this appeared on every channel. Sometimes seen five times a day. This alerted the viewer that he'd have to take potluck because: (1) the sponsor pulled out and we can't find a new one; (2) we never had a sponsor and the station can't pay for the program anymore; (3) the program we planned is so stupid that even *we* couldn't foist it on you; (4) who the hell can come up with ideas this fast? But trust us. We'll pull something out of the hat at the last minute. The outcome of "To Be Announced" was a surprise to the audience and a shock to performers, who didn't find out what "to be announced" was until ten minutes before airtime. (This could explain why programs went on the air as performers were still rehearsing or were half dressed. "We're on the AIR? Shit!")

# 7 / News Flash

"No audience is going to sit there for a half hour and watch someone read the news!"
—Max Fleischer, head of a New York school for broadcasting

As a newscaster, I have a million things to say about news on TV. But you're lucky—I'm only going to mention a few. When we started TV news there were no image makers. We made ourselves in our own image. So we can take part of the blame for starting the image business that developed what Fred W. Friendly has called the talking end of a teleprompter. . . .

It's easy to imagine that in one station programming conference after another in 1947 or 1948, a guy would probably croak, "Hey, what are we going to do about the news?"

"News?" somebody else would say. "Are we planning to do news?"

"Sure," another person would say. "We're probably going to do some."

"What does the FCC say about news, anybody

know?"

"Oh, they probably say we have to do so some."

"Yeah," says the first guy. "But who knows anything about doing the news on television?"

"Yeah," the room choruses. "You gotta have pictures."

And one really sad voice adds, "And they probably better be *moving* pictures, too."

Believe me, that's a pretty accurate description. Television news went through the most rigorous metamorphosis of any element in the news business. And it was a nasty quandary, too.

Money, of course, and how much you could spend, was key—as usual. Most of the little independent stations, after putting in modern structures and technology, had zero dough. For them the answer was to get a guy who could, with some grace, read news copy on camera and hope for the best. And don't put the news on too many times during the day, either. It's 1947 or 1948, the war is over. Nothing's happening. So who wants to see the news? Sponsors want action—like wrestling.

Now, if you're a bigger station you could purchase newsreel film and show that. But like the newsreels in the theater, it would be events that are two, three days old—or more.

So somebody gets a crazy idea: let's put on still pictures. Sounds simple, but it isn't. You check with your technical director about the best size photos to get. Then you buy photos from the various news services. Next, you paste them on cardboard, write a script describing each picture in order—and you're ready to hit the air.

Oh, but you better pray, too. Under the heat, some pictures get craggly. On TV they look like the surface of the moon. Others have too much glare. And if you don't powder these down with a white substance you'll get a good shot of a blur. And if the camera focuses on a photo too long, the picture image can burn into the lens and appear superimposed over the next photo up, turning your newscast into a ghostcast. But your most fervent prayers must extend to the guy off camera whose hands change the pictures as you are reading the news.

This guy is human, remember. So sometimes the picture appears on the screen tilted. Sometimes his hand appears in the shot. And sometimes, when you're describing the arrival of a dignitary, the picture he's holding up is the winning horse in the eighth race. Even the horse knows this can't go on.

Once the paste-and-show technique was conquered, news entered a more sophisticated stage: the slide show. You made slides from your still photos and projected them from master control. No more crinkly pictures, no more blurs, no more disembodied hands . . . but until the projectionists got interested in showing "fillims," as they called them, you still had as many mismatches between the announcer's recitation and the slide subject.

Against these potential horrors, is it any wonder that hardly any persons who can remember the late 1940s identify with a newscaster?

With few exceptions, newscasts were done by any announcer available. Requirements were a full set of teeth and a full hairline. Some stations were so blasé about the news that they threw on a slide that said "NEWS" and had someone do off-camera reading. (I know—I was the invisible midnight "Sanka" newsman at WPIX, Channel 11, in New York.) The director considered himself a genius if he created a few zippy titles like "Girlie News," "Kiddie News" or "New News." It should have been called "Bad News."

You can see that the trek was long and hard to arrive at the Cronkite stage, the Huntley–Brinkley stage and the Howard K. Smith stage. And here let's talk of some of the heroes who brought TV news out of the torture chambers and into the light.

John Cameron Swayze, closely identified now with underwater Timex watches, looked every bit a hero on TV. Classic face, wide-set eyes, properly coiffed hair. The smoothness of an English squire's voice, and diction to match. His voice could tinkle with joyous news or resonate accompaniment to a somber story. So appropriate was his image, audiences must have wondered if he'd ever been a kid. But yes, he certainly was—and in Kansas City yet. In fact, this paragon of sophistication toughed it out in a rough-and-tumble newspaper job on the *Kansas City Post* for ten long years. But this image of ultra-refinement . . . where did it come from? John Cameron says, "Thanks to Mother . . . she insisted I take elocution lessons, and drama and literature, bless her heart." Then the newspaper tied in with a local radio station and several of the writers were assigned to deliver newscasts. Swayze squeezed through the door of opportunity to a microphone.

Several years later, he landed at WNBC-TV in New York City. First big assignment: cover the 1948 presidential conventions in Philadelphia. But by now TV had depressed our man to a point where he didn't think it had any future. All of us in these 1947–48 days felt depressed. TV was one technological screw-up after another. Were enough people watching to make it all worthwhile? (Was *anyone* watching?) Our salaries came in dollar bills. Work hours were endless. And we couldn't see ourselves. Who could afford a TV set? (Author's note: without the technology of videotape or kinescope, I didn't see myself for the first two years. And when I finally did, I was glad I was still young enough to start another profession.)

So Swayze's state of mind was not what you'd call ebullient as he reported from Convention Hall. One evening he's in a cab going from his hotel to the hall. He's dour as a Dane. But the cab driver leaps out, opens the door for Swayze and says, "I saw you on TV last night, Mr. Swayze."

Somebody's actually watching? Swayze can't control himself. "You did? You did? How was it?"

"Oh, the wife and I have seen you every night," says the cab driver. "Wait till I tell her who rode in my cab!"

Swayze tips extra-generously and rushes to call Mrs. S. in New York. "Dear, I'll be on television tonight. Ask the neighbors if you can watch me on their set. I want you to tell me what I look like." That's how much faith Swayze has in this TV—he doesn't even own a set.

He does a good job that evening—intelligent and crisp. But when he calls his wife, Tuffy, she's strangely cantankerous.

"Well?"

"Terrible," snaps through the wires. "You look like a corpse. Dead. You look dead."

Image? Does that come first? Image, shmimage—this problem he can handle.

Swayze thinks back to his audition for NBC, which was more like trying for a modeling job than news announcing. He wasn't asked to speak a line. He sat with four other men in the studio, a camera scanned them all and then they were told to go home. Six days later, he was hired.

After the convention, Swayze molded his new image for TV, reaching back to his schooling in drama and speech. From the deadly plaster cast-like substance makeup people threw on his face, he switched to only a light powder. From a nondescript shirt to a high-fashion widespread collar. From a forgettable tie to one that was honored by the term "cravat." Add a flower in the lapel —and John Cameron Swayze was born.

Swayze's makeover was right on the boutonniere. Nobody could compete with him and, aided by Camel cigarette sponsorship, he became the quintessential newscaster. The public coveted the perfectly turned-out newsman. One evening, unable to get a fresh flower, he appeared bare-lapeled. A few days later he received a bunch of exquisite artificial flowers handmade by a little handicapped girl. A note explained that now he would not have to be without a flower again. (If ABC television executive Roone Arledge had been old enough to work in television then, John Cameron Swayze would never have happened. Thirty-five or so years later, Roone magisterially pronounced that an audience could not "relate" to an announcer wearing a pocket handkerchief. Think of what he might have said about flowers! P.S.: Ever wonder how a guy can have the chutzpah to declare what you can and cannot "relate" to?)

Perhaps because it was the beginning of things. Or perhaps it was because John Cameron Swayze's voice and image were so striking that during his greatest popularity he was approached by countless businesses with proposals to turn out every kind of product with the Swayze imprimatur. He chose only two. The Milton-Bradley board game company turned out an educational game simply named "Swayze." (It was called "The Only News Quiz Game That's as New as Today's Headlines.") And a manufacturer turned out "Swayze" ties. It marked the first, if not the only, time that a newsman reaped such popular perks.

Meanwhile, over at another local station, an Alabama choir boy who had yearned to be a pop and gospel singer and who had performed on the radio was now about to be imaged into television news. Fellow Alabaman John Tillman had persuaded singing Doug Edwards to try announcing. What the hell, you could make $25 to $35 every week! Edward's deep, resounding voice seemed just right for the excitement that news directors craved. Came a series of small station jobs and once more Doug's

Confederate friend interdicted: "Hey, buddy, come to New York. There's an opening at my station."

Southern ex-gospel singer packed his bags, rattled up to the big town, auditioned successfully, and at WCBS (then called WABC) began his image process. It took time. His early requests to be moved from radio to the station's newly acquired TV operation were continually turned down. Doug saw himself ultimately as a television newscaster, but he couldn't convince anyone. The fact is, he didn't have the background for news, and WABC must have been thinking about the extraordinary list of experts it had hired during the war.

But you can't beat image. Doug Edwards had dark good looks, and a countenance reflecting both earnestness and leadership. To listen to him and to look at him, you concluded that somebody was at the helm. And you certainly can't beat good fortune. Opportunity opened the door a sliver at this station—the guy who was doing TV news hadn't made it in one day. Enter substitute Doug Edwards and the beginning of "Douglas Edwards with the News" for the next forty years or more. To his credit, Doug early on acquired the mantle of CBS news-broadcasting integrity. It is he who single-handedly changed early television's ridiculous precept that the lead news stories should be only those for which they had accompanying pictures or film. Edwards insisted that the importance and quality of news must come before any and every picture—always. He also railed against newsmen having to do their own commercials. He was eminently correct.

Ten blocks southeast of Doug Edwards was his Alabama buddy, John Tillman. (You met John earlier as the Alabama Assassin and the "Parliament" commercial cougher. Actually, John's major role in early TV turned out to be as a newsman.) A good, solid thinker, Tillman had left his staff announcer's job at WABC, where he was really lost in the mélange of top-drawer voices, and got himself hired at Channel 11. He was one of five announcers hired before the station went on the air. The others were Jack McCarthy, Joe Bolton, Rex Marshall and myself. In fact, I was the first one hired, by a month or two.

With his clean, straight, soft features, dark hair and lean look, Tillman appeared to be directly the opposite of his pal, the more rough-hewn Edwards. He had served as a page boy in the U.S. Congress; his father was a legend as a doctor (incidentally, many Alabama blacks carried the first or last name "Tillman" to honor the doctor who broke tradition and insisted on treating black patients).

Aided by the power of the *Daily News*—by its money, by its tremendous experience—John's image became perfectly wedded. Elegant, slightly Southern in speech and with a good delivery, he reigned at Channel 11 for more than three decades and won numerous awards. But before Tillman could even begin to succeed, the management of the *Daily News* imposed on all its newscasters the most preposterous rule in TV history: No newscaster could give his name on the air. It was believed that the paper's newswriters were jealous of us TV announcers—now getting all the viewer attention. I had been on TV for two years and was the first to receive angry mail inquiring why I was now too arrogant to identify myself. Additionally, the viewers hammered away at the station for being "absurd," "petty," "stupid"—and "setting communication back 3000 years."

The station finally capitulated—and just barely before the formation of the announcers' union (AFTRA), which would have demanded an identification, anyway.

Like Swayze, Tillman had sartorial smarts. But sometimes image gets in the way of the news. While the rest of us were buying our suits off the $40 racks, Tillman had his custom-made. One day he nattily did the news in his newest, a bouclé suit—bouclé having a distinctive nubby weave, which motivated a viewer to write: "You have the worst case of dandruff I've ever seen! It really detracted from the news. Fix it." The suit was retired.

Tillman's image was unflappable, and he even survived the following:

Interviewing the wife of golfer Sammy Snead prior to an important tournament, Tillman inquired, "Do you have some personal ritual you go through before Mr. Snead's golf tournaments?" "Why, yes," came the instant response. "Before every match I pray over his balls."

I move on to Philadelphia, where news names like John Facenda and Gene Crane are emerging. Facenda, by the way, literally invests in his career. He buys five minutes of airtime from WCAU-TV. That's how badly he wants to be a newscaster—and how strongly he believes that he'll succeed. A Philadelphia copy of John Cameron Swayze, Facenda is sauve and smooth, with a deep, creamy voice. Crane is warm and friendly in the image of the City of Brotherly Love, and serious in dark-rimmed glasses. But no matter how serious . . . early television found a way to make it impossible for us to take ourselves too seriously.

This one day, Crane's news set is sharing the studio with an animal and bird show that appears about an hour earlier. Ten minutes before airtime, the animal crew is about wrapped up. One little catch. The mynah bird evidently wants to catch the early news. He's a big Crane fan. So he flies up to the rafters of this high studio. Crane sits at his news desk and concentrates on his script. He doesn't even hear the commotion of twenty stagehands, floormen and carpenters trying to coax the big beak down.

Program begins. Then, at a certain point, Crane knows something is wrong. Everyone is staring at him. They're laughing, whispering, pointing upward. Crane's annoyed, but keeps his cool. Now they're pointing at him. Crane thinks, "Well, if my fly's open at least it's hidden under the desk and to hell with anything else." Crane learns it's truly something else during the commercial break. Midway through the newscast, the mynah bird leaves its perch and makes a perfect landing on Crane's shoulder. From his vantage point the mynah alternately checks the script in Crane's hand and peers at Crane's face—probably picking up a few pointers. The incident helped make Gene Crane one of TV's most enduring personalities. But the little winged benefactor resigned from newscasting and never appeared again.

Switch to KTLA out in California, where Stan Chambers is giving a moving news story of a beached whale. Enunciating in fine style, he has his newscaster's mouth open wide when a fly flies in. Stan's viewers may see a speck on the screen, but they don't see the fly. They see Stan all choked up and coughing—but of course he can't stop delivering his lines. The next day he receives compliments about his involvement in his stories: "Mr. Chambers was so moved by the plight of the whale that he was in tears, God bless him," one woman said.

And just what kind of an image does a newscaster have when he has to do his own commercials? You can't argue Edwards's point that it can compromise his integrity as a newscaster . . . but you also can't argue the fact that at smaller television stations it was compromise or close down!

As Chambers and Crane and all of us looked birds and other problems of newscasting in the eye, TV news was changing. It had to develop beyond the slide shows and movie newsreels in order to succeed. These newsreels couldn't compete with TV's immediacy. Using on-the-spot reporters, a television station could give its viewers local news every day. "I'd rather have a good auto accident in Queens than an oil-well fire in Iran," said Channel 11's station manager. And with the state-of-the-art new marvel called the Houston Developer, Channel 11 was able to live up to its motto, "First on the Scene, First on the Screen." The Houston Developer took film from the reporter's camera and prepared it for the television camera without having to make a negative first. In minutes, a story was ready for the air. Not only did this scoop the newsreels, it made mincemeat of the newspapers.

But speed didn't solve the problems encountered in shooting night film. To get sufficient light, cameramen had to lug battery packs weighing 10 pounds or more on their backs. And the quality of night film wasn't up to what was shot in daylight, as news director Walter Engels was bemoaning one day in his office. Pete Frezzilino, a part-time electrician, heard him. "Mr. Boss," says Frezzilino in his Italian accent, "let me try to help. Will you give me two days off?"

You ready for this? As Engels tells it, Frezzilino—a tinkerer, a genius—goes home to his workshop. He lays his hands on some 6V batteries that he uses to soup up 30V floodlight bulbs. Together these are much lighter than the 10-pound backbreakers. Now, Frezzilino goes to his local grocery store and borrows some reflectors they use in their displays. He ties these onto the floodlight bulbs. Presto! Fifty feet of beautiful, strong light light. Results are incredible. Television can show events happening twenty-four hours a day. (After Channel 11 had used Frezzilino's contraption for a while, Sylvania bought the idea, called it the Frezzi Sungun and made millions.)

The growth of newscasters and technological advances notwithstanding, the public was moved by crisis events: fires, floods, wrecks, rescues. Less physical but exciting on a different level were criminal investigations.

The Kefauver Hearings on Crime in 1951 were almost better than a movie. And the New York hearings targeting underworld figure Frank Costello were the first time television was allowed in a courtroom. From start to finish, it was an image fight. First, there almost *was* no telecast. The hearings were to be in the New York Federal Court Building in Manhattan, wherein presided Judge Learned Hand. Judge Hand had a thing against cameras, which he had developed when news photographers still used the old-fashioned gunpowder for their photographs. The gunpowder was ignited in a spreadpan to make an explosion in order for the photo to be taken. The sound and the flash gave the Judge the willies. He banned cameras from his courtroom for eternity. No use arguing with him that TV cameras didn't use gunpowder.

Channel 11, panting to be First on the Scene, First on the Screen, wants to cover this story so they can score big against the networks. Engels happens to know Washington columnist Ruth Montgomery, who knows everybody in Washington, and he asks her for help. What can she do? Ruthie knows that to politicians, getting their picture taken is better than sex. Getting on TV virtually *is* sex. And Estes Kefauver, the Senator from Tennessee running these hearings, wants to run for president next year. Montgomery informs him that the Judge, by outlawing the TV cameras, is doing Kefauver's political campaign dirt. He needs these hearings to create his image of a fearless crimefighter of presidential timber.

So Kefauver zooms up to New York City and reminds Judge Hand that the Federal Building is government property . . . and that as a Senator of these United States of America, he, Estes Kefauver, can have a television camera in there every day to keep the American public apprised of this critical investigation into a canker that threatens the very fabric of society. The Judge can just put that gunpowder in his pan and smoke it.

Well, the Judge can't say no to this earnest request. In come the TV cameras, which sets the stage for what will be some of the most dramatic images to come out of early television: the shots of Frank Costello in the courtroom. But here's the true story:

Channel 11 had set up its master control in the men's room closest to the courtroom. (I know, I know, it seems that bathrooms figure pretty big in early TV.) Director Ted Estabrook and station manager G. B. Larson are getting ready for the broadcast when two gents straight out of *Guys and Dolls* lumber in. Hats over their eyes, jackets down to their knees, sneers on their kissers and hands in their pockets.

Hood #1: "We got a message for you. You don't show Mr. Costello's face on the TV. Get it?"

Estabrook (the staff at Channel 11 is notorious for pulling stunts, and he can't believe these jokers are real): "Look, pals, I'm the director and I say Costello's face goes on screen."

Hood #2 (pulls out a gun): "This says it don't."

Larson: "You're right. It don't. I mean we won't. Believe me!"

Hood #1 (pulls out his gun): "I wanna believe you, but I hope I don't get disappointed. You get me?"

Hood #2: "Look. You tell anyone about this and you're two dead television twerps." (He points the gun at Estabrook.)

Estabrook: "We won't. It won't. He won't."

The hoods leave. Estabrook is weak at the knees, shivery at the bladder. How the hell can he telecast the hearings and not show Costello's face? Oh, my God, thinks Estabrook! The thug only said "face." No face on screen. They didn't mention hands or feet or ass—just face. "Hey, guys, get a shot of Costello's hands."

The public sees Costello's hands sweating, twisting, kneading. It's art! Revealing a man's soul through his hands—brilliant! Estabrook wins an Emmy, an award from *TV Guide* and another from *Look* magazine.

"And," he says smiling, "I owe it all to crime."

Skip down the road a few years to 1954, the sensational Army–McCarthy Hearings—and the first PR stunt on television. The hearings are more news in the making. But this time an image is being un-made as millions of viewers watch Senator Joe McCarthy finally get what he deserves—censure. For years the Senator had been the "star" of one of America's darkest periods as he conducted his witch-hunt for so-called Communist sympathizers. By the time the Senator himself was on the hot seat in April 1954, he had ruined the lives and careers of countless innocent men and women. The hearings were noisy affairs, with McCarthy often shouting, "Point of order! "Point of order!" and pounding on the table. By the time they were over in June, McCarthy himself had become a joke. Which leads us to Al Rylander, PR man extraordinaire for Columbia Pictures.

Like all successful PR men, Al has a talent for bringing improbable elements together. In this instance:

1. Columbia's *The Caine Mutiny* with Humphrey Bogart. (It was passed over at the Academy Awards, so Al wants to give it a boost.)
2. Senator Joe McCarthy.
3. Senator McCarthy's right-hand man, Attorney Roy Cohn. (Keep that last name in mind.)
4. Senator Carl Mundt, one of those involved in the hearings.
5. Television.

Rylander convinces Mundt to make a certain announcement on the following day. Then he talks privately with McCarthy.

The next day, Mundt stands and says to the hearing

room: "I'm proud to announce that tomorrow evening we're throwing a cocktail party for all assembled here, and there will also be a private screening of *The Caine Mutiny.*

Whereupon Senator McCarthy leaps up, bangs his show on the desk and yells: "Point of order! Point of order!"

Mundt recognizes McCarthy, who says: "Pardon me, Senator. Did you say Caine Mutiny? Or Cohn Mutiny?"

Rylander's achievement stands unmatched in television newsmaking.


I want to wind up this chapter on a personal note. I was possibly the first newscaster to editorialize on television. I had the background, with my degree in Political Science and an interest in politics and history that began at age five, when my father took me to my first political rally. Even as a sportscaster, I was interested in sorting out the *why* of a story. Now the VIM radio and TV chain, the biggest chain of its kind in the country, hired me to analyze news. And I delivered it often opposed to *Daily News* editorial policies. Why did they let me continue? Maybe a sense of integrity. I do know they needed the money. Take your choice.

*Arguably the "First Lady of the Screen," large and small: Gloria Swanson, doing a domestic turn on Channel 11.*

247

Brothers Gene and Fred Kelly
before Gene goes to M-G-M and
Fred begins directing in TV.
(Photo courtesy Fred Kelly)

Director Fred Kelly giving a few dance
pointers to Garry Moore
on "I've Got a Secret."
(Photo courtesy Fred Kelly)

The scary guy? None other than Bela
Lugosi, Count Dracula, who switched
to chilling audiences on TV in 1948.
Little screen or big screen . . . brrr!

248

*Classic star of the screen Wendy Barrie: one of two of Hollywood's best who captured New York audiences in 1948. The other was Gloria Swanson.*

249

Can you find movie star Elliott Gould in the above photo?
Look for his laughing face, far right, second row. Fellow kiddie
performer Leah Breier (front row, far left) grew up to be an
award-winning magazine editor. (Photo courtesy Leah Breier)

Bad boy Dennis James probably getting
a well-deserved spanking from
Julia Meade on the "Okay, Mother"
show, 1950. (Photo courtesy Photofest)

Believe it or not, the first swimming
instruction show on television—
and we did it all without water.

250

*The tall man in the center is Ed McMahon, on a WCAU (Philadelphia) informational program, circa 1948. At left, famed anchorman John Facenda; at right, sportscaster Jack Whitaker. Seated is Phil Sheridan. (Photo courtesy Photofest)*

251

Daily News *columnist Ed Sullivan on his WPIX gossip show, the forerunner and training ground for "The Ed Sullivan Show." (Photo courtesy WPIX)*

With former heavyweight champion Gene Tunney at left, assorted
athletes and I rehearse for our TV show in conjunction with the
Boys' Club of New York.

253

*Yup, that's Soupy Sales before he put on flesh, emceeing his first TV show with guest singing star Fran Warren. (Photo courtesy Soupy Sales)*

*In center: big Hollywood star Joe E. Brown debuting his Channel 11 TV show, 1950. That's me at left.*

Top: *Ray Heatherton, singing bandleader turned highly successful kiddie show host, 1949. He's blond Joey Heatherton's dad. (Photo courtesy Photofest)* Bottom: *Olympic star Buster Crabbe and his son, Cullen, in their TV series "Captain Gallant of the Foreign Legion." The return of his popularity through TV is still unmatched. (Photo courtesy Photofest)*

255

*Filmdom's Roscoe Karns is "Rocky King, Private Eye" in TV's first whodunit series, Channel 5. (Photo courtesy Marvin Pakula)*

*Despite protests from certain sections of the country, CBS may have launched the first black TV star: singer, actor, gifted pianist Bob Howard (right), seen here in a still from a Hollywood production. The man on the left is Pigmeat Markham. (Photo courtesy Photofest)*

256

*TV's best-loved hostess, Ruth Lyons, with June Allyson and Dick Powell on her Cincinnati talk show.*
*(Photo courtesy WLWT, Cincinnati)*

*My turn as kiddie show host: "Cowboy Guy."*

257

*New York City's first TV couple—Pat and John Tillman hosting "Night Owl Theater," 1948. (Photo courtesy John Tillman)*

258

"We'll be the grandest couple in the Easter Parade" . . . Barbara
Walters' first appearance on TV, circa 1949, with announcer
John Tillman covering New York's Easter Parade from
the steps of St. Patrick's Cathedral.
(Photo courtesy John Tillman)

259

*Was this the first co-anchor team?*
*Newsman Gene Crane of WCAU*
*shares newscast duties with a news hawk.*
*(Photo courtesy Gene Crane)*

*In the early 1950s, young Douglas Edwards (right) carries the CBS news*
*traditions into TV. Don Hewitt, genius of "60 Minutes,"*
*is at left. (Photo courtesy Photofest)*

*Debonair John Cameron Swayze wearing his trademark carnation and cravat—TV's best-dressed newsman. (Photo courtesy Timex)*

261

*Erudite newsman Stan Chambers (in light suit) starting four decades of diverse service to KTLA, Los Angeles. (Photo courtesy KTLA)*

262

*Station Break:*

# She Was Dying to Be on TV

Some girls broke into television smiling next to appliances or showing off quiz show prizes. No such cushy jobs for this young actress, who merits a page of her own because she was known as "The Most Murdered Girl on Television."

She was throttled on "The Plainclothesman," shot on "Famous Jury Trials" and poisoned on "Rocky King"— and after that they thought of new ways to finish her off. She was dropped on her head, she was stabbed and suffocated and she was even drowned. Then, when they ran out of methods to kill her, she became a murderess. But she wasn't as talented a killer as she was a killee. She was so squeamish about hurting the actor playing her victim that she barely placed her hands on his throat for two seconds. "You call that strangling?" demanded the director. "Grab him by the throat—and squeeze, hard—

264

*Joyce Randolph, 1946, "The Most Murdered Woman on TV"*
*before she became Trixie on "The Honeymooners."*
*(Photo courtesy Joyce Randolph)*

*Joyce Randolph*

265

and for longer than ten seconds. And try not to look as though you're scared he's going to bite you. *You're* the attacker!''

A life of crime was not for our heroine. She gave it up for a life in Brooklyn. As Ed Norton's wife, Trixie, on "The Honeymooners," actress Joyce Randolph helped create some of television's most enduring comedy. Thanks for going straight, Joyce!

# 8 / The Lord Giveth . . . but TV Keepeth

**SANTA CLAUS ON YOUR TV SET**

—title for article on quiz programs in *TV Guide*

"Don't give any prizes away tonight," ordered my producer.

I didn't.

In two sentences you have the essence of TV quiz shows: arrogance, deception and greed.

The little scene here occurred way before 1959, when the quiz show volcano finally erupted. Under government questioning, Carl van Doren, a contestant who had won $129,000 on "Twenty-One" in 1957, admitted that he had been fed the answers beforehand. Other contestants, including well-known show-business guests, confessed that they too had been coached. More quiz programs emerged as fakes. The public learned that it had been sucked in—again.

This chicanery had been going on for years. Everyone in the business knew about it, whether they took part or not. So why didn't someone blow the whistle? Whistles were being blown all over the place, but their sounds were overwhelmed by the high acceptance of the audience, which couldn't get enough of these shows.

Like much of television, the "giveaway" came from radio, where duping the public had been a hallowed tradition. The abuses were so blatant by 1949 that a trade daily coyly reported, "Some of the contestants on a certain giveaway show are coached and given answers to questions several hours before they go on the air. It's done just to make sure that a certain percentage of contestants come through as big winners—the theory being that all the world loves a winner."

The Federal Communications Commission, not in on the lovefest, attempted to ban these giveaway shows. This was not received well by the broadcast industry: What? Curb our freedom to be dishonest? The industry got an injunction against the proceedings and the shows continued—and slimed into television. *TV Guide* columnist Bob Gardner fumed that this type of program was "only a cheap, easy way of putting on a show. It caters to greed. It has no entertainment value. It builds nothing but jackpots . . . radio and TV sets are not bought to win money."

Easy for you to say, Bob. But the public didn't turn down the chance when it came along! Answer a question and win? Everybody played! You could appear as a contestant on the air or simply get lucky and get a phone call at home. "Hello, is this Mrs. Plintchlikin? This is YOUR lucky day! YOU are on 'Guess That Answer!'" The papers were full of dramatic stories about winners just like Mrs. Plintchlikin. Catch this one:

### PARKCHESTER COUPLE
### WINS $2,000 JACKPOT

"It was like a gift from heaven," gushed the recipient.

And this headline:

## MAN HITS $8,120 JACKPOT—HE
## FINDS OUT HE'LL SEE AGAIN

Hey, could you ask for a better scenario than this? A retired fireman, practically blind, can now afford the cataract operation he needs, thanks to a quiz show.

Stories like these—and there were plenty—would have you think that quiz shows were not merely television programs. They were forces of good in the world.

Bullshot.

More shows than the industry wanted to admit were a setup for the producer to get something for nothing. Some of these sleazeballs furnished their entire homes with items that should have been won by the public. Their wives had a mink coat for every day of the week. They ate free in restaurants. They vacationed in the best resorts. They could even steal a car or two. And to make extra cash they sold prizes to stores at jacked-up prices. One producer's basement was jammed with so many bottles of aftershave he planned to sell that if there'd been a fire—which his staff prayed for nightly—the house would have gone up like a rocket.

Anyone connected to the show, or to someone connected to the show, was a candidate for gimmies: the station manager, the advertising man, the producer's tax accountant, the advertising man's daughter, the show host, the producer's nephew . . . ad infinitum. "Yeah, yeah, it looks great," said an advertising man watching the audition of a new quiz show he intended to contract. "But what's in it for me? Gimmie the list of prizes." The hell with the show!

I worked with some of the biggest crooked creeps in the business. There was producer Albert Black, the godfather of quiz quackery. And here's the strange thing. Black was really talented. Very talented. In fact, he produced and directed the first dramatic show ever done outside a studio, starring Rod Steiger. Critics commended him for his genius in using the streets of New York City. But like a lot of other guys, Black got his kicks from working in the dark corners of the business. Misappropriated prizes. Payoffs. Phony shows. Above all, give the IRS nothing.

And when a kid on Black's staff tried to prevent him from conning an elderly black contestant, this producer threatened to have him beaten up. Yeah, some of his friends were goons.

Then there was . . . let's call him Norby "Fat Man" Kling, whose name still causes the shakes in those who worked for him forty years ago. As a matter of record, the bum still owes me salary. By now, Kling has probably written a best-seller on how to get rich at the expense of others, but I'll explain his "gimmie" methodology anyway. Kling paid his rent, telephone, electricity. Everything else was "So sue me." I can't honestly say that Kling never gave me a paycheck. He did, every week. That was the brilliance of his scam. But before the check could hit his bank Kling had phoned Mr. No-Cash, the assistant bank manager, who was secretly in his employ.

"Listen, No-Cash," barks Kling, "when LeBow's check comes in, don't pay. Mark it 'uncollected funds.'" I didn't catch on until Kling owed me four thousand bucks. To recover this dough in a lawsuit would take three years minimum. So I corner him face to face. "Oh-my-God," he screams. "How can the bank have done this? I'll write you a new check right away." Of course he does. But the new check is no better than the previous twelve.

With my back against the wall, I go to my union, the

organization to which I pay dues so it will protect me in cases like these. But Kling is paying for protection by the union. With the absence of restrictions by the FCC, the loose control by incompetent broadcast department heads and the presence of wild greed, the muck of the giveaway has reached the announcers' union. Members past and present allege there was a mole in the union, whose purpose was to stonewall complaints made by members against their employers (one of them being Kling).

Unaware of this, I take my tale of woe to this heinous character, who assures me, "Don't worry. I'll make sure you get paid what you're owed." (For other performers in other circumstances he has other lines: "I'll make certain they honor holidays" or "I'll straighten it out. I'll get your job back.") The net result of this guy's efforts is zero. It took years for AFTRA to catch up with his operation. And when he felt the heat of pursuit, he quit his AFTRA job—no notice—and the next day went to work for a station he had only recently opposed as AFTRA representative.

What could I do? Shoot Kling? This same question was asked by hundreds of Kling victims like me. Which is why, even though he's now a highly respected million-aire, Kling doesn't go out on the street very much. He'd better not. As for Kling's quiz shows, we believe that no contestant beyond the inner circle of his family and friends ever won anything. If a legit contestant answered correctly, he was declared a "winner," but never saw his prize.

Black, Kling and their fellow sharks figured out how to produce a quiz show with no money (except payoffs when necessary) changing hands. Here's how it worked. (To get in the mood, pretend *you're* a crooked producer.)

*STEP 1:* Find a manufacturer or company willing to trade

its goods for exposure (free advertising) on your show. Suddenly you've got sewing machines. Or refrigerators. Pianos. Vacations. Boats, if you're lucky. Dinners. Cars. Minks. Perfume. Watches. Aftershave. Jewelry. Airline tickets.

*STEP 2:* You promised the sponsor exposure. Therefore you must feature his products on your show . . . but do you have to give them away? And to strangers? God forbid.

Rest assured this can't happen if: (a) you adjust the difficulty of the question to the intelligence of the contestant: the dumber the contestant, the harder the question; or if (b) the show is conducted by telephone, you give correct answers to your relatives and friends and order the host of the show to call only these people. In the very early days, telephone quiz shows were a cinch for gimmie-producers. The audience was unable to hear the contestant's answer, so any quiz show host who valued his job could interpret the answer any way he chose—usually in favor of the producer.

A note of caution to beginners: Do not give prizes away until you have fulfilled your contract with the manufacturer as to the number of shows on which you will advertise his product. You can profit from the near-disastrous experience of a fellow we'll call Gay Below:

Gay is married and he has a girlfriend. She wants a fur stole. Gay wants to buy her one, but it's against his principles. He hasn't actually bought anything for anyone in the last ten years. So he dreams up a new telephone quiz show and finds a furrier who gives him two stoles for exposure on four shows. One for the show and one for the girlfriend. Gleefully, Gay gives his girlfriend the mink stole. But tragedy follows. In two short weeks, the show is canceled, the furrier wants his stoles back. One had gone to a winning contestant, but the other was now virtually implanted on Gay's girlfriend's back. The furrier is screaming, "I'll sue you, you son-of-a-bitch stole stealer." He threatens letters to Gay's wife, bombs under his car and lye in the face. The standoff ends when Gay does the unthinkable and actually parts with cash—$1,000—to shut the guy up.

The moral is this: In early television when you joyously signed a thirteen-week firm contract with an advertiser, you had to read the P.S. This stipulation, which they all insisted on, allowed them to cancel the show after only two weeks. So much for the firm.

Sometimes, when a producer got lightheaded, there was a real winner. ("All right. You can give away one freezer tonight, but I need the other for my mother-in-law.") But as you well know by now, John Q. Public often never laid eyes on that prize. Then there was the due bill dupe. Due bills are certificates for discounts or freebies. A due bill given to a TV winner could be a certificate worth "an unforgettable dining experience where you and the Mrs. will enjoy only the finest cuisine and attentive service." So Mr. and Mrs. go to this classy restaurant, order the best in the house, and when the check comes they present the certificate. "Oh, Christ, you should have presented this when you came in," says the owner. "We don't accept these anymore." So Mr. and Mrs. have to pay out of their wallet. And when they call the station, they hear, "Gosh, we had no idea that the restaurant would do that. But I'm afraid it's out of our hands now." Actually some restaurants backed out of the deal without informing the show. But here's the more likely case: the producer called and slyly asked the owner not to honor the due bill, so *he* could get the free meal.

There was other due bill duping. Lots of it. "An exciting all-expense paid vacation to Bermuda for two!" often began and ended at LaGuardia Airport, when the airline said nix to the certificates. Or worse, when a lucky winner of that "romantic trip to Hawaii" found the due bill didn't work at the hotel where he had just stayed for an "exciting six nights and seven days."

As TV losses mounted, more nonsensical quiz shows replaced good entertainment. Channel 9 scraped the bottom. One of their shows didn't even have a live host. All they showed was a slide of the prize you could win, with the explanation given by the booming voice of an off-screen announcer. Now on this particular show, a just-out-of-college kid named Len Jacobs got the job as assistant producer by answering a newspaper ad: "DO YOU WANT TO GET IN ON THE GROUND FLOOR OF TELEVISION? HERE'S YOUR CHANCE TO START CLIMBING THE LADDER OF SUCCESS!" "It wasn't the ground floor, it was the sewer," Len says. His boss, the producer, flim-flammed the staff as well as the public. Len's paycheck was put off week after week. Living in his sparsely furnished studio apartment the size of a shoebox, he was down to peanut butter and beer when there was a knock at the door one Saturday. Surprise! Len himself had won the grand prize on his own giveaway show: in lieu of wages, the producer sent him a grand piano. Now Len could consider his studio fully furnished. Nothing else could possibly fit in.

Len's next career move was down, down to a show that was so poor it gave away parakeets as prizes. Len was again associate producer, but in this case it was a fancy term for birdkeeper. He was responsible for feeding the birds and changing the water. And because there was no room at the TV studio, Len had to take his work home with him. He kept the birds in his apartment, where they flew around and made birdie doo on his grand piano. Each night when he arrived home, another birdy had fallen to the floor, its spirit now making birdie-doo in parakeet paradise. Len was too softhearted to throw the birds in the garbage, to say nothing of too tired. So each night he placed a dear departed in his refrigerator. True to form, Len's boss never permitted any winners. Good thing, because by the end of three weeks, Len's fridge was a birdie morgue with twelve little stiffs belly-up and claws clenched. Len quit the business when his boss called and said, "Oh, Len, I'm kinda short this week. Instead of pay, tell ya what: I'm lettin' ya keep da boids."

Parakeets and slide shows were, however, small-time stuff. Columnist Earl Wilson reported on a professional contestant racket. He chose not to identify names, but the facts were these: A talent agency furnished actors as contestants on a TV show. These actors split their prize money with the agency and probably someone involved with the show. The host revealed that the agency had offered him a deal: he could have one of his own relatives on the show to split the take. But he turned it down. Another host was told that he could keep all the money left at the end of each of his shows. So he had his staff pick the most stupid contestants they could find. But a couple of weeks later, contestants were answering all questions correctly—the host wasn't taking home a dime. He did a little detective work and discovered that he'd been double-dealed. His loyal staff assistant had started selecting only the smartest contestants and splitting the take with them. The host lamented, "You just can't trust anyone these days."

So, I ask again, why didn't we blow the whistle when producers ordered us to rig quiz shows? Well, we were young. We went along with what we thought was in the tradition of entertainment. After all, we were made to believe—and it was probably true—that station managers, program directors, directorial staff, all were in on it. And the reality was: Blow the whistle and the only thing you'd do in television again was turn your own set on and off.

I'll say this in defense of TV emcees of quiz games. They would have preferred that every show be on the up-and-up. (And of course, some were.) To be a host on camera under the pressure of making sure that no one won the loot the producer wanted was one hell of a job. For reward, nothing could compare with hosting an honest show. Possibly the first telephone sports quiz ever on television was named "Sport of Call." I was the host. Only small gifts here and the pride for any contestant of knowing he pierced a sports question. Letters rolled in with requests to be contestants. A young girl wrote that her ten-year-old brother watched my show every day, but had never been picked as a contestant. "He's very ill with cancer," she explained. "He doesn't care to win anything. He just wants to prove how much he knows about sports." I couldn't help thinking that if ever there was a reason to "fix" a show, this was it. That week I called him, a squeaky-voiced kid, absolutely ecstatic with happiness. I had prepared some extra-easy question, but believe me, he didn't need my help. He knew sports backwards and he won on his own.

The lovely Longines watch he had earned went out the next day . . . and came back the next week, with a letter. The boy's sister told me, "Tommy died before the watch could reach him. As I told you, he didn't care whether he won. He wanted to show what he knew about sports. And that afternoon, he was the happiest little boy on earth."

Finally, I see that I've omitted a major player in the freebie free-for-all: performers, Even Big Names like Godfrey found ways to latch on to a new suit or an expensive pair of shoes, a hat or just a wristwatch. Prime among them were the comics, who laced their routines with brand names, whether it worked or not: "So this guy walks into a bar, wearing a new Hart Shaffner and

Marx suit, and he says to the bartender, 'You got the time?' The bartender looks at his Timex watch—a real beauty—and says . . ." (And here the audience falls asleep.) Or, "Say, I got all dressed up to come here tonight." (Comic opens jacket to show shirt.) "Hard to believe that a guy wearing an eyepatch could design these handsome Hathaway shirts!" (Hahaha?)

All the viewers had to do to escape this idiocy was to turn off the television. But why did they have to be subjected to it in the first place? Eventually the stations fought back too. In the fifties, one station took a stand against the freebie-loaders by making an example of Gene Baylos. Baylos is a comic genius who is known in the business as the "comedian's comedian." But like just about everyone else, he tried slipping in a few plugs. During his monologues on one show, Baylos had mentioned a brand of rainboots, a vodka and a bourbon. (Not all in the same monologue. Too obvious.) Station executives retaliated by threatening to charge Baylos at commercial rates for the the time he'd spent mentioning each product! They figured he'd used ten seconds for each plug, at $225 per ten seconds. "Let's see, they said. That's $225 × 3 = you, Gene Baylos, owe us $775. We'll deduct it from your $1,000-a-week salary." "You guys gotta be joking!" Baylos protested. They found out they were when their lawyers informed them that they had no right to make Baylos pay. But the point was made.

After all this subterfuge and thievery and gimmie-gouging, you may find it impossible to believe that there was an honest way to get something for nothing, especially for announcers. But many companies couldn't give us enough—and they didn't ask for a thing in return. All we had to do was use the product.

We got clothed in style. One day a box with six Van Heusen shirts arrives at the station. I get a little warm under my Hathaway collar. Van Heusen doesn't sponsor my program. So what the hell are they going to ask me to do? Nothing. Van Heusen sent announcers across the country six brand-new shirts every month. There was never a requirement for a plug. And many of us received our first-ever tuxedos from a company called "After Six," suits from "Eagle Clothiers." Clothing manufacturers loved to see television emcees wearing their expensive duds.

We got invitations from every resort in the Catskill Mountains. No plugs, please! Just show your well-known face at the lunch or dinner table. Order whatever you want. Bring the family!

We got gifts from our own sponsors. My modest four-room apartment in Jackson Heights had no closet space for clothes—it was filled with Monet jewelry, handbags, perfume, men's aftershave and watches. And one day I get that old knock at the door. Two immense deliverymen are grinning at me. They're holding an outboard motor from my sponsor, Evinrude. "Here ya go, Guy!" they say heartily. Shit. I don't have a boat. I live miles from the water. And where am I going to put this monster? The only available space is in my son, Steve's, room. Steve becomes the first kid on the block to have an outboard crib.

P.S. to I.R.S.: I can't believe you jerks never put the pinch on us!

Per usual, eventually the Big Crackdown on Freebies occurred with investigations, scandals and government committees. The word was: No product gets on a show free or as barter. I got a telegram to that effect from the general manager of WOR, where I was producing a bowling quiz show full of freebies as prizes: "CUT ALL FREEBIES FROM PROGRAMS IMMEDIATELY STOP OR YOUR SHOW WILL BE CANCELED IMMEDIATELY STOP."

The telegram was sent from a cruise ship. This son of a

bitch and his family were on that cruise ship getting a tan and having a great time that *I* had freebied for them just before it became illegal. But I can be officious too. I shot back a telegram that read: "THANKS FOR WARNING STOP BE CAREFUL—UNDERCOVER GOVERNMENT AGENT ABOARD SHIP INVESTIGATING FOR FREEBIE EVIDENCE STOP TRY TO ENJOY TRIP STOP."

*Station Break:*

# Freddie B.

Why a special chapter on Freddie Bartholomew? Because of all the personalities I met and worked with in these early times, Freddie B. stands out in my judgment with undisputed extraordinary characteristics. This man-boy of cinematic memories—loving, heroic and charming, and sad, in his portrayals in *Lloyd's of London, Captains Courageous, David Copperfield*, etc.—somehow enriched and nurtured the lives of people around him despite his personal travail and the reality of the world around him.

My family swore I was a movie buff before birth. My mother started taking me to the movies twice a week in her third month. She never quit, and I continued the practice after she died. Freddie Bartholomew was my number-one child actor favorite. Fie to Shirley Temple. Boo to Jackie Cooper. And tolerance for Mickey Rooney.

Maybe because I grew up on the nether side of good speech. I always wanted to speak just like Freddie and say, "Mother dear," instead of "Hey, Maaaa," "onte" for "aunt," and "I appreciate your kindness, Madam," instead of "Thanks, lady."

The details of Freddie Bartholomew's life, which read like a series of Charles Dickens stories, are left to his autobiography. There will be the account of the rape of his movie fortune by his relatives and others, depriving him of millions and leaving him broke. There will be the memories of illness, injuries, unemployment and living the desperate life of a "legend that Hollywood forgot."

Never dimmed, however, was the nobility of this gentle person, nor his love of laughter; and those traits to me are the highmarks of his persona.

I first met up with these points standing outside the stage door of the Loews Capitol Theatre on Broadway in New York City. Inside, Freddie, about age thirteen, had made a personal appearance for one of his major films. When the giant curtains retreated, revealed was Freddie, no bigger than a New York City fire hydrant. "Thank you, all my good friends, for the way you have loved my films. I thank you all—and goodbye." The packed house raised the roof.

So I marched out with many others to get a glimpse of Freddie coming out the stage door. The slick, shiny black limo panted at the curb. And the young movie star, smiling that four-dimple smile, was pushed through the crowd. As he settled in the limo's backseat, a gruff, burly guy thrust his head inside the open window and grunted, "I still like Mickey Rooney better." Those of us who could hear this bird with no couth were stunned. But young Bartholomew, with the manner befitting his ancestral Knights of the Round Table, said softly, "That's really fine, sir. So do I."

I met Freddie Bartholomew close-up about twelve

years later. I was host of a motion picture program on Channel 9. I was stunned. The earnest, smooth, innocent baby face was drawn, haggard, troubled. I asked him typical movie star questions. He was untypically taciturn and even resistant about personal achievements, but enthusiastic and anxious to cooperate about other film people. You had to be a block of wood not to note that Bartholomew had firmly lowered a curtain on his Hollywood career. He wouldn't discuss any phase of it whatever. Period.

But his observations—and his honesty and charm— overflowed the time I was to give him on the air. Until the program director slipped me a note saying, "If you take any longer with Bartholomew, we'll have to cancel our coverage of the World Series—and this is only February!"

Program over. Freddie and I head for a quiet restaurant. I still can't believe I've got my childhood screen hero in my car. At my table. And as we talk I can't believe what is becoming plain. Bartholomew is experiencing hell. His fortune has been spirited away. He has outgrown his screen image. His good looks have been disarrayed by nature and problems. A bad marriage. And he is broke. Earlier that week, Ed Sullivan had introduced him to a large audience at a motion picture benefit. The applause had been tumultuous. The reality was that he had a total fortune of twenty-three cents as he hit the cold winter air.

The foregoing was not poured out, you understand. Rather it was dribbled and squeezed and uncomfortably squirmed out over a five-hour period. And because I was relentless. Freddie declared over and over he was through with acting. Somehow, though inexplicably, I felt my own self was equally imperiled if Freddie gave up on the business. Probably a good shrink could explain how movie fans of the thirties and forties associated their lives with their screen favorites. Through this maze of introspection I suddenly heard myself saying, "Listen, Freddie, how about trying TV? You'd make a great director. You know more about lights and performing than anyone at Channel 11. Let me talk to the boss about you." More startling than the baldness of my question was the swiftness of his answer. "That sounds interesting, Guy. But please, DON'T PUT YOURSELF OUT."

I waste no time. The next morning it takes fifteen seconds to get the general manager's enthusiastic O.K. on Bartholomew. A meeting is swiftly set, but unfortunately the general manager has decided that Freddie should be interviewed by Program Manager Warren Wade, TV's philandering pariah. Quite believably, Wade tries everything to discourage Freddie. The hours are too long . . . directorial work too strenuous . . . boring . . . demanding . . . highly responsible . . . terribly pressured. And it pays only (the bastard has the gall to offer him only) 50 bucks a week. Later, Freddie tells me he understood that Wade didn't want him around. Wade perceived Freddie as a talent heavyweight with a potential for replacing him. "I was so intimidated," Freddie recalled, "I would have taken the job for no money and cleaning the toilets besides."

And so began the TV career of child star Freddie Bartholomew that was ultimately to lead him to the highest echelons of TV directing. Several years later, about 1954 or 1955, Bartholomew began to produce and direct soaps for advertising agencies, one step upward after another eventually leading to Senior Vice President of TV productions of Benton and Bowles. Once again to that rarefied atmosphere of highest achievement.

But at Channel 11 Freddie left a legacy of accomplishment behind and in front of the cameras. Until he came, carrying the experience of years of Hollywood motion picture making, we performers had worked in comparative ignorance.

"Don't place cue cards to the side of the cameras," Freddie warned us. "Reading looks natural if you place it under the lens."

"Never have a camera lower than your face. Either slightly above or at face level for best angles," he advised.

"Don't move hands, head or body too quickly. Do these things with a smooth, even rhythm."

"Put key lights directly on face."

No wonder Wade was worried about Bartholomew. All Wade ever did esthetically was to raise or lower bodices or hems. Freddie even taught us how to take professional still pictures. And for fifteen years at least, my own still portraits were chosen by him.

Going back to the early times again, events show that Bartholomew was immediately and eagerly accepted by the Channel 11 staff. And loved by most everyone. As he settled in among his new colleagues, his own defenses slowly gave way and he returned love and loyalty in heaping amounts, to say nothing of laughter. And ultimately a penchant for practical jokes—a "must" on every Hollywood set.

One late evening while Freddie was in charge of station operations, a staff film projectionist privately showed him a five-minute clip of explicit sexual action. What led Freddie to his next move we innocent but interested bystanders will never know. At 12:30 a.m. the station signed off and played the National Anthem. At 12:34 a.m. Freddie had the fornication film put on the air. And so appeared television's first pornographic show. Several viewers wrote enthusiastic letters. But until this day, Channel 11 executives think it never happened. The viewers' letters only prove what disoriented old jerks the execs really were. Even now, they won't believe the bare facts of the bare. TV executives believe only what they make up.

On another occasion, Freddie tinkered with the weather reports. Weatherman Joe Bolton couldn't memorize all the temperature figures, so an hour before he went on the air, he wrote them on the map with a red pencil. (Remember: red didn't show up on TV.) During the actual telecast, he merely traced over the red with a black grease pencil. But on this night Freddie changed the red figures when Bolton left the studio. Showtime and Bolton breezily reported, "Brr, it's going to be an icy one in Alaska . . . 98 degrees . . . a scorcher out in L.A. at −4 degrees . . . and 40 degrees in Miami— . . . Uh . . . I think we'd better break for a commercial," he said. It took three commercials for him to rewrite his numbers.

No one was safe. Directing a show that investigated local Communist activities, Freddie laid his hands on an official Communist Party membership card. And he decided to scare one engineer half to death. It was during the infamous Senator McCarthy days and even Mickey Mouse was under the Senator's watchful eye. So Bartholomew seeks out this red-haired Irish, devout Catholic patriot. Draws him aside and whispers as he flashes the Commie card, "I'm a charter member and I've been told to contact you because you're a new recruit. Welcome."

"Who, ME?" cries the startled engineer. "Not me. You got the wrong guy."

"Aw, come on," says Freddie, now at his best acting technique. "I hear you're bringing in the whole engineering staff."

Now the engineer is sweating. Wringing his hands. "I got the word," Freddie insists, "from Moscow itself."

"Oh, my God, NO!" sobs the engineer. "I'm innocent. I only belong to the Police Athletic League. Call Moscow. Clear me!"

"Don't worry, don't worry," soothes Freddie. "I'll fix it up for you."

But the way he fixed it up for our universal nemesis,

Top: *Rated by many as the finest child actor developed in Hollywood: Freddie Bartholomew. Bottom: Movie star and TV director Freddie Bartholomew (left) signing autographs at a reception for this author (I'm third from right).*

288

Warren Wade, may have been Freddie's finest hour. He never forgot or forgave Wade for the noxious treatment he had received at their first meeting and for several years after that. Then he evened the score for himself—and the rest of us. Wade the womanizer was at the Waldorf-Astoria. His booming voice holding court among industry giants, he was accompanied by his definitely demanding, suspicious and uncomely wife.

Into this pleasant scene strolled an immensely attractive young redhead covered completely in mink.

"Hi, Warren," she cooed, as she stroked his face, "Am I late, baby? M-m-m-m, I love the new coat you gave me . . ."

Wade was sputtering. Mrs. Wade was slobbering. The luscious redhead went on, "And, baby, I came just the way you wanted me to."

She opened her coat and closed the show. She was not even wearing her pubic hair. The total production conceived, produced and paid for by Freddie B.


If my own career can be termed successful, I accord certain credit to Freddie. This decent person who lived with grace and dignity among the famous and infamous was a lesson in human strength and humanness at its best. There was a time when Channel 11 management and I had problems. We performers had joined the union, AFTRA (American Federation of Television and Radio Actors). The other announcers elected me shop steward, and I took my appointment seriously. But I believe now that they took advange of me and virtually daily sent me into management for small and silly gripes. Naturally I became a target for managerial hostility.

On a certain Saturday in late spring, the Channel 11 vice president, Lev Pope, complimented me repeatedly for my cooperation and versatility as a performer. An emergency had arisen that day and in the space of two hours I had—with only seconds to make clothing and logistic changes—hosted a news, then sports, then weather, then variety talent program. Despite this and despite the fact that I had the most commericals of any announcer, and was the best known (I had written two best-sellers, was vice president of the Sports Broadcasters Association and television director of the March of Dimes), I was fired the following Monday morning.

The charge was that, over the weekend, I had performed a freelance program for ABC-TV without notifying Channel 11. The fact is, I had notified an executive, Alice Cook, on Friday. But when asked about it at a subsequent union hearing she denied my talking to her. Maybe she forgot. Anyway, in a political time difficult for labor, Channel 11 hit the jackpot and the shop steward was gone.

During the union arbitration hearings not one announcer—neither Joe Bolton, Jack McCarthy, John Tillman nor Kevin Kennedy—had the courage to stand up for me. They probably would have been fired. But this didn't frighten a guy who had struggled for years to find himself and stabilize his life. Freddie Bartholomew was now married, again with real "responsibilities." But he pleaded and begged me continuously to allow him to testify in my behalf. But I was just as stubborn. I didn't want Bartholomew to be fired on my account. Please believe his willingness to sacrifice himself for me. His display of unwavering loyalty ultimately did more for me than getting my job back might have.

Freddie Bartholomew was and is the most unusual character I have met since I saw him on the screen at age nine.

Freddie, I'm so glad I knew ye.

# 9 / We Had to Call 'Em as We Saw 'Em

"I work hard all day taking care of two children and doing the housework. In the evening after feeding the family and washing the dishes, I would love to relax and watch a good TV program, but friend hubby must have his sports. I often have had the urge to give him a shot in the head but have restrained myself."

—housewife interviewed by the *New York Post*, 1952

TV without sports? Come on! But the two had a hard time getting together—in fact, the 1947 World Series almost didn't make it on television because it couldn't find a sponsor.

But before I get to that, I want to hop to a year later. . . .

The Giants were beating the Pirates 10 to 8. Baseball games usually run about two and a half hours, but with the heavy scoring and the relief pitchers, this one was stretching into three and a half. I was in the studio waiting to do my post-game show when program manager Warren Wade waddled in.

"WHAT THE HELL IS HAPPENING?" he foamed. "I have a kiddie show scheduled to go on at 4:30 and it's 4:15. Get that game over NOW."

It was some piece of work explaining to Wade that baseball is played by innings, not by the clock. A week later I headed him off as he was phoning the Garden to demand that a hockey game be finished "without ONE MORE interruption." Time-outs? Fights? Injuries? They meant nothing to Wade.

How could he be ignorant of what six-year-olds know these days? He wasn't the exception, he was the rule. In the late forties, multitudes of otherwise red-blooded Americans hadn't had much exposure to sports. Many hadn't even seen a pro game. And most women hadn't witnessed the endearing personal habits of the athletes. The first full season of Yankee telecasts in 1947 brought stacks of angry mail to the Dumont network:

"My ten-year-old now spits constantly," wrote "A former Dumont fan." "He has picked up this disgusting habit by watching your players. You can count one less household among your audience from now on." A "shocked and concerned mother" informed us: "If your boys continue to touch their private parts in full view of the public, I cannot allow my son to watch your station. You should be ashamed of fostering depravity among our nation's youth."

This mom didn't have a clue that the players were one-hundred-percent innocent, just adjusting their jock straps and their cups to prevent them from cutting into their testicles. Meanwhile, at Little League games, pint-sized players were stepping up to the plate and giving themselves a hefty yank, just like they saw the real guys do on TV. We did report the complaints to the team manager, who relayed them to the "boys" . . . who said they would try to cut down on spitting, but they'd be damned if they'd risk castration for TV.

It was a whole new ballgame with sight—for every-one. Not just for virgin viewers, but for players and owners and stadiums and announcers. And for the sports themselves. Television changed sports irrevocably.

Radio was a different planet. The audience couldn't

see the game, which was an advantage for team and stadium owners, who exerted control over what announcers reported. God help us if we described a play as "sloppy" or reported a player's obscene gesture. Ted Husing, generally regarded as the greatest sports announcer of his time, was banned for life from broadcasting Harvard football games because he criticized the team. And I almost got canned my first night doing hockey from Madison Square Garden. "I wouldn't believe this crowd unless I was seeing it with my own eyes!!!" I shouted with enthusiastic banality. "They're hanging from the rafters!!!" It was true. Kids had even lashed themselves to the top rail by their belts and were suspended perilously over the rink.

"You want the Fire Department to close us down?" queried the Garden VP, Ned Irish, after the match. "Cut the pictorializing crap and just call the game, LeBow." Irish's real beef was that the Garden had again oversold tickets in violation of the fire code. And that after a number of tragic fires in nightclubs, the pressure was on to enforce it. My sterling reportage was like setting off an alarm to the entire NYFD.

But announcers could work this invisibility in our favor—or try to—when we screwed up. The eminent Bill Stern should have won an Emmy for this slick recovery: Stern somehow called the wrong receiver on a pass and galloped the guy down to the 10-yard line before he realized his mistake. No problem for Bill, who was notorious for his tall tales. He had his guy lateral to the actual ball carrier just in time for the touchdown. I call that talent. The press derisively labeled it "inventive announcing."

Still, you could get caught in the same trap as Stern, innocently enough. I was the play-by-play man on a hockey game at Madison Square Garden. My color man was Bud Greenspan, now famous for producing films of

Olympic games. His job was to give the opening lineups before I took over; I usually followed along, reading my own program. Suddenly, tonight, something's wrong. He has just announced the defenseman on the opposing team as "Roger Crago."

"Roger Crago?" I scribble a quick note. "Who the hell's Crago?"

Bud whispers, "Tell you after the National Anthem."

He better. And I can't wait for the Anthem to end.

"Cover for me," Greenspan pleads frantically. "I dropped my program out of the booth."

"You out of your head, Bud?"

"Goddammit," Greenspan hisses. "Get him into the game somehow or we'll both get fired!"

These days, in a more relaxed broadcast atmosphere, Greenspan could have noted that he'd dropped his program. Those days, being kids, and trying to get a foothold in the bigtime, we would have covered up murder just to safeguard our reputation for perfection.

So, I got Crago on the ice, and because we had invented him, he was going to be a star. He checked with menace, skated with alacrity, assisted with adroitness—but, God forbid, never scoring. Are you nuts? Bud and I would have had to interview him! Postscript: the next day I got a special invite to see our boss, Bert Lee, Sr., a crack hockey announcer in his own right. He welcomed me with what's called a knowing smile. Uh-oh. But all he said in his ominous, trumpeting voice was, "LeBow, I understand Boston fired that new rookie Crago because he didn't do any scoring. I guess we'll never hear about him again." As I slunk out, I muttered, "Never again. Not ever again." About ten years later, an actual player named Roger Crago turned up and joined a hockey team. Guess you can't keep a good phantom down.

But television yanked the wires on this flim-flam. It was an impeachable but promiscuous witness. We weren't prepared for what it could pick out—everything —and we had to figure out procedure with each situation. Starting unhappily with "live" death.

In this tragic circumstance I was broadcasting a basketball game, St. Francis vs. Seton Hall. I'm launching into first half stats when, across the court, on camera, a referee collapses. Medical help rushes in from everywhere. They work on the poor guy for maybe fifteen minutes. No response. Meanwhile, on screen, we're showing commercials and other things to distract from the tragedy before us. And as they carry the referee past me, 10,000 fans and I know for sure he's dead. But I still think like a radio man. Whatever else happens—invasion from Mars, attack of Killer Bees, indigestion—don't let anything interfere with the flow of the event.

"Ah, there seems to have been an accident," I say. "The referee has just ah . . . fallen . . . ah . . . but he's probably going to be O.K."

It was a dumb call. I never realized that his family and friends might be watching and taking solace in my announcement that he would be all right. And understandably, in their pain, they punished us with threats and severe criticism for misleading them. A few days later, management called a full staff conference—not to skin me alive, but to hash out policy. We decided that while I shouldn't have announced the death, I shouldn't have brushed over the incident. From now on we would confront even the worst situation. And what about injuries? How long should the camera concentrate on the injured player? Many people can't stand seeing someone in pain for too long. And isn't the victim entitled to privacy? We decided to focus on the injury for a short time and assure the viewer that we would report back . . . and then cut to something else. Would that something else be a commercial? Another dilemma: Is the scheduled commercial the best one to air after an injury?

Is *any* commercial? TV executives and sponsors are still divided here. Ask yourself what sponsor can see a benefit for his product at such a time. By 1952, General Motors had its answer: no commercials following a downed player. Unfortunately, very few followed this wise, and empathetic, path.

(I have to admit that after that conference with management, I felt like seasoned mike man Steve Ellis after his notorious goof. He was broadcasting a football game when a slip of paper was waved in front of him. He pushed it aside. The paper reappeared; again he shoved it away. Only when the director insisted did Ellis grudgingly announce: "Folks, the Japanese have attacked Pearl Harbor. Yes, they have done that dastardly deed. . . . And now back to the game." At least Ellis had an excuse: he didn't know who or what Pearl Harbor was.)

If the natural course of events wasn't confusing enough, announcers also faced the grandiose plans of directors. We had a feel for the action. The director had a feel for pictures. And not necessarily of the game. Say it's two outs, one man on first. Coach signals for a steal to second. Player takes a healthy lead. Pitcher turns to throw and . . .

. . . I hear the director's voice over my earphones: "Camera Two! Broad with boobs out to third."

This is my cue to drop the steal and pick up the girl. (Mel Allen often stated to me that this was a constant irritation when he first began to telecast baseball.) You can thank those directors and their spectator shots for breeding a pest that multiplied faster than the cockroach. This was the fan who made idiotic faces for the camera, and who was called the "lens louse." The Garden tried to exterminate them by refusing to sell them seats in camera range, but as you know, it didn't succeed.

Directed into the stands, the camera was like a loaded gun that could go off any time. We got a celebrity in our sights—the reigning musical comedy actor—and nearly blew his personal life to bits. "What luck!" I oozed. "The very entertaining and DISTINGUISHED William Gaxton, star of such Broadway hits as *Of Thee I Sing*. And oh . . . we just doubled our luck, folks . . . because he's with the very beautiful and VERY young-looking Mrs. Gaxton."

So sue me. The perky beauty was everything I said except for that part about "Mrs." Immediately came orders from the head office: Directors better read the gossip columns so they know who's who, who isn't and who shouldn't be. (This voyeur called a camera never stops. I recall a few years ago, a major New York station aired a story that included a street scene showing a hand-in-hand couple. They were married, but not to each other. The handholders sued the station. I think the camera won.)

The head office—in our case, the program manager— harbored his own glorified visions of television sports. "I want you to go out there and bring back the humanity of the team," exhorted Wade. "I want to feel what the players feel. I want to be intimate with the coach. I want to see what I can't see out on the field."

Per orders, next afternoon at the Polo Grounds one camera panned the Giants dugout. I'm at the mike prepared to describe this privileged view. As the camera swings from left to right we see a water cooler . . . a long bench . . . a doorway and—oh, God—Leo Durocher on the can, wiping his ass. I keep quiet. Some pictures are worth a thousand words—to say nothing of an announcer's job. Leo later evened the score by assigning his wife, screen star Laraine Day, as co-host on post-game shows. While I asked players about boring macho stuff like strategy, Laraine handled the feminine angle. "Tell me," she purred, fluttering her lashes (Laraine always batted 400), "how did you FEEL when you knew you had hit a home run?" Some sycophant dubbed her

"Hollywood's gift to baseball," but the TV crew altered that to "Hollywood's kick in the balls." If she thought we didn't hype "her" team enough, or if we forgot to kiss her . . . uh . . . feet, she tattled to Leo. The crowning blow came when she won the award as "Baseball's Most Charming Wife" for her show. I liked it much better when I was teamed up with Curt Gowdy or Jackie Robinson.

After Leo's leak, the Giants dugout was off limits. The announcers felt vindicated. We knew damn well that these problems wouldn't occur if the camera stuck to business. There was plenty of bad blood between directors and announcers. The first season Mel Allen did television, the director wouldn't give him the shots he considered important. Mel didn't speak to the guy for the entire season. I, on the other hand, took the confrontational approach. I went head-to-head with my director in Wade's office. "Both of you boys are eminently . . . harrumph . . . correct," said Wade. "We want to show the action, but of course we . . . harrumph . . . want to be entertaining."

Looking back, I have to admit we were too rigid. But we were also correct—when cameras aim off the field there's the risk of losing an exciting play.

I wonder if the announcers, including myself, appreciated the intelligence and planning that went into figuring out how to televise a game. That deserves a note here. The top sports director in the country was Jack Murphy, who started at the Dumont network. There were no rule books or teachers when Murphy came along. He doped it out himself. (In fact, Murphy trained the man who became the dean of sports directors, multi-Emmy winner Harry Coyle.) Murphy knew baseball—and that was half the battle.

I'll give a for-instance: The toughest play to cover is one with critical action in several places simultaneously. Like the cutoff play. Let's say there's a runner on third. Normally the camera would follow him to home plate—if the ball goes to the outfield. But what if the action wouldn't be at third because the outfielder, seeing he had no chance to make a play at home, would attempt to get a runner on his way to second or third? In this case, the outfielder would throw to the infield instead of to the catcher. Where will the cameras focus now? It's up to the director to decide from these factors: How far in the outfield was the ball hit? How good is the arm of the outfielder to whom it was hit? How fast is the runner at third base?

In less than a split second, the director has to give orders to the cameramen and the engineers inside the trucks and the technical director.

A director might have three cameras to work with. Each camera had four lenses, which in the early days cameramen had to turn by hand. It's relatively more simple now. When the order came for, say, a shot of the infield, and the camera was focused on the catcher, the cameraman had to crank a handle to change the lens. It was clumsy, inefficient and mistake-prone, but it was all anyone had until the invention of the Zoomar lens, which redefined baseball coverage. Now the camera could show pictures from close-up to infinity.

Speaking of that, once and for all here is the truth about the famous Al Gionfrido catch that robbed Joe DiMaggio of his home run in Game Six of the 1947 World Series. I was on the broadcast team of that game. Since there was no Zoomar lens on the cameras, there was no way this catch could have been captured by a TV camera close-up. Only one newspaper, the *Daily Mirror*, had a still camera with Zoomar lens, but they missed the catch. So how come you see close-up photos of that play?

It's hoaxed. I know because I was there the day of the catch—and the day after, when the press called Gionfrido out in the field well before the start of Game Seven. Then, what you *now* see as Gionfrido's famous catch was carefully staged. Over and over, someone tossed him a ball, trying to match the trajectory of DiMaggio's homer the day before. Over and over Gionfrido received directions: "A little to the left, Al." "A little to the right, Al." "Look intense, Al." They kept throwing the ball and Al kept leaping and looking INTENSE until they got the producer's memory of the catch down perfect. Then they shot stills of it as well as film. That day the phony photo found its way into the papers. And I saw it again in a magazine celebrating the fiftieth anniversary of TV and countless other times. Which leads me to ask why no one has exposed it before—and to wonder how many other famous plays in other sports have been replayed after the fact?

I've got another record to set straight. The instant replay. I read recently that it was invented in 1963. Bullshot. The instant replay came into being quite a bit earlier than that at Yankee Stadium, the brainchild of engineer Otis Freeman, when he was on Jack Murphy's Channel 11 crew. (You remember Otis—the guy who opened the window for horse racing on TV?) Outfielder Norm Siebern had just failed to catch up with a ball hit in his direction that broke up a no-hitter being tossed by Yankee ace Ralph Terry. Immediately controversy broke out as to whether Siebern should have made the catch.

Listening to Mel Allen, Freeman heard him say, "Wouldn't it be great if we could see that play again, folks!" It happens that WPIX was one of the first stations to use videotape; it routinely taped most baseball games it carried so that certain plays could be inserted in newscasts later that day. Freeman had a knee-jerk reaction. There was a quick telephone call to the control room, a rapid conversation with director Murphy, orders to the tape editors on the spot to find the outfield hit and replay it. Virtually all was done before the next batter was retired. And thus was instant replay to change—and not always for the better—the whole business of transmitting and watching sports.

Directors. Spectators. Executives. Heartless cameras. These were small change compared to the disturbing challenges facing every sports announcer. Now we had to be accurate or we'd look like fools. When the famous Friday-night fights began simulcasting on NBC-TV, the video commentator, Jimmy Powers, was so inept—and sometimes prejudiced—that viewers turned down the sound on their sets and switched on their radios for Don Dunphy's expertise. More confusion. What the audience saw and what Dunphy was describing sometimes were not the same. Dunphy's exciting voice and machine-gun delivery often persuaded TV audiences that he was juicing up the fight if it got dull. But Dunphy would probably claim that no fight was dull when two professional battlers were in the ring. The truth is, you often felt Dunphy's delivery made the fighters seem faster, more adroit, more spectacular. No gainsaying Don had his problems when TV came in.

There is one more obligatory remark I must make. Now that we have instant replay determining the outcome of controversial plays in football, we have learned that even cameras don't always tell the unvarnished truth. Even when eight cameras are shooting detail from every angle on a play, there often is much disagreement on the final ruling. So it may even be that Don Dunphy saw some things the cameras missed.

As we sportscasters went to work in those antediluvian days, we prayed that the cameras stayed in business. They often went out three or four times a night. But when cameras worked, you couldn't deliberately bullshit the viewer. Do that and they would blow a fuse to your career. Something like that happened to Jimmy Powers, a biased son of a bitch who didn't conceal his ethnic and racial prejudice. His on-air slurs were so brutal that Italian-American Patty DeMarco vowed he wouldn't fight at the Garden if Powers was at the mike. Nevertheless, as sports columnist for the *Daily News* and a ubiquitous commentator, Powers swung a lot of clout. But there was a day when Powers wrote a *News* column that was datelined Miami. And the day he claimed to be in Florida, millions had watched him on their screens as he did a fight from the Garden. His credibility evaporated.

And now that the audience could see everything, what was our function as announcers? The old-style narration was passé: "He swings . . . That ball is going . . . going . . . It climbs over the fence . . . It's a home run!!!" Big deal. Any seven-year-old squinting at his seven-inch TV screen at home could see that.

How much of the action should we describe? What else do we say? When? There was almost as much press on how announcers should announce as on the events. Everyone had something to say about what we said, including Arthur Godfrey. What did this talking teabag, famous for his Lipton commercials and ukelele plucking, know about sports? Nothing. Did that stop him from calling us "windbags" who were merely window-dressing for most televised events? But Godfrey was KO'd by TV. I was calling a fight and the sound went soundless the first few rounds. When it came back on, I gave a recap of the action during those minutes. Here's what popular critic John Lester said in his daily TV column: "It wasn't until he [LeBow] had finished that I fully understood what I had been watching when the sound was off. An announcer can make a fair fight (or any other event) very interesting with the right kind of commentary and background discussion." He headed his column:

## GODFREY OFF THE BEAM
## IN DIG AT ANNOUNCERS

Godfrey retired from bashing sports announcers after that.

Forty-two years later the "right kind" of sports gab is still controversial. I have never wavered from my original premise. When the play-by-play announcer has an important point to make, even if a subtle one, say it. The audience will appreciate it. Today's best announcers in my opinion follow that theory, particularly Al Michaels, Ernie Harwell, Jack Buck and Marv Albert. To many of the others, there is an inclination for viewers to say: "SHADDUP!"

But there were some more problems. It wasn't only *what* we said, it was *how* we said it. Ted Husing's sophisticated, slightly tony delivery worked over the radio. But it didn't match what the camera revealed. Once the audience got an eyeful of those Palookas spitting and crotching and nose-picking, Husing's elevated style sounded foolish. A cruel critic said, "Ted Husing's method of sportscasting went out with the Lindy Hop." Ted never could reach the level of the mass audience either. He called them "Ladies and gentlemen" instead of "folks" or "fans." When CBS replaced Husing with me at boxing matches, they felt I related more to boxing fans.

However, from time to time the TV audience would accept some way-out delivery, at least for a little while. Ex-country-boy pitching star Dizzy Dean was the first jock to make it big in broadcasting. Old Diz didn't know a syntax from a federal tax. His vocabulary was just large enough to order beer and vittles or curse out the batter he couldn't strike out. The language on his "colorful" broadcasts was so ungrammatical and so awful that educators, teachers and parents demanded that he be removed. But Diz kept them at bay for a number of years. His prime retort to his critics was "Them that ain't sayin' 'ain't,' ain't eatin' every day." Sometimes it was hard to argue with that.

But most radio guys were something. Radio was a demanding medium. They had to command rich vocabularies. ("Pow," "swish," "bam," "oof" and other grunts didn't adequately describe action.) They had to know their sports from the turf up. They had to convey the action—no matter how fast it went—enunciating clearly. And they had magnificent trained voices. There was boldacious Bill Stern, Mel Allen, whose mellow Southern tones won him thousands of female admirers. Russ Hodges. Hearty, easy-to-listen-to Bill Slater. And behind these voices were trained intellects. Slater was a West Point graduate and former teacher. Allen was a lawyer. Stern had been assistant stage manager at Radio City Music Hall, which produced the most spectacular stage shows in the world.

With these role models, we younger guys breaking into radio had to aim high. Way out there was the possibility that we might earn the privilege of being called "ace sportscaster"—a term the press used only if we satisfied all the requirements I stated above. So a break for us was when TV came on the scene. Most of the giants—Allen, Barber and others—stayed put in radio, leaving a vacuum for lesser lights like Bill Mazur, Marty Glickman, Jocko Maxwell (the first black sportscaster) and me to wriggle in. TV's future was dubious, pay was dismal and the prospect of being on camera added another danger. Now we'd have to concentrate on the action, the direction, our delivery *and* our photographability. Let me assure you, one minute of ad lib on television and you'd sweat. Two minutes and you'd grab for Valium. That could have accounted for Mel Allen's goof at the stadium one warm, sunny afternoon. Women sitting in the box seats had draped their coats over the railing in front of them, posing a possible problem if a ball hit the clothes. I heard Mel's deep voice over the PA system: "Would the ladies in the front boxes please remove their clothes?"

Although pay and prestige were low to start, standards for broadcasting TV were as high as radio's had been. To win a berth on the Dumont team for the 1947 season at Yankee Stadium, each candidate had to audition for one week as assistant to Bill Slater—one of the few radio biggies who'd jumped to TV. Did it matter to Dumont that I was already doing boxing for them? No, I had to prove myself again for baseball! And since I was up at bat first, I wouldn't be able to profit from someone else's mistakes.

How the hell was I going to make an indelible impression on Slater? The sports trades called him "the guy who makes you see what you are supposed to see." He also personified the versatility that TV demanded: talent that could give the news, host a film, interview a politician or a film star and call a game. One of his shows was "Luncheon at Sardi's." On days with an afternoon game, he had to race from that mike to his Yankee broadcasting booth uptown in the Bronx. So to impress him, I turned into his personal desk reference, crammed with stats, stories about the players, the history of baseball, the league. Every time Slater tossed me a query, he couldn't shut me up. But he couldn't do without me. When my week was over, he said wearily, "I don't have the strength to audition anyone else. You got the job. Now get out of here and let me rest!"

Getting out was easier said than done. TV broadcast facilities were at the Sorry!-state-of-the-art. When stadiums decided to go with television, they had to knock something together practically overnight. Forget glassed-in booths, cushy lounges and elevators. At Yankee Stadium the TV announcer's "booth" was a makeshift gondola hanging from a balcony rail in the stands. To get into it, we climbed into the stands, hopped over the rail and dropped down into the booth as 60,000 to 70,000 fans cheered us on.

Not easy for me, with a leg affected by polio. I couldn't maneuver that leg over the rail. But the TV crew invented a solution on the spot. One engineer was assigned to hoist me up until I could sit on the rail and thrust my leg over to the other side. Then he would jump down into the gondola and lower me into it. I was a good 180 pounds and the lone engineer, Millard Dickerson, was a good-natured 140, if that. Later we picked up another helping hand. A Ford executive with a box seat just behind our gondola one evening had dropped his wallet with 500 bucks. I returned it to him the next day and as a reward he volunteered to join my human hoisting crew. Too late for Dickerson, though. He'd already developed a hernia.

To no elevator, add no toilets. The architect of this palace forgot that announcers have two active ends. To get to the bathroom, we had to climb out of the gondola and double-time it down the stands to a men's room—and usually there wasn't time. God, those double-headers. "I've got a doubleheader" became announcer's code for "I-gotta-go!" As a matter of record, a score of early television sports commentators developed kidney trouble from this setup. Even my strict pre-broadcast regimen—no water, no liquor, take a piss—didn't help when I had to guzzle the sponsor's beer for commercials. And football season was the worst. My sponsor was an orange juice company that insisted I guzzle on camera. "MMMMM! There's nothing like a refreshing glass of orange juice before, during or after a game." It was true. In cool weather, there's nothing like juice to make you pee like a baby.

Any wonder the radio fat cats were staying put?

But fans were defecting from radio to television. As I said before, many of them had never seen a game or a playing area or equipment. Few knew or understood the rules of the game. Guys like me around the country saw a way to hook them: we not only announced the game, we taught it.

We gave them their money's worth. We took viewers behind, inside and underneath uniforms. We showed them football pads. We discussed the protective cups that boxers wear around their testicles. My station manager went on record that this was too daring, but he let it on the air because station ratings were zooming. Fans watched soccer players breaking in their shoes by putting them on and submerging them in buckets of lime. They saw batters practicing swings in front of a mirror. Come to think of it, have you seen any of this stuff on TV lately? Is everyone born knowing everything about the games today? Or is it that people aren't interested anymore?

Sometimes I did my best spontaneously. One night I grab a Ranger for an interview as soon as he steps off the ice. He opens his mouth—and the viewers see he has no front teeth. The guy gums his answers and lumbers off. I explain that hockey players get their front teeth knocked out by the puck, so they wear falsies. But why ruin a good pair? So the players remove them before the match. Walk into a locker room and you'd see a neat row of drinking glasses, each filled with water and a set of choppers. (It's a good thing for the audience we didn't have smell-o-vision. Hockey stinks. Scientists haven't discovered what evil chemical reaction occurs between the player's sweat, the ice and their uniforms. But like sportscasters, they know it could classify as a lethal weapon.)

During the hockey broadcasts we slipped in little-known facts, from the weight of hockey equipment and how it affected different players to how the puck was kept frozen before the game—in an icebox. American hockey audiences heard for the first time why the puck was changed from two pieces glued together to one solid puck. Here it is, for hockey nuts: During one game a puck split in two. Half went into the net and the other sped into the stands. You make the call . . . a goal? Or not? The referees ruled that this was not a goal. The rule book specified that the entire puck must cross the goal line between the posts. Dissenting fans nearly rioted. The next season, the puck was transformed into one piece of vulcanized rubber.

ABC chief Roone Arledge has been given hosannas for introducing the personal association between the athlete and the television audience. Roone certainly embellished it. But back in 1947, we TV sports announcers began it. We thought it was impossible to describe athletes in only two dimensions, so we expounded on their education, their aspirations, their problems. One particular case was that of Carl Brissie, a pitcher for Philadelphia, returned from World War II duty with a wounded leg. Although the tibia had been destroyed, the ankle was intact and by wearing a brace Brissie could still use his leg. Viewers saw the brace through Brissie's uniform, but unless they were told, they wouldn't know why he wore it. I profiled the injury, Brissie's rehabilitation and his dramatic return to the major leagues.

Most stories weren't so theatrical, but that's not the point. It was the engrossing combination of reporting human interest announcing that helped win fans at stations from coast to coast. And it was part of the reason, I believe, that the *Daily News* tapped me as outstanding sportscaster in 1947. Viewers were starved for information. At every station I worked, we received thousands of letters of appreciation and requests for even more detail. But we couldn't take all the credit for the surge of fans. In 1947 and 1948, thousands of them watched us in taverns. They sure weren't going to walk away from free entertainment! The taverns with televisions reported a surge in business. In fact, some up by sixty percent. No wonder one beer sponsor decided to yank its money from radio and put it into TV. TV has always been where the drinkers are.

It seemed as if the challenges in television announcing would never end. Simultaneous with the emergence of TV, blacks were beginning slowly to enter major sports. Their situation in other aspects of life at this point was untenable. They couldn't take advantage of "no-down-payment-for-vets" housing going up in the suburbs, because of discrimination there. Most big hotels in New York City didn't accept blacks as guests. Famous black entertainers like Lena Horne weren't supposed to sit at a table in the very room where they'd just performed. And do you see black faces in photos of the pre-1947 teams? (Sports shouldn't pat itself on the back. In the mid-fifties, an organized group of announcers, including me, had to mount a crusade and fight like hell to get a championship bout for Archie Moore. The promoters insisted that a black wouldn't draw a big enough gate. Archie turned out to be a top fighter and a top draw for the next ten years.)

With the start of the 1947 season, and with Jackie Robinson already having entered the National League, Bill Slater and I still had to face the debut of the first American League black ballplayer, rookie Larry Dobey with the Cleveland Indians. But a short discussion between Slater and myself solved the no-problem problem. Audiences could see Larry was black. We decided to eschew philosophical comment, stick to Dobey's playing abilities and just provide the background we would give on any other player. I think we set an example, because from that day baseball announcers did not focus on color when new black players kept pouring into the game.

Yeah, we got hate mail—but Dobey toned down the bigots with his bat and his character.

Unless you were there—in the locker room, in the dugout, around the team—you can't understand the courage and character needed for a person to break the color bar in sports. When Jackie Robinson was brought up in 1946, Dixie Walker announced that he wouldn't play a game with him in it. Outfielder Ben Chapman of the A's was even more vile in his denunciation. And after an interview on my post-game show, Enos Slaughter, a Pete Rose "deese" and "dose" type who was well known as anti-black, whined to me: "I don't know why youse guys call me prejudiced. I cudda spiked Robinson when I run to first base today. But I didn't." Robinson, my co-host on this show, was fortunately away that day, shaking hands and signing autographs at one of our sponsor's new Sunset Appliance stores. (The minute I had heard that Robinson had been signed by the Dodgers, I got sponsor Gentleman Joe Rudnick to snap him up as a spokesperson. Then I got Channel 11 to sign him for my show. No, I didn't introduce him as the "first black co-host on a sports show.")

The taunts and barbs spewed at blacks from the dugouts injured these men worse than Slaughter's spikes ever could have. Robinson ignored them. Instead of making him bitter, his experiences on the field and in the locker room made him more exceptional than he was. And Robinson was everything legend says: serious, gentle, disciplined and introspective. He remains today a hard act to follow for every ballplayer, no matter what his race or religion.

One of the saddest and most disgraceful things is that despite Robinson's tortuous groundbreaking, black athletes ready for the big time still got harpooned. About a year and a half after Robinson joined the Dodgers, Horace Stoneham was asked why he hadn't integrated his baseball team, the New York Giants. His answer stands in my memory as the worst example of prejudice by an owner or any other high official in that sport. Insisting that his remarks be off the record, Stoneham declared to the stunned journalists: "No nigger will ever play on my ball club—as long as I live." Stoneham lived longer than he thought. For the next two decades, Willie Mays was to save his team and make it a great franchise on two coasts.

In a way I've gone ahead of myself, with announcers and directors and spectators. And here's where we pick up where we started out the chapter: television and the sports world having a hard time getting together. Television was competition for the teams it was televising. "Radio whets the listener's curiosity," said one expert. "Television satisfies it."

We had a hell of a time getting stadium and team owners to play ball with TV. They were afraid that we'd eat into their gate. Owners sat on fortunes, but they yelled poverty when they had to sacrifice paying seats for the TV crew. They saw doom when fans seated behind the cameras got nasty. "I paid for this seat and I can't see over the *&!###??** cameras, and some !$%?##* watches the game free on television. I want my money back!" Some owners demanded huge sums for televising rights. Others tried to cover their ass with protective stipulations in contracts, such as no TV unless the bleachers were completely sold out.

But what did we expect? A ticker tape welcome? TV disrupted arenas and stadiums. We were noisy, undisciplined. We invaded sacrosanct territory, such as the sidelines of football fields. And the medium itself caused games to change. For television's priorities, both football and baseball proceeded too slowly. So to speed the pace, the amount of time the quarterback was allowed to call a play, and the length of time given the pitcher to deliver the ball, were shortened. In hockey, the red lines demarcating zones didn't show up well on TV. To compensate, the center line was painted as broken lines —like the ones on highways. The numbers on the players' jerseys were so small they didn't show up on screen. The owners had to order bigger numbers. At Yankee Stadium, Mel Allen battled General Manager George Weiss until he convinced him to install a camera in centerfield. This would show the viewers the pitcher delivering the ball. Until now they had seen only the catcher and a profile of the batter. Manager Weiss opposed this for a long time, saying that if the TV audience could see a game better than the live audience, they wouldn't come out to the ballpark. Allen wore him down, but that led directly to another situation: One of the leagues traditionally stationed its infield umpire directly around second base. He often blocked the TV audience's view of the pitcher. TV had to persuade the league to reposition the umpire—and that took a whole season.

To make television more acceptable to the stadiums, the Sports Broadcaster's Association established an annual award to the most cooperative. This didn't impress the pro stadiums. They didn't think that any award could make up for the trouble we caused them. They left the field open to the Big Ten stadiums, which usually won. Actually, television was only getting the same sour deal the stadiums had given radio when it started out. Owners had begrudged radio broadcasters good seats, giving the newspaper boys first choice. The press was treated like royalty: free food, sometimes showers and other comforts. It wasn't until the star radio announcers moved to TV that stadiums were more cooperative.

If we were a pain in the neck for the stadiums, they returned the favor. I swear that Yankee Stadium tried to sabotage the Dumont broadcasting team by refusing to seat us behind home plate. We had to guess at what kind of ball the pitcher had thrown. The ten-inch monitor kept conking out and we depended on the umpire's signals as our lifeline. So maybe we made a few miscalls —could you blame us? The press did. Sportswriters viewed us with the same malevolence that owners did. They predicted we'd cause their readership to decline. They were right. It's easier—and more entertaining—to watch a game than read about what it looked like. And once viewers saw things for themselves, they began to argue with the highly vaunted writers.

To get even, some writers really laid into us when we made a mistake. Pulitzer Prize winner Red Smith launched an unprofessionally vitriolic attack on us in *TV Guide* in 1953. I think it was because a TV camera caught him in an unflattering shot. He called us fakes, claiming we could not see or determine the nature of any pitch— from curve to screwball. The Sports Broadcaster's Association assigned me to zip Red's lip with a rebuttal of our own in *TV Guide*. (You can read our exchange in the Appendix.) I crammed in enough scientific evidence to earn a Ph.D., but I don't know whom baseball fans believed more. I do know this uncontestable fact: baseball announcers can call differences in pitchers' deliveries. These days, they're even able to discern more subtle curves, like the forkball or split-finger curve.

There was a brief honeymoon between sports and TV. Once we had them on camera, teams couldn't resist the novelty of being stars. We even got credit for upping attendance at live events in some cities such as Cincinnati and Milwaukee. But if gate receipts fell, the owners blamed us. In 1948, advance sales for the collegiate basketball games at the Garden were the lowest in five years. Ned Irish had the foresight to predict: "As TV becomes commonplace, it will reach the great mass of people who previously had no interest in the game." By 1949, the Eastern College Athletic Conference demanded that TV cameras be barred from their events. The following year, the Cardinals called for a ban on TV at all baseball games. PGA championship golf tournaments were off limits to live radio and TV. And there were weird halfway telecasts. Suddenly TV sets showed only the latter half of some events. The Rangers allowed only the last period to go on camera. Ultimately, pro football was sued by the government for interfering with the right to televise. And ultimately football and baseball dropped their case for curbing television. They did this out of fear that the Congress would look into the reserve clause that bound players to their organizations for life. (As you know, in the last few years the courts declared that clause unconstitutional. The owners had merely delayed the inevitable.)

If a team was in the doldrums or the weather had been lousy, you couldn't blame fans for staying home. Whatever the reason, teams and stadiums began demanding bigger fees for television rights. With talk that the Giants might not be televised, a doleful female fan wrote to *TeleVision Guide*:

> . . . have read in the paper they want to take baseball off TV. May I say it seems a shame as I really bought our set mainly for baseball. My husband is diabetic and does

not go any place after he comes home from work. Also have a crippled friend in Lyons Hospital. Have been up there and those poor men can't wait until they can get to see the games. Isn't there something that can be done to keep it up? Say like a TV club? Every owner paying fifty cents every three months. I'm sure that would help. So many old people also enjoy going to a neighbor's home that can't afford to pay or travel. Please tell me who else I could write to.

As sports on TV was threatened, TV got sneaky. At Dumont we put up a ring in our studio and invited audiences in FOR FREE to watch the boxing and wrestling we televised. NBC and stations east to west followed suit. Not long after, a TV network even supported an entire football league.

When owners discovered that rights could more than make up for empty seats, TV turned into a pump that inflated sports into its present obscenely bloated form. This scramble for big money had tragic consequences for boxing. The small fight clubs that I described in "Station Break: 'Announce, Mister'" couldn't compete with the big-name bouts on TV. The clubs began to fold, and boxing's proving grounds for contenders dried up. Promoters brought in boys who were not ready for major fights or had no ability. It was carnage. Controversial sportswriter Dan Parker reported in 1951 that dozens of fighters had died in boxing rings since the coming of television because of this. (Incidentally, Dan Parker refused a $75,000-a-year offer that a prominent beer company had asked me to make to him. Dan said, "I want to feel free to attack TV's role in boxing's demise.") When boxing couldn't find young dupes to take a beating, it suckered in poverty-stricken old-timers who

*Fellow announcer Hal Tunis and I show the TV audience the outboard motor sent to my house the night before. The sponsor never sent the boat.*

317

Jackie Robinson at contract signing for his services as spokesman for the Sunset Appliance Stores and as co-broadcaster on my various sports shows. At center is Gentleman Joe Rudnick, who insisted on superimposing his telephone number on the moon.

**CALL THE PLAY**

**WIN**
ONE OR MORE
$100 U.S. SAVINGS BONDS $100
on WCBS –TV's SPORT QUIZ SHOW
"Call The Play"
SATURDAYS • 6:15
CHANNEL 2
Starring
MEL ALLEN
Your Local Emcee
GUY LEBOW
SPONSORED BY WHITE OWL CIGARS

When one good cigar deserved another, Mel Allen and I teamed up for a CBS sports show.

318

*Dumont television engineer Otis Freeman testing its newest invention, the image orthicon camera at Ebbets Field, Brooklyn, 1946. This signaled the ability to televise without high-wattage studio light. (Photo courtesy Otis Freeman)*

319

could barely shuffle around the ring. To make these pathetic displays appear worth watching, boxing pulled out that magic word: CHAMPIONSHIP. The true meaning of the word has been stretched so far that it's almost valueless. Today there are over two dozen categories with CHAMPIONSHIP in each one.

Going for dollars, the boxing associations didn't care who fought. In the late forties, they brought over a German fighter, Hein Ten Hoff. At this time, the cruelty and destruction of the war was still fresh. Veterans were still returning home from overseas. The Nuremberg Trials were revealing German atrocities. Channel 11 suggested I interview Hoff, who, it was rumored, had been a Nazi. One executive hinted that if I didn't go along with this promotion, I'd be canned. But I didn't budge. Hein Ten Hoff was not interviewed by me or by anybody else in the country after that, as I recall. He returned to Germany, tail between his legs.

I want to make a point about money here. Although money was the driving force, we're not talking big bucks. TV didn't have the sponsors. That's why the 1947 World Series almost didn't get on the air. Baseball commissioner Happy Chandler couldn't get a taker for his $300,000 asking price. With a piddly 500,000 TV viewers projected, compared to the 30 million radio listeners, this amount seemed like highway robbery. By August it was rumored that Gillette, which bankrolled the radio broadcasts, had offered $30,000 for TV. There was even the ridiculous story that TV stations would try to get the TV manufacturers to make up the difference. Game One was scheduled for September 30. By September 26, Gillette was at $60,000 but there was still no joy in TV's Mudville.

Now, that summer, the big sales pitch for TV sets had been the World Series: ". . . Box seats to the entire series —FOR FREE!" Once negotiations stalled, set sales shriveled. And the same customers who had walked out of the stores pleased as punch a month earlier were returning ready to punch the dealer. "You told me I could see the games in my living room. If they don't televise the games, how am I going to see them? Gimmie my money back." Dealers were considering whether to put "Gone Fishing" signs on their stores when, finally, Gillette and Ford agreed to split the $60,000. (Three years later, television rights went for $750,000.)

But hold it. One more impediment. The appointed announcer team almost didn't get on the air. Radio paid about $83 a broadcast for the world series and TV had the same generous outlook. You know the old saw the employer uses when he wants to underpay you: This job is so prestigious you should be grateful for the opportunity. But head announcer Slater wasn't buying it. He, Don Dunphy, Frankie Frisch and LeBow negotiated in Gillette's office for hours. But no deal. We went on strike. That very evening before the first game—it was about 9:30—Bill Slater phoned us all. "O.K., we're on! $125 a game!"

Gillette learned quickly that television was going to boost their earnings over the moon. They and other sponsors grew enormously powerful, quickly. Like no other kind of television program, sports got grafted onto advertising. Claire Bee, former basketball coach of Long Island University, and one of the greats, was color man for basketball telecasts. At the half, he was supposed to demonstrate on a chalkboard why one team was winning. Bee was not one to fill airtime with idle talk. "I guess they're just lucky," he said at last. "That's all I can say, just lucky." Immediately the sponsor was on the phone threatening to have Bee fired if he ever used that word "lucky" again. The sponsor was Camels.

Sponsors horned in with demands for more time-outs to display their product. And before you could say

"Schaefer Beer," basketball and ice hockey developed artificial time-outs to satisfy them. These lasted until the sponsor was ready—referees got instructions via hand signals or buzzers or electronic devices. The momentum of the game was gone forever. But to be fair, I can't blame the sponsors for gratuitous time-outs, because more time-outs were signaled by a certain basketball referee than any rule book called for.

This was the invention of the top collegiate basketball referee, Pat (The Fly) Kennedy. Kennedy usually arrived at the Garden with his fly unzipped. Typically there would be a phony time-out called-in emergency as soon as Pat noticed his open fly. Then, both teams—well coached for this play—gathered around him. Sportscasters were also in on the charade, and we gave fictitious accounts of the cause of the break in play. A few seconds later from the middle of the huddle, Pat's arm swept up in a magnificent arc from his lower body and over his head, and as his hand reached the top of the arc he would roar, "PLAY BALL!" With social propriety restored, it was the opinion of all sports announcers that the scores of games Pat refereed would have been much higher if his zipper hadn't started out so low.

Fortunes were flowing between teams and sponsors . . . but they weren't reaching the guy who was making the money for both sides: the athlete. Except for the few superstars, like Babe Ruth and Joe DiMaggio, it was a sacred tenet of sports to pay athletes as little as could be gotten away with. NHL players made do with $4000 to $7000 a year. Most of them, from backwoods Canadian areas where there was no work, thought this was a fortune when they signed. At least they'd eat. But they couldn't afford much else. Their idea of a big night out was to come to my house for BINGO.

Management got away with this slave system because athletes had no representation and no rights. The reserve clause had turned a man into a piece of property owned for life. Owners put on the paternal act, but they were determined to keep the "boys" in their place . . . which was not at the bank. In the spring of '47, there was a debate about whether the World Series should appear on TV. Larry McPhail seemed against it. He explained that television might cut into gate receipts—which would reduce the take for the boys—and the owners were worried about that. They were only "trustees" for their "boys"; the Series really belonged to *them*.

Puh-leese, St. McPhail.

To beef up their pitiful pay, athletes had to take other jobs—on or off season. It wasn't unusual for basketball players to play for another league on an "off" day, but TV put a glitch in that. An official watching TV on *his* day off spotted a couple of pros from one league playing for another and they were fired. Many businesses didn't want to hire a man just for the winter, so it was difficult for baseball players to find part-time work until a clever man started a part-time placement agency for ballplayers. The ABC Freight Elevator Company in New York made a point of putting on athletes. They hired an ex-ballplayer as their recruiting agent, Max Zavslovsky, the earliest scoring ace in the NBA. Ken Strong, a legend on the Giants football team, became one of the most successful liquor salesmen in the country.

Lucky players got on the spokesperson gravy train. Shaking hands at malls and stores sure beat working! And it was easier than doing live commercials, which athletes tended to screw up. Lou Gehrig's debut was for Post cereals. A hell of a debut, too. He goofed in his first commercial. "I love my Wheaties," he exclaimed, which unfortunately was made by his sponsor's competition, General Mills. Incidentally, the great Gehrig was so underpaid that in the off season he risked life, limb and career by working as a referee in ice hockey.

Getting back to sponsors, though. They were willing to risk having the commercial mangled for the prestige of being identified with the player. Their kick was boasting to friends that MICKEY MANTLE was coming to their house for dinner. Not surprisingly, most athletes balked at being on camera at first. Besides the crew and the lines and everything else, there was . . . makeup. Duke Snider about bolted from the studio when I asked him to put some on. He'd raced over straight from a game, and even for the handsome Duke he looked raunchy, especially with that heavy five-o'clock shadow. "Me? Nah. You think I'm a queer?" I appealed to his vanity: did he want *me* to come off better than *he* would? It worked. "But don't tell anyone," he said. "I don't want this to get around." Next morning I called Snider's wife to ask how she'd liked the show. "Never mind that," she said. "What did you do to my husband? He called me from your studio and told me to buy him face powder at the all-night drugstore. He kept looking in the mirror when he got home and he wouldn't even wash his face before he went to bed. I think he put on more powder before he left for the ballpark."

By the way, Phil Rizzuto recently compared ballplayers' reactions to television when he scooted for the Yankees with TV today. "Guy, you won't believe this," he said. "One of the reasons ballgames take so long now is that players are very conscious of television. In the dressing room they're doing their hair, putting black under their eyes to look more macho, wearing colorful wristbands, gloves and anything to doll themselves up because they know they're on camera. And when they get into the game, all the business they do at the plate and on base and everywhere else that delays the game is something they feel looks good on TV. Holy cow!"

In the early 1950s, the players got a hand with extra money through a PR-man-turned-agent, Frank Scott.

Before Scott we were paying off players with perfume and watches. In fact, Mickey Mantle said he had enough to tell time from his shoulders down. Some of the players made money by selling their loot to teammates. I personally gave Billy Martin his first watch, because he did my show one hour after he arrived in New York from San Francisco, still in his zoot suit and ten-gallon hat. But Frank Scott changed all that, and soon getting a ballplayer meant getting up a hundred or two hundred bucks—per visit. The only way we countered that was by going to the dressing rooms and interviewing athletes there.

I'm closing this chapter with a short tale about a prediction made way back in '48. It sums up how little understanding most of us had about the monetary power of TV. There was one prophet of profits: Mike Jacobs, one of the undisputed great sports promoters, known for his MSG boxing promotions, his shrewdness and his affection for the boxers who fought for him. During a decidedly low period, when television appeared to be diminishing the attendance at all manner of sports events, a luncheon was given to honor Mike, who was in declining health. Frail and with a raspy voice, Jacobs stunned the crowded room by declaring that the ultimate in the business of sports would happen when all TV viewers would pay for the privilege of viewing sports on their private screens. This business would be in the billions, he said, and the money earned by promoters and by athletes would be in the millions.

Mike, I'm giving you the last word. You deserve it.

# 10 / Rustlers, Hustlers and a Few Honest Men

## TAKES TV WORKS

February 1—Police were hunting for a sneak thief who helped himself to the works of a television set on the fourth floor at the Triboro Hospital, Flushing-Hillcrest, Queens. The theft, discovered Monday, was disclosed yesterday by Dr. Alfred Ring, superintendent, who said the set cabinet was left.

*(New York Daily News, 1951)*

Scenario: Customer dials TV repairman.

*Customer:* "Oh, Mr. Repairman, my television set is acting funny. The picture won't stop rolling."

*Repairman:* "Yeah? You probably gotta plane overhead. You see a plane up there?"

*Customer:* "Oh my, you think so? I'll go take a look." (Pause.) "I didn't see any airplane."

*Repairman:* "Yeah? It probably was outta sight by the time you got to the window. Those planes cause a lotta trouble. Atmos-feeric disturbance is what we call it."

*Customer:* "Yes, but my picture is still rolling."

*Repairman:* "Yeah? Well, lady, you probably gotta 'nother plane up there. Or—listen! You gotta ham operator in your neighborhood? They cause a lotta problems. . . ."

Get the picture? Too often the customer didn't—

because he couldn't get an honest or capable repairman (or, in the best of all possible worlds, one that was both). The "atmos-feeric" double-talk was one of the ways a repairman could avoid admitting that he didn't know squat about television sets; or if he was genuine, probably couldn't do anything about your problem. So if he couldn't control the circumstances, how could he be expected to fix the set?

In the late forties and early fifties there was a shortage of trained technicians, but no lack of unscrupulous sharks out to make a quick buck. Not that repair scams were born with television. They'd been plaguing radio owners for years. In fact, one report claimed that Philadelphians had a two-to-one chance of getting a dishonest fix-it job. But with television, the situation became worse. Sleazeballs had the public by the chassis. Who knew how a set *worked*? (Do you know how yours works?)

You had to consider yourself lucky if price gouging was your only misfortune. "Looks like your tuner's on the blink, mister. Think I can get one for you, but with inflation the way it is, could cost you . . . let's see . . . a hunnert-fifty dollars." (Translation: "The price of my greed has gone up since last month, and you're going to pay through the nose for this piddly piece of equipment that cost me peanuts.")

No, the worst crook was the brazen television rustler who rode the TV trail in the late forties. He wasn't your ordinary burglar, who had the decency to steal your set when you weren't home. This villain carried out his act right in front of you. Ostensibly you had every reason to trust him. You got his name through an ad in the paper, or maybe through a friend. He arrived wearing an official-looking uniform announcing something comforting like "Honest Jack's TV Repairs." After poking into the innards of your set, he shook his head mournfully. (I swear those guys took acting lessons.) "Uh-oh. You gotta doozy—a #4 on the fritz. Can't do this baby here. It's gotta go to the shop."

Uh-oh. That was the last you'd see of your television. This guy was as much a repairman as Howdy Doody (who probably knew more about TVs). His plan was to sell your set to an unsuspecting family or a "hot" dealer; or earn even more money by selling the parts separately. You waited unsuspiciously while your set was being "repaired"; he rounded up TVs from more homesteads in the neighborhood, and then he rode off into oblivion.

A couple of ballsy guys actually tried this scheme on New York City firemen. They showed up at a firehouse sprouting a TV antenna, saying they'd heard the set wasn't working. (A safe lie. You could assume any set would have trouble.) The firemen asked to see some ID; the shady duo couldn't produce any, but they still tried walking out with the set to "take it to the shop." New York's bravest smelled smoke, turned their hoses on the guys and the scam fizzled out fast.

But the most ambitious scam by far was the "Havana Hijacking," masterminded by a Cuban named Rubén Planes. His last major business venture had been during World War II, when he sold the Cuban public motor oil labeled as cooking oil, so now you have an idea of how low this creep could crawl. Here's the story:

Soon after the war, Dumont was manufacturing TV sets and equipment, which it continually demonstrated for potential buyers. One day into the showroom walks a nattily dressed gent. It's Planes. The Cuban government is crazy to get hooked up to the exciting new TV industry, he says, flashing a roll of greenbacks. Mucho visits with mucho money-flashing follows, over the next few weeks. Then: "Any chance that Dumont might want to visit Cuba to demonstrate its products?" inquires

Planes, waving more cash. Dumont, in mortal competition with NBC, RCA *et al.* sees a chance to put a whole country in its hip pocket, and so . . . *sí, sí, sí!* Before you can smoke a Havana, a charter plane stuffed with sets and electronic machinery, a crew and a sales force headed by Otis Freeman and John Hunt wings its way to Happy Havana. Planes has gone ahead to obtain for Dumont a permit to show its wares on Cuban soil.

And that's not all he's doing. Truthfully, the Cuban government isn't interested in TV. Truthfully, Planes has formed his own private television company: the Planes World TV Corp. Planes' plan is to use the Yanqui suckers to help him sell stock in his company. They will demonstrate the televisions to the public, which will be led to believe that Planes has purchased all this TV stuff from Dumont. But Planes hasn't told Dumont any of this. *No, no, no!*

So the plane lands and Planes whisks everyone to a massive auto showroom he has converted into the "Dumont Demonstration Hall." Weeks pass. The Dumont gang enlightens standing-room-only crowds on the wonders of Dumont Television. Planes' stock sales soar. But mysteriously, the Cuban government doesn't place one order. Patience, Planes tells the Yanquis. In Cuba, we do business more leisurely. *Sí, sí, sí!*

Then, Dumont must inform Planes that it's *adiós* time because Dumont is committed to televising the lighting of the Christmas Tree on the White House grounds in the United States.

When this sorry news hits Havana's newspapers, Planes' stock sales take a dive. Who wants to invest in a TV company if the equipment is leaving the country? Planes panics. He threatens Dumont with unnamed retribution if they try taking their Yanqui asses off the island before the sixty days are up. But they start packing. What can he do? they ask each other.

Planes? Plenty. Overnight the Dumont equipment disappears. Planes ditto. Freeman and Hunt send everyone else Stateside, but they stay to track Planes and reclaim the goods. It's a Keystone Cop chase with Planes one step ahead, still using their equipment to sell his stock. The police can't seem to catch up to him . . . in the seventeen minutes a day they work. They also can't seem to locate any of the massive electronic machinery. *No, no, no!* In despair, Freeman and Hunt take Planes to court. The case is mysteriously postponed. Is there anything Planes has overlooked? No. Even their phone is tapped. One night, Freeman calls home, talks to director Jack Murphy. Murphy jokes, "Why don't we just assassinate Planes and get this thing over with?" The next day, every citizen in Havana reads these inflammatory words in the paper. But the next day is also the sixty-first day of the permit granted to Dumont and the police magically find the Dumont equipment! Otis and John fly home heroes, leaving Planes to face his hundreds of victims. *Sí, sí, sí!*

But to get back to the good old USofA, where *some* thieves operated with more finesse. Or was it that they had bad backs and couldn't lift a whole set? Like the prestidiginous pilferer who hit Philadelphia eateries and taverns. (Many had installed televisions as a smart business move. The sets attracted new customers who didn't own one; and old customers who'd bought their own would still drop in.) Masquerading as the television manufacturer's representative—"Just doing a check to make sure you're one-hundred-percent satisfied"—he'd fiddle with the set, referring to a technical-looking notebook. ("Our service manual.") But after he left, having enjoyed a drink or coffee on the house, the set never worked as well. Turned out that during his fiddling, he'd stealthily removed a vital inner part of the set. After a half-dozen or so eatery owners reported problems, speculation was that the sneak thief was putting together his own set.

Once the public was alerted to these con games, the crooks had to find a different line of crime and they faded into history. But the continuing nightmare for TV owners was the agony they suffered at the hands of repair shops and service contract centers. At this time there were no regulations, and no licensing. Anyone could hang out a sign that said "TV REPAIRS." Some mishaps were honest mismanagement. A small repair shop owner might not be able to keep up with the amount of work he took in. With no money on the credit side of the ledger, he couldn't order the parts he needed to repair more sets. And with the shortage of electronic supplies caused by the Korean War effort, the parts might not be available. Customers would wait for weeks, months.

However, the hard-core, scandalous abuses were perpetrated by cheats who knew exactly what they were doing: fleecing the public. These heartless bastards removed sets from bedrooms of paralyzed old people and never fixed them. They kept televisions from families for months, returning them—if they did—with defective parts, missing parts or with no work done at all. They sent out "service men" who didn't know the difference between a television set and a radio. They sold service contracts and went bankrupt before the contracts were up.

(Another species of heartless SOB was a certain major appliance dealer. He advertised a phony sets-for-vets drive, telling viewers that if they brought in their old sets when they purchased a new one from him, he would donate the set to the VA Hospital. I know, I did the ad for him, and I believed him. He got thousands of sets, but as far as I know, not one made it to the VA Hospital, even for visiting hours. I kept asking and he kept saying, "They're on their way.")

By 1950, in New York City consumer complaints about TV were glutting the Better Business Bureau. How bad was it? During the first five months of the year, the BBB received more bad news concerning TV than it had for any other single category in its twenty-eight-year history. The BBB and the honest radio/television dealers devised a sales and service code, but by then it was too late for thousands who had been duped, fleeced and hornswoggled. And not just in New York. Chicago and Philadelphia BBBs asked New York for help in fighting their crooks; and who knows how many other devious-minded sorts terrorized the public elsewhere?

The extent of the abuses was revealed when an experienced TV serviceman conducted an undercover investigation sponsored by *Radio Daily, TV Daily,* the most prestigious communications sheet published. Posing as an average Joe just looking for work, this nadir raider was hired by a number of disreputable service companies. At the first company, he had to pass a stiff qualifying exam to determine his technical expertise. The questions:

1. Do you own a car?
2. Do you know what an antenna is?
3. Do you know how to put one on a roof?

He answered "yes" to all three and was pronounced an official serviceman on the spot. But that's only the tip of the iceberg. Before going out to make his house calls, he got stern instructions: "Look, buddy, don't worry about giving the customer a real good picture, as long as he gets *something*. Your job is to get the antenna up. And don't spend more than ten minutes on a repair job. You gotta hit ten houses a day. If the people aren't home, leave a card under the door. That way, they know we were there and can't complain about our service."

Two days later, he was assigned to the firm's repair shop and given a couple of sets to fix. Each needed just one simple tube, but the shop didn't have them in stock. "Nah, we don't order them," the boss said. "You get them from these here," pointing to a junk heap of sets waiting for repairs. Our fearless undercover agent couldn't believe what he was hearing. "But what about the sets I take the tubs FROM?" he asked. "What about them?" was the retort. "So we'll take some tubes out of other sets and put *them* in *these*. Who knows if we'll be able to fix those sets anyway?"

Unwittingly, the agent had stumbled upon the reason so many televisions came home to their owners with missing parts! Actually, this was not always done as a deliberate cheat. A basically honest guy who was too strapped to order more parts might try it a few times, thinking he could make good. But ruthless vultures like these made it a habit to feast off the carcasses of powerless TVs. Somebody always ended up on the short end of the tube—and it was the customer.

Then in the summer of 1950, the public was hit with the most shocking evidence of the need for regulation in the service industry. You want untrammeled cupidity? You want wholesale fraud? You got it. The Capital Television Corp., a service firm, went bankrupt. They'd taken in $750,000 for as many as 15,000 service contracts and lived up to almost none of them. Capital's one aim was to make it easy for the customer to get bilked, and with that credo they opened fourteen handy locations in Brooklyn, Queens, Nassau, Westchester and New Jersey. All service centers were kept understaffed to ensure that the customer's money would not be wasted on overhead. Instead, the hundreds of thousands of dollars that should have been spent on servicemen servicing televisions went into the palatial Capital Television Corp. headquarters in the posh Jackson

Heights area of Queens. Here Capital executives trod on thick carpeting, dictated letters at five-hundred-dollar desks and kept cool with air conditioning estimated at $10,000. Investigation fell to the Brooklyn District Attorney's office, which double-spoke this opinion of the situation: "The firm was guilty of over-expansion without foresight." Come on! That operation took a lot of planning! And as the song says, "The livin' was easy."

So, with the spectre of delays and dishonesty, it shouldn't surprise you that set owners often took repairs into their own hands—a dangerous move. One of Dumont's models was privately dubbed the "man eater" by Dumont engineers. The juice needed to power it was so strong that even when the set was unplugged, it had enough juice left in it to kill you. If I had thought this was just technical scare talk, I had to believe it after a friend of mine, a writer at NBC, was electrocuted as he tried to fix his set WHICH HE HAD TURNED OFF FIRST. From then on, I always called a repairman. But I also always went with him to a second repair shop and had that owner check the tubes the repairman was telling me I needed.

To help consumers, the Better Business Bureau put out a leaflet entitled "Things You Should Know About the Purchase and Servicing of Television Sets." Actually, service headaches were the last in a long line of perils awaiting the public. Trouble began when you first went into the store to buy a TV. Today our biggest headache is finding a set at the best price. But then . . .

First off, the idea of TV was so new to the majority of the public that it was shrouded in mystery and even fear. People worried that this television contraption gave off X-rays or ultra-violet rays that could ruin their eyes. One ludicrous rumor was that a dog had gone blind watching television. (We had all kinds of fans in early TV.) To calm the public, the American Medical Association wrote nine rules for TV viewing, including: "Viewers should not try to watch indistinct pictures." (Indistinct! In that case, almost everyone would have turned off their TVs. On most sets, images came in sequences of four: one original and three ghosts.)

In the store, the consumer was fed a voodoo psychology. Just listen to this malarkey from the owner of Devega, a major TV and appliance chain, in a *New York Post* interview in 1952. (By now you'd think scare tactics would be over.) "Expecting a television set that won't have to be serviced is like wanting a baby that won't have to go to the doctor's. A TV set is a complicated and delicate instrument. When installed it must be inspected frequently to obtain the best results. Then too it is subject to certain abuse in the home, children fiddling with it, visitors who know nothing about a set turning the dials and so on." It was "Them"— the mystics who understood this miracle of modern technology—and "You"—the addle-headed, simple-minded customer. I'll concede this: TV store owners knew zip about their wares. So how did they get to be major retailers? Their success was a direct parallel to how well they could bullshit the public.

To beef up sales, the industry played on guilt feelings of people who had not yet bought a TV. The American Television Dealers and Manufacturers sponsored a below-the-belt sales campaign that sounds like an ad for bad breath. The headline was: "There Are Some Things a Son or Daughter Won't Tell You!"

Among the ridiculous claims about the disastrous effects of *not* owning a TV were: "No, your daughter won't ever tell you the humiliation she's felt in begging those precious hours of television from a neighbor." It gets worse. "You give your child's body all the sunshine and fresh air and vitamins you can. How about sunshine for his morale? How about vitamins for his mind? Educators agree: television is all that and more for a growing child." Eleanor Roosevelt, who had agreed to appear in future ATDM ads, withdrew permission immediately.

Once you entered a store, it was "Buyer Beware." A common ploy was selling secondhand sets as new. One sad story:

It's 1950. A guy buys the lastest-model set. Takes it home. Picture's lousy from the first day. He buys a couple of antennas. Calls a half-dozen servicemen. Picture's still lousy. He has a friend, a technical wizard. Friend checks the set. Uh-oh. The "1950" model was in reality a 1946 model. Its original seven-inch picture tube had been replaced with a twelve-and-a-half-inch tube, but the set couldn't provide adequate power for the larger-size tube.

You could be hit with other false claims. Hundreds of customers in New York City eagerly snapped up sets touted as getting the full range of channels—and found out that either these sets weren't equipped to receive Channels 11 or 13 or that reception was so bad there wasn't any way of telling which channel they were watching. Sets sold as having "wonderful reception" might be great as long as a motion picture was on, but live programs dissolved into a mess of grizzly gray flecks.

Poor reception was one of the most constant gripes from set owners. In doing research for this book, I talked to Ben Blank, the founder and owner of SaveMart Appliance Stores, the largest such chain on the East Coast. Blank was a pioneer, selling sets in his one-room walk-up store in the Bronx in the late forties. "Customers just didn't understand that probably over half their problems—rolling picture, ghosts, vertical lines, snow— were caused by the weak signals from the TV stations, not their sets." It was this kind of misunderstanding that led to excitement and suspense on many a showroom floor. Like at the Monarch-Saffron store on West Forty-fifth Street in New York City. Joe Berger, an honest, earnest young salesman and general manager with an electronics background, sees a customer he sold to last week lugging his set into the store with him. The man huffs over to Berger.

"You owe me a new set," he announces.

Berger knows what's coming. He gets daily calls from customers who think he's their personal television consultant. And he's endured plenty of visits like this one. "What's the problem, Mr. Franconi?"

"This . . . set . . . doesn't . . . work! I can't get a decent picture. It jumps. It snows. It's a lemon."

"The problem isn't the set," explains Berger patiently. "You live in an area that gets poor reception."

"If I had a good set, the reception would be good. You trying to get out of giving me a new set?"

"We don't owe you a new set."

"You sure as hell are going to give me a set that works. I'm standing right here till I get that set."

Game. Match. Set. Which the owner got if he yelled louder, stayed longer.

Two brothers who owned a TV store in Steubenville, Ohio, came up with a slick way to avoid crazy scenes like this. They didn't make any false claims about reception —no, sir. They erected their own booster tower to improve reception on sets they demonstrated and sold. Sales zoomed up, until the Federal Communications Commission stepped in. Seemed that no one could put up a tower without FCC permission and the brothers had overlooked that fine point of law. Sales went down, right along with their tower.

So let's say you do find a set you like. Now you're ready for Waiting List Number One: the Delivery Waiting List. Because, as the salesman might have told you, "We don't have them in stock right now. There's a real shortage of sets." Maybe there is . . . and maybe there isn't. It might be that there are hundreds of sets in the distributor's warehouse. The distributor might hold them back on orders from the manufacturer to drive prices up. Or, maybe the store owner doesn't have the cash to pay for the number of sets the distributor want him to take. Or, maybe he hasn't knuckled under to the Piggyback Scam. This caused a major investigation. When electronics manufacturers found that certain items weren't moving—for instance, the 45 rpm record changer—they forced retailers to buy these changers along with the TV sets. No changers, no sets.

What happens when your name gets to the top of List Number One and your set is delivered? Check it carefully. It could have arrived without the picture tube if these were scarce at the moment. "I said the set would be at your house this week, lady; I didn't promise the tube." (No wonder some people preferred to take their chances and buy a television kit. A firm called Transvision manufactured one for under $200. And Beacon Television, a shop on Third Avenue and Forty-ninth Street in New York, not only sold the kit, but provided space and tools right there for assembling the kit. And they threw in their assistance for free.)

Once you get your set, it's time for List Number Two: the Installation Waiting List. You won't be able to watch your television until it's hooked up to an antenna. You could wait two weeks . . . or you could agonize for four months. The reason is, again, a severe drought in the technical department. Once you are down on this list, you plan your whole life around that date: weddings, birthday parties, vacations—nothing can interfere with that visit. If you miss it, you may have to wait another few months. Even then, the serviceman could be so rushed he'll have time to install only a temporary indoor aerial. You'll have to be satisfied with a crummy picture until he can spare the time to install the outside antenna.

(Speaking of antennas, if you lived in an apartment

house in New York, you had trouble. Many landlords refused to allow tenants to put up individual antennas. Or they slapped an extra fee onto the rent. One name should be familiar to you. Trump. This was Fred, father of Donald. He charged his tenants $50 a year for hooking into a master antenna—even though televisions weren't installed in all his apartments yet! They were fighting mad!)

While you were worrying about your one paltry TV set, there was a war going in the TV industry. The giants were trying to crush each other in the race for sales: RCA, Zenith, Admiral, Emerson, Motorola, Dumont, etc. Miles below these giants were little independent manufacturers. They stood two inches high next to these colossi but they had some crazy light in their eyes that didn't let them see defeat.

When I'm talking small manufacturers, I'm talking minuscule, not the larger small companies like Viewtone. I'm talking Mars. Ever hear of them? This brand was a limited edition in 1949 and '50, but it belongs in the annals of television with giants who always take up all the room.

Mars stands for "Marshall," the son of Myles Breger, who was one of the investors of this brave company. A fellow named Jack Sombre was the genial general manager, and among the salesmen was a wild and crazy guy named Hal Brenner. (Sombre went on to a distinguished career in the television sales field and Brenner became an executive of Cellular Communications for Potamkin Motors, for years a major Cadillac dealership in New York. Both men will tell you that their Mars days prepared them for anything!)

Now, Mars realized it could never beat the bigwigs in sales volume, but it figured out how to use them for its own ends. Through a smart licensing arrangement, they bought the sturdiest, most reliable chassis from RCA: the

RCA 630. (In case you ever come up against this information in a Trivia game, the number "6" stands for the year 1946 and the number "30" is the number of tubes in the chassis.) For picture tubes, they made a deal with Dumont. Using these top products, they put sets together in custom-made, knock-em-dead wood cabinets. They did Swedish modern, they did consoles with bars, they turned out hand-tooled leather and they had a lavish chinoiserie with black lacquer, gold trim and hand-painted Oriental motifs. When your Mars set was delivered to your home, it arrived with a cabinetmaker to smooth out any nicks. This wasn't a set, it was a collector's item!

Mars sets were sold to small places: radio repair shops (many of which were now tinkering with TVs), furniture dealers, mid-size TV stores. There was no way of bringing each model from store to store, so one salesman came up with a surefire sales catalog, which boasted the original boob-tube theme. Inside were black-and-white photos of the Mars line, but the cover anticipated *Playboy* magazine by years. The guy cut out a picture of a TV screen and pasted another cutout of a nude model with her boobs hanging over the edge of it.

SEE THE 15" PICTURE<br>IN A 10" SCREEN

was the title. That was all he needed to get the owner's attention. From then on, it was more business than usual.

Brenner visited dealers all day and didn't even rest when he got home. On Tuesdays he turned his living room into a living showroom. He and his wife invited a mob of TV-less friends and friends-of-friends to watch Mars TV. Brenner bought a concession tray—the kind vendors use at stadiums—and filled it with popcorn and peanuts and handed out eats while people laughed at

Uncle Miltie or cheered for wrestling. Once in a while, he made a sale and drove the set over to the new owner personally.

But nothing was as wild as the sex-for-sets pitch. One Mars distributor couldn't make a sale at a particular retail store, no matter what he tried. (I promised this guy he could remain anonymous. He's now retired, his marriage has lasted for decades and he doesn't want any trouble in that department.) For months the owner had been complaining that his wife was sick and he wasn't getting enough sex. But the distributor didn't catch on. He offered him free show tickets. He flashed cash. A new car. Nothing worked. "I been telling you what I want," the retailer finally said in disgust. "But you never take care of me." Next visit, the distributor showed up with the goods, a blonde with protrusions fore and aft. He snuck her up to the second floor of the store. "Got something for you upstairs," he told the dealer. "I'll watch the floor." Ten minutes later the dealer came back down. "I couldn't believe my luck," he said. "But you dirty bastard, you almost screwed me. There's no furniture up there. We had to do it on the toilet." P.S.: Dirty bastard or no, the distributor moved six sets that day.

But I've reserved the best for last. My favorite news item from those bygone glory days of television:

## TV TOO COSTLY FOR JAPANESE

TOKYO, July 7 (UP)—Jiro Sato, Japan's man in the street, and his wife are eager for television but they are going to have to wait a long time for it. The reason: Nobody can afford it.

Receiving sets are far beyond the reach of the average man. Six companies are making sets on an experimental basis, but these are not on general sale. The sets cost 100,000 yen, or about $275. That's a sum the 15,000-yen-a-month worker would find impossible to shell out. There are less than 300 sets in Japan, all of them in Tokyo.

*(1951)*

# "And Now, for a Final Word . . ."

"Well, the old hand on the clock says it's time to go. . . . So there it is: all I can remember of the early days. Probably I'll think of more later.

Once they asked Kitty Kallen, the famous big-band singer, if she knew she was a legend. Kitty replied, "Gosh, if I knew I was going to be a legend I'd have acted differently." How would you have acted Kitty? How?

Some of us who pioneered the early TV times are also often referred to as "legends." Had we suspected this anointment, would we have acted differently? If we had, might we have short-circuited our freewheeling creativity? All of us in TV hoped to make this new kid on the entertainment block in our own image, with our own ideals—some of us with few ideals and fostering bare-bones sex and rigged game shows and fraudulent commercials and violence. And others of us idealized

346

great drama and music, travel underwater and a trip to the moon, and witness to the world's epochs. But are any of us "legends" satisfied with the way the kid grew up?

Every day we suffer the twin instincts to hug or beat the hell out of our progeny. Go ahead! Ask me again how we feel about TV, the kid we tried to bring up right. Sorry, gang, I'm gonna cop out on the answer. But I got a smart-ass guy who maybe figured it out. It's my friend, the comic columnist Joey Adams, who said, "TV is still an infant. That's why you have to get up and change it so often."

Goodnight and 30.

*Appendix:*

# The Great Debate

From *TV Guide*, July 3, 1953

# HOW REMARKABLE
# CAN YOU GET?

## By Red Smith

Reference was made a week ago to the hawk-eyed commentators on fights who can sit back in the remote shadows of the mezzanine and announce that a boxer's eyes are glassy. These gentlemen have remarkable vision, yet they are not half so discerning as the gentlemen who describe baseball games for us.

The gentlemen who describe baseball games tell us a hundred times a day that the pitch, merely a blur on our screen, was a fast ball outside, a curve ball that caught the corner, a knuckle-ball, a screwball, a sinker (or downer), a change-up, a fork-ball, a palm-ball or a slider.

Had these lads been operating in the day when pitchers threw the emery-ball, the shine-ball, the mud-ball and the spit-ball, they would have identified them just as readily.

As an exercise in keen observation and meticulous reporting, this is pretty good. It borders on the miraculous when you discover that there are many ball players not at all sure that there is such a pitch as the "slider."

Time and again trained professionals stand at the plate, watch the ball from the instant it leaves the pitcher's hand, and cannot tell what sort of pitch it was. Yet up in a booth hung under the grandstand roof, maybe 200 feet from the plate, some ringtailed genius recognizes the pitch as a slider that broke about two inches.

They are absolutely wonderful, these eagles of the air. They are also absolute fakes.

The slogan of sports reporting on radio was, "If they can hear this, they're not watching, and what they can't see won't hurt 'em." With the advent of television, it was thought the boys would have to confine themselves to the truth. This turned out to be wild optimism.

The television camera, good as it is, still can't see a pitch as well as the batter can, or, for that matter, as well as the man sitting in a grandstand seat. And the man in a grandstand seat couldn't recognize a slider or a knuckler or a screwball if it hit him.

Time and again it happens that Mickey Mantle is asked, "What was that ball you hit (or missed) in the seventh inning?" He replies, as honestly as he is able, "A fast ball, belt high and a little inside." At the same time somebody else is asking the pitcher what he threw to Mantle in the seventh. "A curve," he answers.

They aren't sure, but the man under the roof is. He declared it was a screwball which broke across the knees.

It doesn't take long for the man in the stands to realize that the man up under the roof is making it up. Once he has learned that, he ceases to believe that the man upstairs is trying to tell the truth. Then, he begins to wonder whether he can believe anything the man says. Even the score.

From *TV Guide,* September 25, 1953

# SEEING RED

Sportscasters Answer
Red Smith on the Great
Curveball Question

By Guy Lebow
*Second Vice President,*
*Sports Broadcasters Association*


The executive board of the Sports Broadcasters Association, representing its 40 or more members, takes strong exception to an article authored by Sports Writer Red Smith in TV GUIDE.

Mr. Smith, in our opinion, has lashed out in an unwarranted, crass and, we would prefer to believe, unsolicited attack on the sportscasting profession. Because of his method of half-truths, distortion of fact and unbelievably irresponsible use of quotes, we feel he has questioned the integrity of each individual sportscaster.

The author starts off by uttering disdain for any baseball announcer who claims he can differentiate between an inside pitch, a curve or what not 200 yards away. The batter and pitcher, according to Mr. Smith, seldom agree what has been thrown. Here, Mr. Smith lacks the reporter's researching methods. Were he to dig

352

deeply, he would discover perspective is a great factor in focus. Isn't it easier to estimate a dance pattern from the back of a theater? Why not then the curve of a ball or its relation to the batter from a distance? With his obvious desire to create confusion, Mr. Smith quotes a batter as saying he hit one type pitch and the pitcher saying he threw another type. Therefore, if these two differ, how, Mr. Smith asks, can the announcer presume to be right?

Mr. Smith, at first glance, seems to make his point. But the truth of the matter is that most experienced ballplayers, questioned about a ball at which they had swung, preface their answer with: "I think it was . . ." Those few words, you will admit, change the entire complexion. Actually, if the batter could tell accurately what he was receiving, he would get a hit most every time. The baseball announcer sees the pitch after it has completed it mission: curved . . . sunken . . . or sailed.

Usually, the announcer has a "book" on every pitcher in the league he broadcasts. Let's say Pitcher Jones has a fast ball, curve and screwball. He's a left-hander facing a left-handed batter. His first pitch curves into the batter. Result: the announcer concludes logically this is the screwball. He follows this logicalizing in all reports he must make within seconds. But more, Mr. Smith sneers as he berates the broadcaster for daring to call a slider pitch.

It's miraculous, says Mr. Smith, when you discover many ballplayers are not at all sure there is a slider pitch. It's equally miraculous Mr. Smith does not know, or perhaps does not wish to tell, the whole story. And the whole story is that an overwhelming number of players and experts do admit the existence of a slider.

For example, Frank Yeutter, Philadelphia baseball writer and former president of the Baseball Writers Association of America, in his book about Philadelphia Pitcher Jim Konstanty, calls him the greatest of all slider pitchers. Frankie Frisch and Rogers Hornsby, on a recent

TV program, discussed the abilities of certain sliderball pitchers. And, writing for a sport magazine, Casey Stengel said there is a dearth of .300 hitters today compared to 20 years ago because today's young players have not learned to solve—yes, our good friend—the slider. Had enough?

How less ominous the average announcer would have been made to seem if Mr. Smith had admitted the practice of calling pitches originated with the great *sports writers* many years before the invention of radio, instead of being passed off as a poisoned brew dished up to make you, the listener and viewer, more susceptible to beer or cigarets.

Mr. Smith reaches an incredibly low level of journalism when he uses quotation marks around the phrase attributed to sports announcers: "If they can hear this, they're not watching, and what they can't see won't hurt them." Quotes, as every schoolboy writer knows, are used to narrate exact words—not the implication or approximate meaning, but the precise wording.

Which sports announcer, we ask, ever has made such a remark? To our knowledge, no one in the Sports Broadcasters Association, which includes almost every sportscaster and his writing assistant in New York City. It is damaging to every announcer for Mr. Smith to use quotes so wildly. Mr. Smith should name the specific announcer in fairness to all, but then it is obvious nothing in his article can be construed as fair.

For this article is unfair to the vast army of ambitious young men all over the country attending college and private classes, learning the business of sportscasting, striving hard to learn the sports, players and broadcasting techniques, training their eyes and minds for quick accurate assessments, dreaming of entering a dignified and respected profession, looking with understandable awe upon the decent men of the sportscasting profession who occupy high positions of acceptance with their public.

Mr. Lebow's statement is on behalf of these officers and members of the Sports Broadcasters Association: Joe Hasel, president; Sam Taub, first vice-president; Bob Allison, secretary; Len Dillon, treasurer; Bill Ackman, Larry Allen, Mel Allen, Sam Aro, Nat Ash, Judson Bailey, Red Barber, Buck Canel, Geoff Davis, John Derr, Jack Dillon, Jimmy Dolan, Don Dunphy, Bryan Field, Bob Finnegan, Jack Fraser, Major Al Frazin, Marty Glickman, Al Helfer, Russ Hodges, Harold Holtz, Ted Husing, Hal Janis, Paul Jonas, Frank Litsky, Stan Lomax, Bernie London, Ken Lydecker, Jocko Maxwell, Jack McCarthy, Dean Miller, Johnny Most, Harry Nash, Bob O'Connor, Bud Palmer, Kal Ross, Chris Schenkel, Vince Scully, Bill Slater, Tom Slater, Bob Smith, Bill Stern, Art Stockdale, Harry Wismer.